WHAT BEING ~~
AND
WHAT BEING BLACK ISN'T

Jacob Whittingham

HANSIB

Published by Hansib Publications in 2010
London & Hertfordshire

Hansib Publications Limited
P.O. Box 226, Hertford, Hertfordshire, SG14 3WY, UK

Email: info@hansib-books.com
Website: www.hansib-books.com

A catalogue record for this book is
available from the British Library

ISBN: 978-1-906190-30-9

Printed and bound in Malta by Melita Press

For
Frances Ruth Vigors

Dedicated to the Memory of Sunday Essiet

1992-2008

"…Somehow along the way Black life and culture was deemed profitable, and the big great White male took interest and fought over the seven seas of soul. **'Niggativity'**, which was a minority element in the hood, had its DNA corporately extracted…"
Chuck D

"…first you and I got to unify [to]
stop the **'niggativity'** and control our creativity
the rich is getting richer, so why we ain't richer?
could it be we still thinking like niggas?
educate yourselves, make your world view bigger
visualize wealth and put yourselves in the picture!"
KRS-One

'I LOVE BLACK PEOPLE, BUT I HATE NIGGERS'
Chris Rock

"Be proud of who you are! Let's enlighten ourselves and re-educate our fellow Brothas and Sistas of the knowledge of Self. Let's escape **'niggativity'** so we can become who we really are."
Tion Jakely

"Have you been vaccinated? 'cause here comes an Inoculation of Truth, guaranteed to immunize you **'niggativity'** proof. **'Niggativity'** is that deathly, mental disease killing-off the Black Community; making us live like slaves, even though we born free…Here comes that healing cupful of Truth. Bitter to some, but sweet to 'the true'…"
Akil

Front and Back Cover designed by
Inderpal Virdi (heyindy.com), Southall (28 years old)

'No N*ggativity Pure Positivity' logo designed
by Raam, Accra (21 years old)
and
Jesse, Southwark (18 years old)

Website and MySpace designed by
justfix.co.uk Ltd, Southwark (20 years old)

CONTENTS

INTRO...

To everyone reading this book, whether you're just flicking through or you're here for the long haul, let me start off by saying that, whilst we're still getting used to the notion of a Black American President, I think it's a good opportunity to put some things into perspective.

I know that some people would have you believe that Obama signifies a new dawn in how the world ultimately comes to treat Black people, but let's not get carried away with ourselves.

You'll hear the political commentators say that it was a' triumph for all Americans, that the West really has gone colour blind. But let's not get things twisted – we still got a long way to go. Yea that's right, I said it – we got a looooong way to go. You might know that 95% of African Americans, and 67% of Latinos voted for Obama. But what you might not know is that an incredible 57% of White Americans voted *against* Obama. That's right, more White Americans voted for John McCain, and his running mate Sarah Palin – a comedy double act we haven't seen the likes of since Cannon and Ball graced our screens.

Now don't get me wrong, I'm glad that 43% of White people gave a Black guy a chance. But before we get haps, we should also remember that 43% of *all* African Americans live beneath the poverty line, and it's estimated that 40-44% of African Americans are functionally illiterate. We should also remember that Barack made his victory speech inside a bullet-proof glass case, such is the threat to his life by people who can't handle a Black President.

You see the truth is, Obama does not signify an achievement for White people, or for White America, or even for America. Obama signifies an achievement for Black people, and Black people only. Because despite the Western perception of what Black means on this planet – menacing, angry, violent, stupid – a Black person managed to convince a country with one of the worst histories in race relations, that he could run the country better than any other man or woman, and assume the position of 'the most powerful person on the planet.'

However, if you're not Black and you wanna make Obama about you, and you wanna help 'make a difference', then I'm gonna ask you for three favours, primarily to do with young Black people:

1. When you see a batch of kids walking down the street, hoods up, talking loud, play fighting – I'm gonna ask you not to get scared. Try not to get scared because hoods aren't a weapon, they help keep people warm during winter. Try not to get scared because the more you act scared, the more they'll think that they're supposed to be scary, and the more that they'll think that they're supposed to act up to the scary stereotype that you've given them.

2. When you see three or four Black kids in your shop, I'm gonna ask you not to follow them around. I know it's difficult to think of them as having any 'purchase power', after all, the article you read in *The Sun* was about how a gang of youths tore up a jewellery store in Knightsbridge – but when you make them feel like they're thieves, they'll lose faith in their ability to amount to anything positive. In many cases, this leads to a sense of apathy about their predicament – and that's when the drama really begins. So just try, even a couple of times, to trust that these kids might actually be in your shop to shop – legit.

3. And lastly, when you get on a bus, and you've just finished work, and you're tired and you're hungry, but you can hear that there are some kids playing music off their phones, full blast and shouting to each other – I'm gonna ask you to just chill. Try to remember what you were like when you were young. Weren't you a little annoying too? If you badly need them to turn the music down, then please talk to young people nicely, 'cos when you act rough with them, they'll get rough with you.

To the people of African heritage reading this book. We're living in one of the most sublime eras of our history. The most powerful man in the world is Black, and if some political analysts are to be believed, that Oprah is considered the most powerful woman in the world, we pretty much got a monopoly on things right now.

For the first time, we got every reason to brag about the achievements of Black people without talking about Michael Jordan or the Pyramids. For the first time, we got the whole world prepared to accept the positive achievements of Black people. And that's because Obama has shown everyone what true Blackness is.

But as well as we've got Obama, we've got the drama. In the UK, Black people are 10% of all people in mental institutes and there are nearly twice as many Black people in prison as there are at University. From the fact that there are only two Black CEOs in all British blue-chip companies, to the fact that last year only 45% of all Black Caribbean pupils got five good GCSEs – it's important that we don't lose sight of where we are right now.

What is also of paramount importance is that we understand that none of us will achieve anything until we, ourselves, individually, are prepared to say, "I'm gonna do what I need to do, so that I can do what I want to do. And I'm gonna do it without begging anyone to do it for me."

And that's why Biscuit wrote this book. This book is about *What Being Black Is, And What Being Black Isn't.*

Blackness has always been, and always will be, about getting a university degree regardless of the school you went to, taking care of your children despite the estate you grew up on, and being on time, even if you had to ride the bus.

The book is not here to offend, and it's not here to upset – I know that in places it's kinda harsh, and it pulls no punches – but it's time we opened up some of those wounds that we were afraid to look at, and face head-on the problems that exist in the Black community right now – 'cos there *are* problems. You see, I know you might not agree with all of what Biscuit says, but the intention is not to be right. The intention is to open up a discussion.

Like Biscuit says, "Blackness is a responsibility, not an excuse." So let me pass you onto him. In the meantime, stay blessed.

Jacob Whittingham

WHAT BEING BLACK IS AND WHAT BEING BLACK ISN'T

"The world can only be grasped by action, not by contemplation ...
...The hand is the cutting edge of the mind."
Jacob Bronowski

nigg ' a·tiv i·ty n.
[adj: niggative] [ant: positivity]
1: An attitude expressed through an act, a statement or expression made by a marginal faction of Black people exemplified by an extreme detestation for blackness.

2: A state of being, or a mindset made consciously or unconsciously by a Black person that directly or indirectly negatively affects themselves and their community.

3: The unique characteristic of a nigga/nigger.

ster·e·o·type n.
[adj: stereotypical]
1: One of the direct consequences of racism – in that the discriminated become the dupe of a series of rationalisations whereby the power-holders justify their dominant position in the society.

2: A means of social control and repression.

black ' ness n.
[adj: black]
Defined by not only the colour of one's skin, but a reflection of a mental attitude, characterised by the following traits:
i)   The determination to be financially independent of the state.
ii) The desire to be educated (by any means necessary).
iii) The ability to avoid confrontations with Black people.
iv) The courage to condemn niggativity.
v)   To love being Black (regardless of how 'old skool' or unfashionable it might seem).
Source: Mr Biscuit's Revised Unabridged Dictionary

CHAPTER ONE
BLACKNESS

"To rebuke a person, to admonish or to correct a person does not mean hate. When someone will correct you, that is the greatest sign of their love for you. The scripture says, 'He whom the Lord loveth, he chasteneth much ...'"[1] *Unknown*

Last night, I had this weird dream. I remember that there was a room, actually it was more like an office, with a man called Thomas, or Thom, or something. Anyway, this man is sat at his desk when this guy called Nick knocks at his door.

"Come on in Nick, take a seat. Make ya' self comfortable," Thom says, in his southern drawl. Nick walks into Thom's office, takes off his pale green bomber jacket, places it carefully on the spare chair and sits down.

Thom puts his pen down, and waits for Nick to settle in. 'So, how long's it been since ya' last appraisal? How're things?"

"It's sweet as a nut,"[2] Nick boldly replies. He reclines back in his chair and puts his hands behind his head. "It's a blinder being Chairman of the largest far-right political party at a time like this. I'll be honest though, we're not really very active these days," he concedes.

"Why's that? Are you thinking of retiring? Is your party losing support? Has the government tried to ban you again? Have you guys got an Obama too?" quizzes Thom.

"Nah, nuffin like that," Nick responds, quickly dismissing Thom's concerns. "It's just that...well...," Nick searches for a way to break the news to Thom, "...well...these days, Black people are sorta doing our job for us."

"Well knock me down and steal muh teeth! Is you serious?!" Thom yells, taking off his pointy hat and readjusting his seating position, eager to hear Nick's explanation. "Howja do that!?"

Nick comes closer. He pauses, and then whispers, "I know that Black fellas[3] don't openly like to admit to it, but deep down, they know that things are going pretty badly in their community right now.

Geezer, you should see the barmy pony-and-trap that they kill each other over. Blimey, sometimes we actually wonder whose side they're really on?!

A lot's changed since you were last over in England – it ain't like it was a coupla years ago. Back in the old days, they'd make life pretty tough for us. Whenever they got upset wiv the way they were being treated by the 'ol' Bill', they'd kick up a fuss and riot all over the place: like in Brixton, and Toxteth, Tottenham, Notting Hill, and St Paul's, and Handsworth.

If they knew that being Black made it hard to get a job, they'd set up their own businesses. Or better still, they'd go to night school, and get so many qualifications that employers had no choice but to employ 'em.

And when Black people were acting 'niggative', they'd use their loaf. Some of 'em would slap the rest of them into shape, teaching them about their 'istory and stuff, getting 'em to work as a team and all that.

Bloody 'ell, a coupla decades ago, it was all going Pete Tong for us. But now, Black people are kinda like the 'sick man' of the UK – they're off their rocker!

We don't even need to fundraise, recruit or go on those stupid pointless marches anymore. All we need to do is step back and leave 'em to it."

A smirk develops on Nick's face. "What a result. These days, Black people have more to be afraid of at the 'ands of another spade than they do of us!"

Thom interjects. "Dadgumit! That's cuter than grits, 'cos did'ja know it's pretty much the same over here too. Did'ja know that when Obama got elected as president, I was gonna skedaddle lickety split outta this town. Coloured folk was darn near thinkin' that they was gonna rule the world. But sure 'nuff nothin' changed. I was readin' a magazine that said that:

- Despite being only 13% of the population, Black people represent 30% of America's poor.
- 40% of the people on death row are Black.
- A young Black male is more likely to die from gunfire than a soldier was in the Vietnam war.
- White people have a life expectancy that is 6 years longer than Black people.
- 62% of Black families are headed by single parents.

- And 69% of Black children can't read by the time they're 10 years old.[4] You savvy!"

"Are those facts kosher?" asks Nick.

"You betcha sweet bippy! One Black man at the top don't mean that things are a changin' for the rest."

Nick smirks and replies, "You don't 'ave to tell me that me ol' china. On the night that Obama was voted in as US President, a young Black kid, Nathan Douglas was being stabbed to death in Wandsworth, south London! Trust me my son, Obama can't change what's happenin' in Black kids' minds – the only fing that can change that is Black kids themselves.

I mean, listen to this: the 'ava day, me and a coupla geezers I know, Little Smithy and Rich Ed, tried to cut up these two Black guys that we saw standing on a street corner – you know, 'cos we enjoy doing that sorta stuff.

We got tooled up, 'ad our gloves on, wiv our ski masks pulled down. But when we pulled up beside 'em, with our St George's flag clearly visible from our car window, our weapons leaving nuffin' to their imagination, and shouting 'oi oi saveloy' so that they'd know it was us, you'll never in a million years guess what happened?"

"Those jigaboos pulled a gun on you?" asks Thom.

"You're not even close old boy", Nick instantly replies.

"They called the cops?" Thom asks, feigning boredom but interested.

"Not on your nelly. They don't trust 'em."

"They set a trap for ya'?" Thom replies, getting impatient.

"Leave it out."

Thom gets frustrated. "Dawgonnit! Then what?!!"

"They did nuffin'!!! Not a f***ing fing. They didn't get scared, they didn't run for cover and they didn't even flinch."

"Is you serious ol' buddy?!" Thom growls thumping the desk.

"Deadly serious."

Thom looks confused. In all his time volunteering for the KKK, he's never heard anything so incredible.

"Well butter my butt and call me a biscuit!" he says, his face paler than his normal complexion, still reeling from the shock of this revelation.

Nick continues, wanting to explain. "Incredible ain't it? These two muppets were far too busy having a barney wiv each other, than to worry about me and my boys. I mean, there we were, ready to do some damage to 'em, and they couldn't give a monkey's about us. It sanded like one of 'em had stepped on the other's brand new white Nikes and had refused to apologise!

Believe me, I tried with all my might to get a reaction from 'em, but they were quite clearly hell bent on going spare at each 'ava, so they saved us the trouble! What a bunch of spanners.

And that's the way it is these days in Blighty. You would not belieeeeve the amount of aggro Black people 'av with each 'ava – they're more interested in fighting with each 'ava over nonsense than to care about what us xenophobes wanna do to 'em. Crazy ain't it?!

Anyway, since we 'ad some spare time, we went to 'ava a pint or two at our local, The Rifleman. After we 'ad a few drinks, we came to the conclusion that since Black lads were far too preoccupied with knocking ten bells out of each 'ava, we may as well focus on Black birds instead. The plan was to get in our motor, and shout abuse at any of 'em we saw on the street.

But just as we were about to leave the pub, we caught the end of this BBC news story about them.

It said that 25% of African mothers and 50% of Caribbean mothers were single parents, compared with only 10% of White mothers.[5] When I heard this, I felt kinda deflated. I didn't really see the point in insulting coon birds – it seems like once Black fellas got 'em up the duff, they were doing a sound job of w*nkering up their lives instead!"

Thom strokes the few tufts of hair on his head with pleasure. "Well that's as cute as a sack of puppies. Yesseree, you guys must be havin' fun!"

"But trust me, it gets better," exclaims Nick. "Even my little boy says that he doesn't bother starting on coloureds at school anymore. The little nipper told me that last week he heard these two nigglets cuss another monkey about how dark he was: 'You're so Black you look like someone left you in the oven on gas mark nine. You're so Black the barber has to draw a chalk line on ya' barnet to distinguish between ya' face and ya' hair.'

What a bunch of head cases – even darkies accept that their skin colour's mingin'. And what I love is that their insults are way better than ours!"

Thom was buzzing.

"I must admit though, it's getting a bit boring. Take the other day for example, when me and a bloke I know, Hughes, had this pukka idea about releasing a CD filled with songs about how much we hate these Kintes.

But check this: a couple of days after we recorded the album, I heard this tune by a rapper called 50 Cent.

From what I could understand, this gobsh*te only ever called Black people niggers. All his songs rabbit on about killing sambos, getting lairy with the rest, and talking about how to turn Black birds into prostitutes.

And what a result. Apparently this 50 Cent guy's having a blinder in the Black community, selling records all over the place and making plenty of wedge in the process. Now how's that for self-destruction?!"

Nick composes himself. "Na' don't get me wrong, it ain't *all* niggers who've got this attitude, so it ain't game over yet, but it's certainly enough to give us a well-earned break and watch them f*** each other up for a while! Mate, with friends like these, Black people don't need enemies!"

I opened my eyes the next morning. I sat up in bed. I took a deep breath. "Things aren't the way they should be."

Inside I've always known that some things weren't right in my community, but for years I tried to persuade myself that things weren't that out of control.

I suppose I was kinda like that guy who falls from the sky towards the ground and as he gets closer to his death, he keeps saying to himself, so far, so good, so far so, good…"

…'cos every time another shooting made the 6 o'clock news, I'd say to myself, "things are still cool, things aren't that bad…"

You see, when 7-year-old Toni-Ann Byfield was shot by a 33-year-old man in Harlesden, I tried to ignore it.

And when a promising 18-year-old athlete I knew was convicted for his part in the stabbing of a young man in Brixton, I tried to overlook it.

But when the 15-year-old Sunday Essiet from south London, was brutally murdered in Woolwich, I suddenly woke up.

I couldn't make excuses anymore. Some things are truly f***ed. And they've been f***ed for a long time.

I was tired of seeing single Black mums, struggling with a pram and a screaming kid in one hand and a dozen bags of shopping in the other, without a father in sight. I was tired of worrying about my brother every time he went out raving, in case he looked at someone the 'wrong way'. I was tired of hearing Black people complain about racism without ever doing anything serious to challenge it.

I know that Barack Obama's the new President of the USA, and I'm proud of his achievement – 'cos it's damn near incredible – but it doesn't change what's happening on our island, and it certainly doesn't change what's happening in our communities.

'Cos straight up:

- 48% of West Indian families and 36% of Black African families are headed by a single parent – far above the national average.[6]
- Black people typically earn £100 a week less than White people.[7]
- Black people account for around 75% of all the victims of gun crime in London and around 80% of all the suspects involved.[8]
- 62% of all people arrested for robbery in London are Black.[9]
- 31% of all Black murder victims are shot, compared with only 12% with Asians and 6% with Whites.[10]
- 16% of the male prison population, and 31% of the female prison population is Black.[11]
- 80% of Black people live in Neighbourhood Renewal Fund areas – areas targeted in need of urgent regeneration.[12]

This is the reality.

I remember watching a Chris Rock show once: "*...It's like a civil war going on with Black people. And there's two sides...there is Black people, and there's niggers...and the niggers have got to go.*"[13]

It got me thinking... If I, as a Black person, love and respect my Black self, then how can I excuse the f***ed up attitudes that some Black people exhibit? If I, as a Black person, understand what it means to be Black, then how can I defend the 'niggativity' that some Black people exhibit?

I got outta bed and rubbed my eyes. I went downstairs to get some cereal.

I know that if some people knew what I was thinking right now, I'd probably get cussed. I can hear them now: "You don't understand how hard it is for some Black people growing up in this world...You don't know how difficult it is in this country for Black people...You don't appreciate what some Black people have to go through."

Believe me, I understand what they're saying, I understand where they're coming from, and I'm not trying to dis anyone. Really I'm not...

I know this whole situation ain't really our fault. I mean, it doesn't take Steven Hawking to work out that pretty much all the social problems that we face in our community come from one source – from one tiny gang we'll call the Candyman:

...the minority of people who make the decisions that affect the lives of the majority; the minority of people who dedicate their lives to increasing their economic and political power over the majority; the minority of people who dedicate their lives to the accumulation of wealth, at the expense of everyone else's...

...basically, the people who control the means of production in our society – anything which through ownership generates ongoing income for the owner...

...and they are the newspaper editors, the company CEOs, the politicians, the bank execs, the TV director-generals, and the business magnates.

Think it's a myth...? In the UK, over the last ten years, the share of wealth held by the richest 10% of the population rose from 47% to 54%, and the wealthiest 1% saw their share leap from 18% to 23%[14] ... and at the same time, the number of people living below the poverty line has increased, with more than one in four households classed as being so-called 'breadline poor'.[15]

Yep, they're the ones who *loooooooove* to write stories about how dangerous all Black kids are, they're the ones who think that Black people are only good enough to work as cleaners, they're the ones who refuse to invest real resources into the areas where Black people are highly concentrated, they're the ones who cuss off the Notting Hill carnival every year, they're the ones who continue to exploit the civil wars that kill millions of Africans each year, and they're the ones who keep themselves rich, by keeping us poor.

I finished my cereal and got up to brush my teeth. The way I see things, if I spilt a cup of tea in my friend's house, I should really be the one to clean up the mess – you follow?

Well that's kinda like our situation. Since the Candyman caused the mess they should clean it up – which is why we've been waiting for them to sort the situation out. And that's why when people say "Black people need to stop blaming the system", or "Black people need to stop cussing 'the government'," it used to get me kinda mad.

But after last night's dream, the 'Black-people-need-to-fix-up' comments didn't make me feel so mad anymore and I couldn't quite figure out why... and then it suddenly dawned on me... **I ran out of the bathroom and into my bedroom**, the toothpaste still in my mouth. I picked up a book, a book that I'd seen my Dad read called *How Europe Underdeveloped Africa* by Walter Rodney. I hurriedly opened the book and read:

"The colonisation of Africa lasted for just over 70 years in most parts of the continent. That is an extremely short period within the context of universal historical development... The decisiveness of the short period of colonialism and as negative consequences for Africa spring mainly from the fact that Africa lost power.

Power is the ultimate determinant in human society, being basic to the relations within any group and between groups. It implies the ability to defend one's interests and if necessary to impose one's will by any means available. In relations between peoples, the question of power determines manoeuvrability in bargaining, the extent to which one people respect the interests of another, and eventually the extent to which a people survive as a physical and cultural entity.

When one society finds itself forced to relinquish power entirely to another society that in itself is a form of underdevelopment."[16]

I put the book down. I began to see how naïve I'd been. For 400 years Black people have been enslaved, raped, robbed, shot, maimed, beaten and slaughtered. Around 60,000 out of 80,000 members of the Herero tribe were butchered during the German occupation of Namibia,[17] between 50,000 and 100,000 Aborigines were murdered during the European invasion of Australia,[18] 200,000 Kenyans were killed by the British in the 1950s alone,[19] and somewhere in the region of 8 million Congolese were massacred during Belgian colonialism.[20]

And yet for each of those four hundred years, Black people have petitioned, argued, marched, wailed, implored and pleaded for the Candyman to stop. We adopted their religion, we wore their clothes, we changed our names, we spoke their language, we even bleached our skin – and yet none of this changed the way the Candyman treated us.

Even during my existence, I've been hoping that one day the Candyman will ride in on a white horse through the Black community, and, like Zorro, create peace, love, unity and wealth. I prayed that one day the Prime Minister will address the House of Commons and say: *"I'm so sorry for everything that's happened to Black people. So now I'm gonna invest £billions into the Black community to make amends."*

I walked slowly back to the bathroom. The Candyman has never, and will never, change its attitude towards Black people. And this is a fact supported by experience, supported by logic, and supported by history. Every time we ask for a better welfare system, for better schools, for better housing, they roll out the same excuses:

"We're working on it"

"You have to be patient"

"Don't worry, things are better now than they were before."

Why?... because our poverty, lack of education and misery is directly linked with their wealth and success. That's why it's no coincidence that since 1995, in poor areas where household earnings are at around £11k a year, the proportion of young people entering Uni only increased from 0.89% to 1.77%.[21] But in middle class areas, where earnings were around 22k a year, it increased from 10% to 19%, and in richer areas where incomes were £40k a year, the proportion of young people going to Uni increased from 33% to 50%.[22]

Because the worse our schools are, the lower grades Black kids get, the less likely it is that Black kids will go to University, the worse the jobs that they end up with – the easier it is to maintain the status quo.

Now since it looks like they benefit from our poverty, why would they want to change our situation? I mean...would it be logical for Man Utd to loan all their best footballers to Accrington Stanley? Is it in line with human nature for Israel to give Palestine all their land back? Did it ever seem plausible that Lord Voldemort would stop bugging and harassing Harry Potter?

Sure the Candyman *can* help us, but after four centuries of abuse, it's kinda silly putting any faith in their 'good' nature. After all, they are our oppressors... and in case we didn't know, their job is to oppress. Oppressors get the name, 'oppressor', precisely because they are unpleasant, authoritarian, dictatorial and tyrannical people. And that's why oppressors – being oppressors – treat the oppressed in a pretty bad way:

- 33% of Black Caribbean people live in the most deprived wards in England, compared to only 14% of White people.[23]
- In America, a Black baby is more than twice as likely as a White baby to die before its first birthday.[24]
- And in France, unemployment in certain Black and North African areas runs at nearly 40%![25]

Yet regardless of this blatant oppression, we still ask the Candyman to help us!

When I think about it, Roadrunner never ever under any circumstances tried to convince Wile E Coyote that he should stop trying to eat him and become a vegetarian instead. Why? 'Cos it wouldn't have made any sense... being that Wile E Coyote was: a) evil and b) the sworn nemesis of Roadrunner.

And when I think about it, Yoda never tried to set up a meeting with Darth Vader, attempting to appeal to his 'generous' side and talk about a possible peace treaty. Why? 'Cos Darth Vader was the most evil person in the Universe – perhaps with the exception of the Emperor – and if he was prepared to cut his son's hand off, he certainly wasn't a man to be negotiated with. I know that the Klingons did finally make peace with the Starship Enterprise, but we all knew that Captain Kirk and Spock were making a mistake.

You see, one thing that I learnt in GCSE History is that the Candyman only ever relinquishes power to powerful Black people – people like Jean-Jacques Dessalines of Haiti, Cudjoe of Jamaica or Kwame Nkrumah of Ghana.

But to weak Black people – Black people who beg/plead/petition – they give us 'things'…or to put it another way, meaningless crap to stop us thinking about how unbelievably f***ed up our lives are.

In order to make us forget the shockingly bad grades of young Black boys in education, they give us Adidas trainers. In order to make us forget that England imprisons Black people at a rate six times higher than that of White people,[26] they give us *I'm a Celebrity Get Me Out of Here*. In order to make us forget that some of our housing estates look like they were designed by the producers of *Apocalypse Now*, they give us the Olympics.

From wars with countries that most of us can't even find on a map to *Strictly Come Dancing*, the Candyman has for years given us 'things' to put our brains to sleep.

Yep, they convinced us that the next American president, Jordan's latest boob job, the new series of *America's Top Model*, or *CSI*, or *Prison Break* (admit it girls, you only watch it for Wentworth Miller) or Arsenal's latest bid to win the Champions League are the most important thing in our lives. And consequently, the Candyman can plunder and pillage, and do whatever they want, whilst we, in the meantime, are far too preoccupied with the Idiot Lantern (TV), to question anything that's happening to us.

We listen to all those speeches that Labour and the Conservatives make every year about how they embrace multiculturalism, we fill in all those sheets of paper for job application forms about equal opportunities, we see all those Black and brown faces on the news, we see a Black guy sitting in the Oval Office and we think to ourselves, things really are changing. Things really are ok.

As I went to get my jacket and my gloves, I started thinking about my history lessons again. It occurred to me that in times gone by, if the Candyman hasn't been able to think of enough 'things' to keep us preoccupied, and if Black people have ever started to get a bit restless, the Candyman follows exactly the same formula: the Tinkering formula[27]...and boy does the Candyman love to tinker.

Essentially, tinkering is when you fool or mess around with something, but don't actually change anything. In other words, tinkering is what the Candyman does to keep Black people from feeling a little miffed about their depressing situation. They rattle the system a little, pass a couple of laws, but in essence they change f-all.

Stage one is where Black people get vexed about the fact that they're poor, but the Candyman refuses to do anything about it.

Stage two is where Black people start demonstrating peacefully (singing songs like 'We Shall Overcome'), asking the Candyman to give them a better educational system, the opportunity to get decent jobs etc. The Candyman won't listen of course, 'cos singing ain't really gonna convince someone that they should surrender their power and wealth now is it?

Stage three is where a section of Black people get impatient about the non-respondent attitude of the Candyman. They start talking about taking power for themselves and begin rioting.

Stage four is where the Candyman realises that if things continue the way they are, Black people are probably gonna slaughter the Candyman in their entirety and take power.

And as they realise this, the Candyman take sides with the peaceful group of Black people, gives the system a tinker such as giving the Black people an elected official. This marginalises the militant Black people, 'cos now the majority of Black people (foolishly) think that everything's gonna be jiggy.

An example of a tinker was the American 'Emancipation Proclamation' in 1863, giving Black folk their 'freedom from slavery'. It avoided a violent Black revolution, and instead made Black people think that the White ruling class were 'working' on the Black situation, despite the fact that the Black condition remained virtually the same as it was before the proclamation.

And today, 'Affirmative Action' which reserves a certain amount of jobs for African Americans is a tinker. It makes Black people think "wahey, we can get jobs, we can't be discriminated against anymore!" And yet even after the introduction of 'Affirmative Action', Black unemployment is twice as high as White unemployment, just as it was back then.[28]

Now don't get me wrong. I'm not saying that tinkering doesn't make things better. But 'better' is an ambiguous word. I'm 'better' off if someone gives me a cup of soup, but it ain't gonna help me pay my mortgage. In fact, all a cup of soup does is keep me alive…and that's all Black people have been given over the last few years. Cups of soup to keep them alive.

Take the American Civil Rights Bill in 1964 for example. It made racial discrimination in American public places illegal and granted equal opportunities in employment and it helped give people like Barack Obama the opportunity to get involved in politics and ultimately run the most powerful nation on earth. It was a classic cup of soup…'Cos it made things 'better', but only a teeny bit better:

- Today in America, a Black child is five times more likely to live in poverty than a White child and is more likely to die in the months after birth than a Cuban or Chinese baby.[29]
- 69% of Black children cannot read by the age of 8 years old, compared with 29% among White children.[30]
- 80% of America's homeless are Black.
- And despite the fact that there is a Black President sitting on the throne, Black America represents nearly 30% of America's poor – a figure that is only marginally better than when Martin Luther King was assassinated way back in 1968.[31]

Now after reading this, it's hard to believe that anything actually got better for Black people in the United States after the Civil Rights Bill of 1964. In the UK, it's exactly the same. We've had the Race Relations Act in 1965, the *Scarman Report* in 1981, the Human Rights Act in 1998, and the *McPherson Report* in 1999. And it's all failed to put a dent into the misery that is 'the Black British experience'. In the UK today:

- Male Black unemployment is at 14%, whereas male White unemployment is at 5.6%.[32]

- Black people are twice as likely to be a victim of crime in comparison to White people.[33]
- Between 1993 and 2003, the Black prison population rose by 138% compared with 48% for White people.[34]
- And Black people are three times more likely to be admitted to mental health hospitals than the rest of the population.[35]

I put my draw-string bag on my back and walked towards the door, leaving for work. I decided that I was done with asking the Candyman to help me. And in being done with asking the Candyman to help me, I was done with carrying a 'victim mentality' around with me: the belief that everyone but ourselves is to blame for the f***ery that exists in the Black community.

You see, I had been so caught up blaming the Candyman for the things that go wrong in the Black community that I had refused to look at what *I* could do to bring about change for myself. Whenever a Black person was accused of not being a responsible father, I would always say, *'it ain't his fault that he doesn't spend time with his child, it's the government's fault, they've made him who he is.'* Whenever a Black person was charged with murdering someone, I would always say, *'it ain't his fault that he stabbed that boy, it's the media's fault, they're the real criminals.'* But the problem with such an attitude is:

- One: Those Black people who act 'niggative' don't EVER have to check their attitude, 'cos they know that regardless of how f***ed up their actions are, they can always say, *"but I'm Black, I've had a hard life, you don't understand how hard things are for me."*
- Two: Those Black people who hadn't even thought about acting 'niggative' know that it's ok to do so, 'cos they know that they can rely on a number of apologists to back them up.

In my mind I can hear Chris Rock again: *"I see some Black people looking at me: 'Why you gotta say that...it ain't us it's the media...the media has distorted our image to make us look bad...why you gotta come down on us like that'...Please cut the f***ing s***. When I go to the money machine tonight and look over my head, I ain't looking for the media, I'm looking for niggers!"* [36]

Bottom Line: If Black people can't criticise 'niggativity', we remain f***ed. 'Cos from my perspective, a Black person, being Black, experiencing what it's like to be Black, living in the Black community, has the right to freely talk about the attitudes and actions

31

exhibited by other Black people. And a Black person, looking Black, being treated Black, having Black friends and Black family members, has the right to discuss the problems and faults that he/she feels exist within the Black community.

I opened the door and walked out, the cold, fresh air blowing against my face. I have to keep reminding myself that Barack Obama is in America – and we're here – and whilst I love the fact that he's doing what he's doing, he ain't gonna give us a job, stop the police from terrorising us, or build us a nice new house. That responsibility is ours, and ours only. So we in the Black community have two choices. We can whinge about the Candyman all day and all night, and excuse the 'niggativity' that some people in our community perpetrate – and over the course of the next 200 years we will continue to be patronised, the system will be tinkered with, but nothing will change – or we can whinge and then change the situation for ourselves, by changing ourselves.

After all, Blackness is not to run from problems. Blackness is to run problems. It's about time we took that red pill…and it's time we told it like it is.

> "We cannot think of being acceptable to others
> until we have first proven acceptable to ourselves."[37]
> *Malcolm X*

NOTES

1. *The Arsenio Hall Show* (1994).
2. *Cockney Dictionary* http://mariodelgado.com/cockney-dictionary/(accessed 25 August 2008).
3. The Racial Slur Database http://gyral.blackshell.com/names.html (accessed 25 August 2008).
4. Lowe, James B, *The American Directory of Certified Uncle Toms,* (Chicago: Lushena, 2002).
5. Berthoud, Richard, *Young Caribbean men and the labour market: A comparison with other ethnic groups,* (published for the Joseph Rowntree Foundation by YPS 1999), www.jrf.org.uk/knowledge/findings/socialpolicy/N69.asp (accessed 18 May 2008).
6. Race divide on single parents (*Metro* Newspaper 10/04/2007), www.metro.co.uk/news/article.html?in_article_id=44768&in_page_id=34 (accessed 18 May 2008).
7. *Black and Asian workers 'underpaid',*(12/04/2002) http://news.bbc.co.uk/1/hi/uk/

1924907.stm (accessed 18 May 2008).

8. *Black People 'in criminal justice crisis'* (15/06/2007), www.epolitix.com/latestnews/article-detail/newsarticle/black-people-in-criminal-justice-crisis/(accessed 25/06/2008).

9. *Street Robbery: Fact sheet,* (Black Information Link 25/7/2002), www.blink.org.uk/pdescription.asp?key=1021&grp=55&cat=199 (accessed 27/11/2007).

10. McLagan, Graeme, *Guns and gangs – the inside story of the war on our streets.* (London: Allison & Busby 2006).

11. *Black inmate numbers surge in overcrowded US & UK prisons,* 28/04/2005 (Black Britain) http://www.blackbritain.net/news/details.aspx?i=1434&c=uk&h=Black+inmate+numbers+surge+in+overcrowded+US+&+UK+prisons (accessed 27 November 2007).

12. *House of Commons Home Affairs Committee: Young People and the Criminal Justice System,* (Second Report of Session 2006-2007, Volume One p. 9 (published by the House of Commons 22/05/2007), http://www.publications.parliament.uk/pa/cm200607/cmselect/cmhaff/181/181i.pdf (accessed 18 May 2008).

13. Rock, Chris, *Bring the Pain,* HBO (1996).

14. O'Hara, Mary, *Vital Statistics: Mapping the widening UK gap between rich and poor,* (The Guardian 08/02/2006), http://www.caledonia.org.uk/dorling.htm (accessed 18 May 2008).

15. Morgan, Ian, *Gap between rich and poor 'widest in 40 years',* (17/07/2007), www.24dash.com/socialhousing/24471.htm (accessed 18 May 2008).

16. Rodney, Walter, *How Europe Underdeveloped Africa,* (Howard University Press 1981), www.marxists.org/subject/africa/rodney-walter/how-europe/ch06.htm (accessed 18 May 2008).

17. Hochschild, Adam, *King Leopold's Ghost – A story of greed, terror and heroism in colonial Africa,* (Macmillan 1998).

18. Knightley, Philip, *Australia: A Biography of a Nation,* (Vintage 2001).

19. Elkins, Caroline, *Imperial Reckoning: The Untold Story of Britain's Gulag in Kenya,* (Henry Holt and Co. 2004).

20. Hochschild, Adam, *King Leopold's Ghost – A story of greed, terror and heroism in colonial Africa,* (Macmillan, 1998).

21. Hill, Paul, *Class Gap Widens Under Blair* (The Times Higher Education Supplement 02/06/2004), www.timeshighereducation.co.uk/email_friend.asp?storycode=189736 (accessed 18 May 2008).

22. *ibid.*

23. *1999/00 Survey of English Housing,* (DTLR, 1996 English House Condition Survey, DTLR quoted in *Improving labour market achievements for ethnic minorities in British society,* Performance and Innovation Unit, Cabinet Office, 06/2001) p11. http://www.blink.org.uk/bm/manifesto_section.asp?catid=17 (accessed 27

November 2007).

24. Lowe, James B, *The American Directory of Certified Uncle Toms*, (Chicago: Lushena, 2002).

25. Powell, Francis, *A Letter From France: Inside Paris' Suburban Ghettos*, www.human naturemag.com/editions/1_07/frenchghetto.html (accessed18 May 2008).

26. *Re-thinking Crime and Punishment − The Facts*, (29/11/2007), www.rethinking.org.uk/ facts/system.shtml (accessed 18 May 2008).

27. Henry, Conan, *Personal communication*, 28/08/2006.

28. Lowe, James B, *The American Directory of Certified Uncle Toms*, (Chicago: Lushena, 2002).

29. Esler, Gavin, *American Dream Eludes The Poorest*, (21/09/2005), http://news.bbc.co.uk /1/hi/programmes/newsnight/4265454.stm (accessed 18 May 2008).

30. Lowe, James B, *The American Directory of Certified Uncle Toms*, (Chicago: Lushena, 2002).

31. *ibid*

32. *The Black Manifesto 2005 Tackling Male Unemployment*, (The Black Information Link 03/05/2007), http://www.blink.org.uk/bm/manifesto_section (accessed 27 November 2007).

33. *Victims of Crime*, (National Statistics Online 08/01/2004), www.statistics.gov.uk/ cci/nugget.asp?id=1088 (accessed 18 May 2008).

34. *Statistics on Race and Criminal Justice System*, (A Home Office publication under section 95 of the Criminal Justice Act 1991 (2004)), www.homeoffice.gov.uk/rds/ pdfs05/s95race04.pdf Pg.87 (accessed 18 May 2008).

35. *Mental health inequality warning*, (07/12/2005), http://news.bbc.co.uk/1/hi/health/ 4503582.stm (accessed 18 May 2008).

36. Rock, Chris, *Bring the Pain*, (HBO 1996).

37. X, Malcolm, *A Declaration of Independence*, (12/04/1964), www.teachingamerican history.org/library/index.asp?document=1148 (accessed 18 May 2008).

CHAPTER TWO
The 'S t u p i d N i g g e r' Guide:
The Idiots Guide To Stupidity

"Only slaves and dogs are named by their masters. Free men and women must name themselves. But when free men and women name themselves the same names that the master named them, that's cultural genocide." *Nana Asa Hilliard*

Thank you for purchasing *Volume One of The Beginner's Guide To Stupidity*. Designed for busy people who can't find time to study, this fun and interactive course is the foolproof way to being stupid. In just three easy steps, we'll take you through the process necessary to go from a self-respecting member of the Black community, to a complete idiot. Volume One is all about becoming a N – I – G – G – E – R. The reason: because thanks to the small but dedicated number of Black people, who've spent many years striving to perfect the art of utter stupidity, we know that the most proficient way to begin the path to idiocy is to change your name to one that shows the world just how nignoramus you are!

It doesn't matter if you haven't thought of yourself as a nigger before! Intelligent Black people like Randall Kennedy, rich Black people like Eddie Murphy, crazy Black people like Elephant Man, British Black people like Asher D, and tough Black people like Mike Tyson have all made the transition. Whether you're young or old, rich or poor, Protestant or Catholic, Conservative or Socialist – anyone can successfully follow this course.

And we're so confident about the methods employed in this course, that if you still refuse to embrace the name after completing this Volume, we'll give you your money back! That's right, because in just ten minutes you'll be calling yourself and everyone else – be they White or Black – a nigger. All day. All night. On the street. In the home. To your parents. To your children. To your boss. To your employees. To your friends. To your enemies. To everyone.

NIGGER. NIGGER. NIGGER. NIGGER. NIGGER. NIGGER. NIGGER. NIGGA. NIGGAZ. NIGGETTES. So without further ado, carefully read on...and enjoy...

STEP ONE: LET INFORMATION BE YOUR TERRORIST

As far as the Candyman's concerned, the biggest threat to our way of life are Islamic Fundamentalists. But for wannabe niggers like yourself, the BIGgest problem is INFORMATION. The reason: because information kills the nigger in you.

You see, when a nigger begins to think, they start to read. And when a nigger starts to read, they begin to truly understand where the word 'nigger' came from. And trust me, if a nigger ever ever EVER understood where the word 'nigger' came from, they would never ever use it candidly *ever* again.

That's why a nigger's best friend is nignorance, and that's why you need to treat any information on the word nigger like America treats Syrians – as a potential threat to your whole existence. So in Step One, f*** Iran and the Taliban – we're listing the *real* Terrorists.

The Origins Of The Word Nigger (A Nigger's 9/11)
THE FOLLOWING INFORMATION CARRIES
AN ELEVATED TERROR ALERT

Yep, that's right, the origins of the word 'nigger' ain't nice at all! Before 1441, the year that the European enslavement of Africa began,[1] Black people or African people were known by a variety of names – Aethiops, Afer, Moors, Azenegues[2] etc etc – but not Negroes. No, the word 'Negro' only kicked in once slavery kicked in. And that's why in many circles, 'Negro' actually meant 'slave'.[3]

Then, in the late 1700s, out of the word 'Negro' came the word 'nigger'. Some people believe that the term was born out of a *phonetic* spelling of the White, US Southern mispronunciation of the word 'Negro' – but don't be fooled by that – the real reason why White people first used the word 'nigger' was done to cause deliberate offence to Black people.[4] 'Cos at that time (and most times) the Candyman, in their detestation of Black people, constantly searched for new ways to make Black people feel awful about themselves.

One way to do this was to give them a name that showed how pitifully powerless they were. And as a result, the Candyman would *deliberately* mispronounce the name 'Negro', and would call Black people nigger instead. Because when you knowingly and deliberately mispronounce someone's name, it says to that person that:

i) I control what your name is,

ii) I am so powerful that I don't even have to pronounce your name right, and

iii) You're so weak that you can't stop me from pronouncing your name wrong.

Ok... I know that sometimes when someone remixes your name it can be a form of affection. I remember hearing that Kenneth Ley, the ex-Enron CEO (aka the multimillion-dollar fraud man) was tenderly called 'Kenny Boy' by George Bush Sr. But what we need to remember is that this Negro/Nigger remixing was done by slave masters, and during slavery, slave masters had zero affection for Black people. And when I say zero affection, I'm talking about pure badness. And I'm not talking about the, 'my-boss-treats-me-bad' kinda badness – I'm talking about *Hell On Earth* badness. Let me give you some examples:

• **To Make Sure The Slaves Kept Working Like Slaves**

At least one slave every day was hung by their hands and whipped. An average whipping would consist of 30 licks to the back. A slave once wrote that, "in flogging, [the slave master]...would increase his [the slave's] misery by blustering and calling out that he was coming to flog again, which he did or did not, as happened".[5] Afterwards, salt or pork brine was put onto their bleeding backs to increase the pain. The Black person was left there to hang for the rest of the day. As a result, "the yellow flies and mosquitoes in great numbers would settle on the bleeding and smarting back, and put the sufferer to extreme torture...I have seen the sufferers dead when they were taken down. He [the slave master] never was called into account in any way for it."[6]

• **If A Male Slave Ran Away**

The lightest possible punishment was having the words "a slave for life" branded into their forehead with a hot iron.[7] However, more than likely, they would be tied to a tree branch by their hands, and their testicles would be cut off and fed to them.

• **To Deter The Slaves From Running Away**

Slave masters "have cut off the legs or arms of the most wilful slaves, to terrify the rest."[8] Slave masters would also take a random pregnant slave, cut a hole in the ground so that she could lie face down on the earth, and violently flog her.[9] In some parts of South Carolina (USA) they would "drive nails into a hogshead [a large barrel/cask] so as to leave the point of the nail just protruding in the inside of the cask".

They would put the slave in the cask, "and roll them down a very long and steep hill."10

• **If A Slave Did Something Wrong**

They were "chained down in a log-pen with a 40lb chain, and [made to]…lie on the damp earth all night. In the morning [they would be] tied…to a large barrow, which is usually drawn by a horse, and…drag it to the cotton field for the horse to use."11 Alternatively, the slave master would "tie a rope round a slave's body, and suspend him from the ground. A fire was kindled over him, from which was suspended a piece of fat pork. As this cooked, the scalding drops of fat continually fell on the bare flesh."12

• **And If A Slave Asked For A Break**

Then you could be looking at a truly severe punishment. A newspaper recorded what happened to an 8-year-old Black slave girl back in 1845:

> "*After coming home, her constant request, until her death, was for [a] break, by which it would seem that she had been starved as well as unmercifully whipped. The body exhibited evidence of the most cruel whipping and beating we have ever heard of. The flesh on the back and limbs [were]…beaten into jelly – one shoulder-bone was laid bare – there were several cuts…from a club on the head – and around the neck was the indentation of a cord, by which it is supposed that she had been confined to a tree.*"13

Now these are the people who created the name 'nigger' – not nice huh?! That's why if you wanna be a nigger, whenever you hear people talk about the origins of the word, we advise you to act like an American who's been asked to sit on a plane next to two guys named Baddar and Ziad…

…Run for your life.

The Real Definition Of The Word 'Nigger' (A Nigger's 7/7)
THE FOLLOWING INFORMATION CARRIES
A HIGH TERROR ALERT

Back in the days of slavery, slave masters had a multitude of names that they employed to degrade Black people. But after a while, it simply became too time consuming and tiresome to have to think about which insult to use – Porch Monkey, Jigaboo, Sambo and Coon all carried the necessary abuse – but it was far more efficient to stick with one that was tried, tested, and which possessed the greatest effect. Nigger, in view of its fantastic success in causing offence to Black people, won hands down as the verbal weapon of choice for the slave master. And as the word 'nigger' was propelled into the premier insult for Black slaves, after a while, the word 'nigger' actually became another way of describing a slave. Now, since a slave was a lowly, filthy and substandard creature it became logical to use the word 'nigger' to cuss anything that was lowly, filthy and substandard. So for example:

- Instead of saying something like "I f***ed up", you'd say, "I niggered up".
- Instead of saying "I ruined my pair of trainers", you'd say, "I niggered my pair of trainers".
- If you left a 'nigger tip' at a restaurant, it meant you left a small tip.
- A 'nigger steak' was a slice of cheap meat.
- 'Nigger luck' was undeserved luck.
- And if you were doing 'nigger work', then you'd be doing a poorly paid job.

Now if any present day 'nigger' knew this, they'd probably stop using the word immediately – even if their record label told them to…which is why if you want to be a nigger, you need to think of this information as if it were strapped to a suicide bomber…Stay well clear.

The Love That Racist Folk Had For The Word Nigger In The 19th and 20th Century (A Nigger's 21/7) THE FOLLOWING INFORMATION CARRIES A SEVERE TERROR ALERT

Despite the so-called US 'emancipation' of slaves in 1865, cussing Black people was over-regular. In fact, it was soooooooo regular, that the word 'nigger' soon went mainstream. There were products called 'Nigger Hair Tobacco' and 'Niggerhead Oysters'. Brazil nuts were referred to as 'Nigger Toes', there was a puzzle game called 'Chopped Up Niggers', and even a colour called 'Nigger Brown'.

Right up until the 1960s, over 140 place names in the US contained the word 'nigger', like 'Nigger Bill Canyon', 'Nigger Hollow' and 'Niggertown Marsh'. Although the US government changed these names in 1967,[14] many varieties of flora and fauna are still commonly referred to by terms that include the word 'nigger', such as the 'Nigger Head Cactus'. Even in Britain, the word 'nigger' was normal, so for example, on a dock, the Black iron post that ships would be tied to was called a 'Niggerhead'.

To put it in today's terms, it's almost like a packet of biscuits being called 'P*kibix', or a town named 'K*keville'. Yet this is just how normal it was to use the word. That's why if you hear anyone discuss the information above, react like you would if you got on a train with a man carrying a backpack with electrical leads hanging out of it...walk away, keep well away!

So To Recap...Forget Osama bin Laden, the information featured in this section is far more dangerous to niggers than Al-Qaeda ever was. **Remember**:

— *Stay away from Books...*
— *Stay away from anything on the History Channel...*
— *Keep away from intelligent Black people...*
— *And never ever watch anything that mentions slavery.*

STEP TWO: TAKE BLACK SELF-RESPECT OUT AND PUT NIGGER DIS-RESPECT IN

Now that we've shown you what information you must avoid and forget, the next step is re-education. And that's because no nigger can expect to be a nigger if they still feel proud to be Black. So sit back, play the CD enclosed, and let these words transform you from a self-respecting Black person, into a 'niggative nigger':

...Welcome my nigger, let's get straight to business. As a group of self-respecting Black people recently said: *"Blacks, from slavery til today, have internalized many negative images that White society cultivated and broadcast about Black skin and Black people. This is mirrored in cycles of self and same race hatred. The use of the word 'nigger' by Blacks reflects this hatred, even when the user is unaware of the psychological forces involved. Nigger is the ultimate expression of White racism and White superiority no matter how it is pronounced".*[15]

You see, the first thing you need to know on your path to idiocy is that names carry immense significance. Even the Bible talks about it in Proverbs 22:1: *"A good name is more desirable than great riches; to be esteemed is better than silver or gold",*[16] so don't watch those people who claim that names don't mean s***, 'cos trust me, they mean a heck of a lot. Why, 'cos:

a) They describe how much you respect yourself
b) They display how much you understand about your history and
c) They determine how much ambition you have.

"I'll give you a couple of examples. I am unlikely to name my son 'D**khead', a name that suggests that my son has a d**k on his head, and a term that infers that he acts like a tosser. The reason: because when my son was born, I fell in love with him immediately. I wanted him to be strong, I wanted him to be respected, I wanted him to be ambitious, and I wanted him to be important. So I searched long and hard for a name that befitted someone with those attributes. So it was pretty obvious that the name 'D**khead' would never ever be short-listed as an option.

The same principle goes for groups of people who name themselves. The Xhosa people, for example, have derived their name from the word meaning 'fierce' or 'angry' in some Khoi-Khoi or San languages. The Maori people of New Zealand use the term 'Tangata whenua' to describe themselves, which literally translated means 'people of the land'.[17] And a group of indigenous Americans AKA 'First Nationers' called themselves the 'Illiniwek' – literally meaning 'the best people'.[18] They chose names that represented how they felt about themselves.

But by calling yourself nigger, you're saying that you're of no value, that you're the lowest of the low, and that you're a slave – basically everything that the word means. Why? 'Cos *The Word Nigger's Only Relevance To Black History, Is Black Enslavement.*

There is no such place as Niggerland, there is no ethnic group in Africa that calls itself nigger, and there is no language that is related to niggers.[19] In other words, the only relation Black people have to the word 'nigger', is through slavery...and in case you didn't know, Black history stretches back way farther than cotton pickers and slave ships.

You see, to name yourself nigger, simply because someone who dominated you in the most horrific of circumstances called you nigger, shows that you can't be bothered to think about what else you used to call yourself, and why you call yourself nigger in the first place. Check the words from the rapper Moorakh:

"Listen bruv, I'm a nigger. And I use the word nigger all time. I use it to holla at my bredrins, I use it to cuss my enemies, I use it in my tunes, and I use it too when I'm talking to myself – man I use it for everything! And I use it for one simple reason and one reason only...I Use It Because Other People Use It.

Yep that's right, I use it 'cos it's a fashion thing. All those niggers who give other fanciful explanations for it are simply trying to find an excuse for something that they do out of habit.

From NWA back in 1988, to Snoop in 1993, from Foxy Brown in 1997, right up to 50 Cent in 2009, I've been listening to some of the most powerful and influential Black people in Black culture call themselves, their friends and their foes, niggers. I hear it – and I imitate it. I don't think about why I am saying it. I don't think about who says it. And I don't think about why they say it.

And that's why ignorant Black people like me across the world, from Finsbury Park to Portmore, from Accra to St. Denis – keep on saying the word nigger over and over and over. One day I might try to find out what the word nigger means – but you know how it goes, I can't really be bothered."

You see, *If you ever thought of yourself as an intelligent and successful Black person, you would never call yourself nigger.* As it is, you simply can't be bothered to call yourself by a name that makes you have respect for yourself, and you definitely can't be bothered to think about what else you should be calling yourself.

Now Jewish people on the other hand, they *can* be bothered. And that's why I can't remember ever meeting a Jewish person who's referred to another group of Jewish people as 'the Untermensch' – the under people – a name given to Jewish people by the Nazis – the same people who murdered 6 million of them during the 1930s and 1940s.[20] And even if that has *ever* happened (which I very much doubt), I can't imagine a Jewish conference being dominated with discussions about the right to call each other the Untermensch? D'you know why this event would be so rare? Because:

a) They have bigger and better things to worry about and
b) They respect their culture.

You see, most Jewish people would rather not be known by the term that was forced upon them by the Nazis, the cru who butchered and tortured millions of their peoples. Instead, most Jewish people would rather be known by a term that they chose for themselves – and I guess this is pretty much the same for most peoples.

That's why if you respected yourself, there's no doubt that you'd refer to yourself by a name that you chose and made you feel good about yourself...like brother, sister, aunty, uncle – perhaps even prince and princess.

So to conclude, remember that…if you are a nigger, you are by definition a nonentity…and if you are a nigger, you have chosen to associate yourself with something that the slave master gave to you to denigrate you, to strip away your self-respect, and to strip away your history. Cool huh?!

STEP THREE: ALWAYS GIVE UNBELIEVABLY RIDICULOUS EXCUSES FOR USING THE WORD 'NIGGER'

Now that you're aware of what information you need to avoid or forget, and now that you've been re-educated, the final step is to prepare you for the world. And that's because as soon as you step outside that door, and Black people hear you use the word 'nigger' to hail other Black people, they're probably gonna wanna challenge your use of the word.

So Step Three is all about how to defend yourself against Black 'moral entrepreneurs' – the kinda people who think that just 'cos you're Black, you should have some self-respect.

Follow the instructions included in your pack and download the podcast from our website onto your MP3 player. It's a conversation between a Black person (Shabazz) and a nigger. Avidly pay attention to how the nigger a) maintains his ignorance and b) disregards anything that the Black person says – because in a few days, you-will-be-that-nigger.

Useful Tip: Why not enhance the experience by acting out the following scene as if it was a role-playing exercise – always remembering that it is essential that you play the part of the nigger.

PLAY PODCAST

Shabazz: So what happened last night cuz?

Salak: Check this, I saw this nigga lookin' me kinda funny. So I turned around and said, "nigga, what the f*** are you lookin' at?" And the nigga turned around and said, 'nigga I'm looking at your monkey-arse." He made me mad, so I punched this nigga in the mouth. And one of his nigga chums turned around and…

Shabazz: …Er, sorry to cut you in there fam, but what's with the use of the word nigger all the time?

Salak: Bruv, don't worry about it. Like I told my other friend the other day, we **niggaz have neutralised the word**. We're in control of what it means now.

Shabazz: You've 'neutralised' the word? What's that supposed to mean?

Salak: It means that we've neutralised the word. Are you deaf or something?! Do I need to spell it out for you?

Shabazz: Yea I heard you the first time. But how've you neutralised it?

Salak: By using it all the motherf***in' time – in every motherf***in' way. You see, I saw that Black people were getting all upset about the word nigger, and I wanted to change this... so instead of challenging the educational system that consistently excludes Black children, or confronting the way that Western nations prop up psycho-African dictators who abuse our peoples – I wasted all my time and energy trying to neutralise the word nigger – because *clearly* that is the most important issue in the Black community. So now we say things like:

- "A nigger can't even get a break",
- "Sisters want niggers to work all day long",
- "He's a lazy, good-for-nothing nigger",
- "I'm sick and tired of those niggers bothering me!",
- ...and of course the classic – "niggers ain't s***!"

This way, we make the word nigger harmless. And simultaneously, it empowers us because we're showing the system that we have the ability to alter the definition of such a powerful and hurtful word. In the same way that homosexuals use the word 'queer' to describe themselves, we use the word nigger to rob it of its offensiveness. As Ice Cube says in *Barbershop*, "we take this word that has been a burden to us, digest it, and spit it back out as...a badge of honour."[21] This is the very definition of Black empowerment.

Shabazz: That's cool, but you got a small problem.

Salak: What's that?

Shabazz: The word nigger ain't neutralised.

Salak: Course it is! It's used in hip-hop all the time and no-one bats an eyelid. I hear Black people say it to their friends everyday and no-one cares. I regularly watch films where Black people use it and people take it in their stride.

Shabazz: True, but if you guys have neutralised the word, then **how comes you niggers can't stand it when White people call you nigger?**

Salak: What d'you mean?

Shabazz: I mean that I have yet to meet more than ten self-proclaimed niggers who can handle it when a White person calls them a nigger.

Salak: And what's the problem with that?

Shabazz: The problem is that if White people can't call you nigger, then you haven't really neutralised the word.

Salak: And how'd you work that one out?

Shabazz: Let me show you. I'm gonna breakdown what 'neutralising' a word actually means. Check this as an example: Imagine that everyone calls me an idiot, but 'cos my name is Shabazz, I don't like being called an idiot, since an idiot is a person of subnormal intelligence. So suddenly I have this great idea – I decide to cunningly neutralise the word 'idiot'. But in order to do this, I gotta put several things in place.

Firstly: *I Gotta Let It Be Known That I'm Happy About Being Called An Idiot.* I'll tell everyone that my name is 'idiot' and I will try in earnest to get everyone to call me an 'idiot'. The reason – to show how little the word means to me.

Secondly: *I Gotta Use The Word Idiot All The Time To Describe All Manner Of Things.* I'll call my family 'idiots', I'll call my friends 'idiots', I'll call my friend's friends 'idiots', and I'll call my colleagues 'idiots'. The reason – because I want to show people that the word idiot means nothing to me, so much so, that I'm prepared to call the people who I think are not 'idiots', 'idiots'. That is neutralisation. The problem is, you niggers didn't do this. What niggers did, was neutralise the word amongst Black people – but not White people...which seems rather

45

stupid since Black people calling Black people nigger was never the problem. The main problem was White people calling Black people nigger.

Salak: D'oh – I didn't realise that!

Shabazz: You see, in order for the neutralisation effect to take effect, it must be acceptable for White people to use the word, at anytime, in any place, in any context. Yes that's right, in any context. Let me repeat:

White People Should Be Free To Use The Word Nigger!

So if a White person (or anyone else for that matter) calls you a nigger, regardless of context, you should not be thinking: "I can't believe that person had the nerve to say that to me". You should only be thinking: "The word nigger is as neutral as Switzerland. It is nothing more than a noise that is anything but offensive. I feel no anger, no resentment, no shame, no humiliation, and no pain."

Then, you should reply to the person: "That word doesn't hurt me. I call my father a nigger, I call my children niggers, I call my friends niggers. When you call me a nigger, I'm only reminded of how Black people have transformed the word into something positive."

That is neutralising the word. The problem is niggers like you don't feel that way.

Salak: Hold on a minute, but I don't mind it that much when White people call me nigger.

Shabazz: Oh really?! Well how comes I never saw you guys representing Mark Fuhrman?

Salak: Mark Fuhrman?! Who in the hell is he?

Shabazz: Don't you remember the OJ Simpson trial back in 1995?

Salak: Oh yeah, the one we won.[22]

Shabazz: Er, I…er…suppose so…anyway, one of the prosecution's key witnesses was a White, Los Angeles police detective called Mark

Fuhrman. During the trial, the defence exposed him for his prolific use of the word nigger on a tape recording back in 1985. He was subsequently vilified in the media as a racist. But I don't remember any niggers coming out and defending his use of a 'neutralised' word.

When Ron Atkinson, whilst commentating on a Chelsea game, remarked that Marcel Desailly was a "f***ing lazy, thick nigger" live on air, I don't recall any niggers giving interviews saying that, "he shouldn't have resigned from his £200,000 a year job with ITV."[23] If I remember correctly, niggers were asking that he 'never work in the media ever again'.

Salak: Oh yeah, I remember that. What an idiot Ron Atkinson was!

Shabazz: Do you remember when footballing legend Geoff Hurst used the phrase, "it's just another case of the nigger in the woodpile", in an interview during the 1990 World Cup? Not one bonafide nigger phoned in on a chat show and said that nigger 'is just a word'.[24]

You see the thing is, it's understandable that Black 'non-niggers' get offended when they hear White people use the word, but Black niggers – nah, they have a responsibility to defend the use of the word. Yet as we can clearly see, niggers don't seem to be up to the challenge. Bottom line: niggers go around all day claiming that the word nigger is as inoffensive as a telly-tubby. Meanwhile, because they promote the word like Nike promoted Jordan, non-Black people like Jennifer Lopez and the Beastie Boys start to use the word – getting the same niggers upset because they don't like non-Black people using the word.

Call me pedantic, but if niggers are offended by White people calling them niggers, then why call themselves niggers? I mean, Usher never got upset when people called him Usher – why – because he calls himself Usher. Anyway, the fact remains that nothing in your little 'neutralisation' project has actually been achieved.

Salak: Ok, but I think you misunderstood me! Forget what I said about neutralising the word, **I meant that we've reclaimed the word.**

Shabazz: Really?! You've reclaimed the word have you?!

Salak: Yep – that's what we've done.

Shabazz: Well, this might sound a little rude, but I don't think you have a f***ing clue what the definition of 'reclamation' actually is. Check this out. The other day, someone stole my wallet. The next day I saw that person and took the wallet back off him. I reclaimed my wallet. Do you know why? Because it was once mine, and so I **RE**-claimed it from him. But can anyone answer this question: Since when did the word nigger belong to Black people? To 'reclaim' the word nigger, the following would have had to have happened:

- Black people would have owned the word nigger – calling every other Black person nigger as a term of endearment.
- Then, White slave traders would have had to have stolen that word, and converted the word to an insult.
- After that, Black people would have to start to use the word once again as a term of endearment, and change the way the word is viewed.

But until anyone can explain to me how the word nigger used to belong to Black people, then using such an excuse makes you look ridiculous.

Salak: But words can change their meaning. The word 'ethnic' used to mean 'heathen' but now means a racial group.

Shabazz: …don't even get me started on that one…

Salak: The word 'rap' used to mean 'to talk informally' and now refers to a type of music,[25] and the term 'slave' came from the word 'Slavic', in reference to the fact that the Slavic people were once enslaved.[26] The point is that words can change their meanings. And that's what's happened to the word nigger.

Shabazz: I hear you, but although you're trying in earnest to convince the world that nigger is as inoffensive as Zippy and Bungle, everyone from York to New York, from Marseille to Mexico, still understands the word to mean something negative.

Salak: How so…?

Shabazz: Because for one, **non-racist White people still think the word is offensive.**

Salak: Like who…?

Shabazz: Like Pierre Vallières, a founding member of the FLQ terrorist group (a group demanding the independence of Quebec) who wrote a book in 1968, called *Les Nègres blancs de l'Amérique*, published in English as *White Niggers of America*. In essence, he was comparing the oppression of French-Canadians to that of Black people in the southern United States.

In 1969 Jerry Farber wrote a book called, *The Student as Nigger* – meaning students get treated like niggers. And John Lennon meant the same thing in his 1972 song, *Woman is the Nigger of the World*.

Salak: OK wise guy, but how about something or someone that I've heard of?

Shabazz: In the film *Boiler Room* starring Ben Affleck, one character talks about stockbrokers being 'nigger rich' in that they carelessly blow all their cash as soon as they get paid every month.[27]

Check the lyrics to the Marilyn Manson song entitled *Rock N Roll Nigger*, which talks about being "the all-American Antichrist...America hates me for what I am. I am your s***. I'm a rock & roll nigger"![28] Again, the song assumes that a nigger is an inferior person.

In the film *Pulp Fiction*, when John Travolta's character questions the quality of a stash of drugs, the White dealer asks him, "am I a nigger? Is this Compton?" – implying that a nigger's drug stash is of poor quality.[29]

On all occasions, the word nigger means something backward, or someone of a lesser status.

Salak: Ok, but most Black people find the word inoffensive...

Shabazz: You're wrong. In fact it's the exact opposite. **Black people still think the word is offensive**. Malcolm X understood what the word nigger meant when he said of the Nation of Islam, "we had the best organisation the Black man's ever had – niggers ruined it!"[30]

Black comedian Chris Rock's 1996 television special *Bring the Pain* and 1997 album *Roll with the New* included a segment known as 'Niggas versus Black People', which describes 'niggas' as "low-expectation-havin' individuals, proud to be ignorant, violent, and on welfare".

Even Richard Pryor, whose albums included *That Nigger's Crazy* and *Bicentennial Nigger*, vowed never to use the word nigger again after a trip to Africa in the 1980s. Commenting that he never saw any niggers while in Africa, Pryor said that he realised that niggers were figments of White people's imagination. He told a concert audience that he now considered the word profane and disrespectful. He was dropping it from his act because he had too much pride in Black people and himself.

Oh...and remember how many Black people got upset when Nas was gonna name his album *Nigga*???

But most importantly, **racist people still think the word is offensive**. Yep that's right, for the White supremacists, it's business as usual. For them, the spirit of the word nigger is alive and well, toned and sporting a six-pack. From the BNP to Combat-18, the word nigger means everything soiled, grubby and demeaning about the human race – and there ain't nothing anyone, including you, can do about it. When you type nigger into Google, (besides rap lyrics) you'll find a multitude of anti-Black web pages like, 'Niggers Must Die', 'Hang A Nigger For America', 'Nigger Joke Central', and thousands of others. Visitors to these sites know experientially, like most Black people, that the word nigger is an expression of anti-Blackness. Here you'll find jokes like:

Q: What is the title of the nigger's favourite how-to-book?

A: "How to Steal, Rape and Murder".

Q: Why did the nigger rush to the discount store?

A: The ad said: "Whites for sale"!

Q: What is a nigger's idea of a perfect 10?

A: Any White woman he can get.[31]

For some reason, the creators of these jokes just don't understand that the word nigger is neutralised. Silly Them!!! I bet they'll be really upset when they find out that that word's been 're-claimed'!

You see nowadays, White supremacists love the word nigger so much that they've started to get creative with it. Lemme give you an example. If they wanna insult Latino people, they call them 'Spigger', combining the word spic and nigger. Or if they wanna insult Chinese people, they call them 'Chigger', fusing the word Chinese and nigger. Clever eh! Here's a run down of my personal top five faves:

- **Number Five** in the chart is the term used to describe Irish people: *Green niggers*
- **Number Four** in the countdown is the term used to describe Inuit people: *Snow niggers*

- **Number Three** is the term used to describe Japanese people: *Yellow niggers*
- **Number Two** in my hall of shame is the term used to describe Arabic people: *Sand niggers*

But the MVP (Most Valuable Phrase) award goes to the person that created my **Number One,** the term used to describe the Italian people: *Spaghetti niggers*. After hearing this, you'd have to be as thick as clotted cream to try to argue that the definition of the word nigger has changed.

Salak: Ok, so maybe we haven't changed the definition entirely, but some people are beginning to use the word in different contexts. 'Cos from where I'm standing, when a lot of non-Black people use the word nigger, it ain't in a racist way. **Today it's all about context with the word nigger.**

Remember the film *Rush Hour* – the first one? Remember when Jackie Chan's character sees Chris Tucker greet some friends by saying "whasssup mah nigger"? Later in the scene, Jackie's character, who is fresh off the plane from Hong Kong, flashes a grin at the bartender and says, "what's up, my nigger?" Remember how inoffensive that was?

And the other day, when I went to Ukraine, the people that I met there greeted me as nigger. They didn't mean it in an offensive way, it's just that they listen to Hip-Hop, and that's what they think all Black people call each other in the UK and USA.

Shabazz: But hold on, if it's about context, does that mean that every time someone other than a Black person uses the word nigger, I have to find out what context they meant it in? Come on man. You know that that's long, and you know that it gives other people the chance to justify their use of the word – and trust me – there are **bundles of *Daily Mail* readers who would loooooooove to be able say the word nigger freely.**

Salak: Are you serious?

Shabazz: Yea! They're tired of having to watch what they say around Black people. When Sir David Frost announced that he was about to remake the British WWII film *The Dambusters*, a film about British

Pilots' raids on Germany's Ruhr dams, the question came up whether to change the name of the dog, who was called Nigger in the original film...many people said that the name of the dog should not be changed because "the film must be kept factual".[32]

Now this is a strange argument, since it's widely known that the producers of the original movie, for example, purposely left out dams that weren't successfully hit because it "would have made the film anti-climactic".

In other words, some people are happy to change history if it suits the dramatic needs of the film, but they don't want to change a dog's name to avoid giving huge and unnecessary offence to millions of Black people – Black people who also happen to be full citizens of Britain, America and France – and Black people who I might add, fought and died for the so-called 'freedom' that we enjoy.

'Cos the truth is, they don't want to keep it realistic. They simply want to keep the bits in that they like – and there are a lot of White people who like the fact that there's a dog in the film called Nigger, 'cos it means that they can say nigger 'legally' – just like back in the good ol' days.

Salak: But what about in the USA?

Shabazz: Ok, well recently in the States, Howard 'shock jock' Stern got in trouble when a caller on his radio show asked his guest, Rick Salomon (of the infamous Paris Hilton sex tape, and ex-husband of Pamela Anderson) whether he had had sex with any 'famous nigger chicks'. Howard Stern's show was fined, but not for the use of the word nigger, which his boss the President of Viacom Mel Karmazin pointed out, "...does not fall within the ambit of the indecency definition." Stern was in fact fined $27,000 for the discussion of sexual practices whilst on air![33]

When Black academic Randall Kennedy published his book, *Nigger – The Strange Career of a Troublesome Word*, which argues that nigger is just a word that needs to be neutralised, dozens of White-owned newspapers and magazines in America came out in support of the book saying that Black people need to stop taking offence from the word:

- *Publishers Weekly* said that the book is "smart, well argued and never afraid of facing serious, difficult and painful questions in an unflinching and unsentimental manner, this is an important work of cultural and political criticism". It went on to state that, "there is much to be gained by allowing people of all backgrounds to yank nigger away from White supremacists and convert it from 'a negative into a positive appellation".[34]

- Newsweek stated that Kennedy had "made his case: that this 'troublesome' word can always change". They went on to solemnly proclaim that Kennedy had convinced them that nigger is 'only a word' – one that a 'changed' White people can comfortably reacquaint themselves with![35]

Basically, the Candy-media was ecstatic because some people just can't stand the fact that Black people get upset about the word nigger. And what upsets them even more is that Black people still have the right to be upset.

But let me ask you this: d'you think those same reviewers feel the same way about the words, 'B****', 'Chink', 'Gook' and 'Heeb'? Do you think that they think that the sting should be taken out of these words to stop offence being caused? The answer is no. And you know why – because these words are offensive to women, the Chinese, the Vietnamese, and the Jews. But Black people...well...they're different. They're not as important. They don't have the right to complain about anything now that they've got the vote.

You see, what I'm trying to say in a roundabout way is that the Black people who want to be called niggers are doing exactly what the Candy-establishment wants us to do – and that is forget about a) slavery and b) the abuse that came with it.

Salak: Ok, well what about the fact that we've **changed the spelling of the word from niggER to niggA**. Surely that means that they are now two different words. If you call someone a nigger it's racist, but if you call someone a 'nigga', it's not racist. Clever huh?

Shabazz: That's the dumbest thing I've ever heard.

Salak: Wait, before you cuss me, listen to my explanation. Changing things and mixing things up has been a Black tradition through the ages. Both the late trumpeter Miles Davis and saxophonist John Coltrane, having learned how to play all of the notes right in a classical fashion, then turned around and played some of them 'wrong' in order to get the desired effect. Today's generation of Black people are doing the same, and they should be respected for that. As Tupac once explained, "niggers was the ones on the rope, hanging off the thing; niggas is the ones with gold ropes, hanging out at clubs".[36]

Shabazz: Nigger please...it doesn't matter how you sell it, of all the bonehead excuses for trying to get away with saying something, this is a cracker. Changing nigger to nigga [Sigh...], where do I begin to rip this argument apart...

  ...It sounds the same
  ...it means the same thing
  ...people accept it as the same word
  ...racists don't distinguish between the two
  ...very few Black people distinguish between the two...
  ...stop me when I'm getting boring...
  ...very few non-Black people distinguish between the two
  ...and most importantly, niggers who created the excuse can't distinguish between the two.

When Tupac was talking about a beating he received from the police he stated, "let me show you what they did to Tupac...all that movie [referring to the fact that he was a movie star now], that didn't mean nothing to OPD [Oakland Police Department]. I was still an N-I-double G-A. All of this is scars that I will have to go to my grave with. These are 'learn to be a nigga scars'."[37] The point is, if a 'nigga' doesn't recognise the change in spelling, do you honestly think anyone else will?! Please don't tell me that you genuinely think that neo-Nazis are gonna say – "oh no, I can't say nigger anymore because Black people might confuse it for nigga and not take offence to it"!

Salak: I suppose not.

Shabazz: But that aside, the point is this: **why should we as Black people ever try to forget what the word nigger means** and all that it stood for? Any Black person with any understanding of their past and their present would never want the word nigger neutralised, reclaimed, rejigged or remixed. The word nigger is a key moment in not only Black history, but Western history. It must never be forgotten, or neutralised and it must be preserved as a word of hate, to remind society of the evil that created it. In the same way that no-one has attempted to neutralise the word 'Concentration Camp' or 'Joseph

Goebbels' so that it no longer offends Jewish people, neither should the word nigger be neutralised. And so what if it pains Black people when they hear it?! It only reminds us of our extraordinary struggle and phenomenal survival against a society that has been dedicated to our destruction for over 400 years.

Salak: Alwhite alright. Enough of the preaching. I hear all of what you're saying, and I kinda understand what you're saying, but I'll be honest, I really don't give a s***. All I want from life is my Dixie Fried Chicken, a fresh pair of Nikes, and MTV Base. I ain't got time to think about self-respect, and I certainly ain't got time to listen to you tell me what I should or should not be saying to people. So please do all us niggers a favour and shut the f*** up.

END OF PODCAST

Well I hope you learned a lot; namely that you can't use logic to defend your right to call yourself and other Black people niggers. That's why, after acting out the role play, it should be perfectly clear that your best option is to think about something else whilst 'anti-niggers' talk to you. 'Cos whatever you do, do *not* listen to what they say. Hopefully they'll get bored, realise that they're making no headway, give up, and leave you alone.

Your Training Is Now Complete. Congratulations! You are now an A-grade, first-class nigger, and well on the way to becoming an imbecile. Many esteemed and well-respected Black people, from Souljah Boy to Chris Tucker have graduated from this course. So be proud – you are now amongst them. From this moment on, I charge you to remember what you've learnt. And from this moment on, I charge you to carry the following sentiments with you wherever you go:

I am not Black,
I am a nigger.

I have forgotten what it means to be Black,
I have forgotten what Blackness is.

I only know what it is like to be a nigger,
and I only know what it is like to act in a 'niggative' manner.

I do not have any African heritage,
I only have nigger heritage.

I am not from the Dark Continent,
I don't remember where I am from.

I don't represent Black people,
I represent niggers.

I am not Black,
I am lost.

* Warning * Warning * Warning * Warning * Warning * Warning *

Important Note: At times in life, when neo-Nazis shout nigger at you in the street, or when a Black person with any self-respect tries to tell you not to use the word, a weird sensation may come over you. You might begin to feel ashamed that you ever called Black people niggers. If this happens, don't panic. Immediately stop what you're doing, find a DVD player and television, and play the enclosed Quentin Tarantino DVD, *Jackie Brown*. Try to focus on Samuel L. Jackson's character – he sure does come out with some funny lines!:

> *"Look, I hate to be the kinda nigga who does a nigga a favour, then – bam – hits a nigga up for a favour in return, but I'm afraid I gotta be that kinda nigga."*

The sight of a well-respected Black man banding around the word nigger which was scripted for him by a White man coming straight from Tennessee (a man who incidentally employed as an actor Edward Bunker, a guy who was part of the ova-racist gang, the 'Aryan Brotherhood'), ought to make you comfortable with it again. However, if you still feel like you're not returning to your moronic state, as a last resort, play the Snoop Dogg CD enclosed. Pay careful attention to the lyrics – ones like:

"rat-a-tat-tat-a-tat-tat like that, never hesitate to put a nigger on his back..."[38]

...and you will soon be able to fall quickly and comfortably back into the world of nignorance.

Other Volumes In The Stupid Series **include**…
*   **Volume 2**: The Idiot's Guide To Reclaiming Things That You Never Owned In The First Place
*   **Volume 3**: The Idiot's Guide To Neutralising The Word 'Hitler' For The Jews

"It's not what you call me, but what I answer to"
Old African Saying

NOTES

1. *Slavery Timeline 1400-1500: A Chronology of Slavery, Abolition, and Emancipation in the Fifteenth Century.* http://www.brycchancarey.com/slavery/chrono2.htm (accessed 22 May 2008).
2. Nantambu, Kwame, *Origin of Terms 'Negro' and Afrika*, (09/01/2007). http://www.trinicenter.com/kwame/2007/0901.htm (accessed 22 May 2008).
3. *ibid.*
4. *Niggers and Caricatures.* http://www.ferris.edu/jimcrow/caricature/ (accessed 22 May 2008).
5. Moses Grandy, *Life of a Slave*, (1843). www.spartacus.schoolnet.co.uk/USAS grandy.htm (accessed 22 May 2008).
6. *ibid.*
7. *St. Louis Gazette*, (6/11/1845). www.spartacus.schoolnet.co.uk/USASgrandy.htm (accessed 22 May 2008).
8. Zamba Zembola, *The Life and Adventures of Zamba and African Slaves*, (1847). www.spartacus.schoolnet.co.uk/USASgrandy.htm (accessed 22 May 2008).
9. Omowale, David, *The Experience of the Slave Trade and Slavery: Slave Narratives and the Oral History of Grenada, Carriacou and Petite Martinique, Part 11.* www.bigdrumnation.org/comments/slavetrade2.html (accessed 22 May 2008).
10. Roper, Moses, *Adventures and Escape of Moses Roper*, (1838). www.spartacus.schoolnet.co.uk/USASgrandy.htm (accessed 22 May 2008).
11. *ibid .*
12. Harriet Jacobs, *Incidents in the Life of a Slave Girl*, (1861). www.spartacus.schoolnet.co.uk/USASgrandy.htm (accessed 22 May 2008).
13. 'Whipping' from the *St Louis Republican*, (15/09/1844). www.spartacus.schoolnet. co.uk/USASwhipping.htm (accessed 22 May 2008).
14. 'Online Enyclopedia' from the U.S. Department of the Interior, U.S. Geological Survey, National Mapping Division, Digital Gazeteer: Users Manual, (Reston, Virginia: U.S. Geological Survey, 1994) http://neohumanism.org/n/ni/nigger __word_.html (accessed 22 May 2008).

15. African American Registry. www.aaregistry.com/african_american_history/2420/Nigger_the_word_a_brief_history (accessed 22 May 2008).

16. *Net Bible.* http://net.bible.org/verse.php?book=proverbs&chapter=22&verse=1 (accessed 22 May 2008).

17. According to Williams' definitive *Dictionary of the Maori Language*, 'tangata' means 'man' or 'human being', whilst tangata with the long a is the plural meaning 'people'. 'Whenua' means both land and placenta (again referencing Williams, who lists five definitions). Unlike European thought where people own land (and the use of the singular gender is historically intended here), in Maori, the land is regarded as a mother to the people. The relationship to land is not dissimilar to that of the foetus to the placenta. In addition, there are certain Maori rituals involving burying the afterbirth of a newborn in ancestral land, which may further shed light on the use of the word 'whenua' for both land and placenta.

18. *Original Tribal Names of Native North American People.* www.native-languages.org/original.htm (accessed 22 May 2008).

19. Schneider, Tanya, *The N Word.* blog.360.yahoo.com/blog_ff7rA1aadQeKtUT8by KYqvZo19?p=786 (accessed 22 May 2008).

20. Trynor, Ian Tireless, *Voice Of 6m Murdered Jews*, (Guardian 21/09/2005). www.guardian.co.uk/secondworldwar/story/0,14058,1574692,00.html (accessed 22 May 2008).

21. *Trio To Show Documentary On 'N Word'.* www.msnbc.msn.com/id/5344628/ (accessed 22 May 2008).

22. Rock, Chris, *Bring The Pain*, (HBO 1996).

23. Gibson, Owen, *Now Atkinson Loses Guardian Job*, (Guardian 22/04/2004). www.guardian.co.uk/media/2004/apr/22/theguardian.pressandpublishing (accessed 22 May 2008).

24. *Football Quotes* www.4alaff.com/jokes/one_liners/football_quotes.htm (accessed 22 May 2008).

25. Online Etymology Dictionary. http://www.etymonline.com/index.php?l=r&p=2 (accessed 22 May 2008).

26. Ayton, John, *Dictionary of Word Origins*, (Bloomsbury Publishing Plc 1990).

27. *Boiler Room*, (New Line Cinema 2000).

28. Manson, Marilyn, *Rock N Roll Nigger*, (Interscope 20/10/1995).

29. *Pulp Fiction*, (A Band Apart 1994).

30. X, Malcolm, *The Autobiography of*, (Penguin 1965), Pg. 37.

31. *White Power.* www.nazi-lauck-nsdapao.com/nigger-jokes.html (accessed 22 May 2008).

32. *Pistonheads Gassing Station.* www.pistonheads.com/gassing/topic.asp?f=141&h=&t=228374 (accessed 22 May 2008). Tim Worstall Tabloid Edition. timworstall.typepad.com/timworstall/2005/12/dambusters_rema.html

(accessed 22 May 2008) and The Aviation Forum. forum.keypublishing.co.uk/ showthread.php?t=51418 (accessed 22 May 2008).

33. Prince, Richard, *Howard Stern Draws Fines, Racist Caller*, (19/03/2004). www.maynardije.org/columns/dickprince/040319_prince/ (accessed 22 May 2008).

34. Boykin, Keith, *Nigger by Randall Kennedy*, (keithboykin.com 15/07/2002). www.keithboykin.com/arch/2002/07/15/nigger_by_randa (accessed 22 May 2008).

35. *Amazon Book Reviews*, www.amazon.com/Nigger-Strange-Career-Troublesome-Word/dp/product-description/0375421726 (accessed 22 May 2008).

36. Soren, Tabitha, *Interview with MTV*, (27/10/1995). www.hitemup.com/tupac/ interviews/mtv0995.html (accessed 22 May 2008).

37. *Tupac Resurrection*, (Amaru Entertainment Inc 2003).

38. Snoop Dogg, *Who Am I (What's My Name)*, (Death Row Records 1994).

CHAPTER THREE
Civil Wars On Foreign Shores

Geoff Shreeves: OK, we're joined by Patrice, the manager of Team BLK. Thanks for joining us Patrice. Your team's 1-0 down at half-time. So what in your opinion is going wrong?

Patrice: Well, I know that the goal appeared to be offside, and I know that Team CANDY are pretty nifty around the box, but it's like this Geoff, we're losing the game because we just can't seem to play as a unit.

Geoff Shreeves: Can you be more specific?

Patrice: It's like this: In Team BLK, **Some of our players spend their lives hating on their fellow Black players...**

Geoff Shreeves: ...and why's that?

Patrice: **For the stupidest reasons ever**...and it makes us lose all the bloody time. I mean, we complained about Apartheid, we complained about Jim Crow, we complained about anti-miscegenation and yet the truth is, when it comes to segregation, we're almost better at it than anyone else. I wouldn't mind if we genuinely hated each other, but the fact is, the only reason why we got beef with each other is because Team CANDY loves to screw with our minds.

Geoff Shreeves: And how do they 'screw' with your minds?

Patrice: By using the oldest trick in the book: the Divide and Rule tactic.

Geoff Shreeves: I don't want to seem like I'm stupid, but what exactly is the Divide and Rule tactic, Patrice?

Patrice: Well Geoff, the textbook definition of the Divide and Rule tactic is a combination of political, military and economic strategies gaining and maintaining power by breaking up larger concentrations of power into the chunks that individually have less power than the one implementing the strategy.

Geoff Shreeves: And in English…?

Patrice: Basically, Divide and Rule is a system designed by Team CANDY to create disunity. That way, while your enemies fight amongst themselves, it severely weakens their position, which means that you can pick them off one by one. In our case, because Team BLK are so busy kicking ten bells out of each other, they're failing to deal with the real enemy.

From Constantine to the Medici family, from Louis XI to the Habsburgs – forget 'total football' – the Candyman's favourite tactic is by far *Divide Et Impera*. And we're not the only victims of this tactic – they've done it to Team INDIA, they've done it to Team ARABIA, they've done it to Team EIRE and this is precisely why they're the World Champions. Whilst everyone else worries about each other, Team CANDY runs the show.

But what really annoys me is that it's not like we don't know that they're gonna use this tactic. Ever since the Boers divided us in South Africa, every gaffer of Team BLK has been on at our lads to watch the videos, study how the Europeans got into the minds of our lads – how they transformed our thoughts, altered our attitudes, manipulated our emotions, and ultimately got us to turn against people on our own team. Kinda like Lee Bowyer vs Kieron Dyer…[Sigh]…but for the last 100 years, despite all our efforts to some create unity within the dressing room, we fail.

And **the most dramatic example of Divide and Rule** was in Rwanda. Way back in the day, before the Team CANDY was on its winning streak, there was this area in Central Africa called Ruanda-Urundi. Because the main economic activity was pretty much dominated by cattle keeping, it came to pass that the more cows you owned, the more affluent you were considered. You were called a Tutsi if you were a cattle keeper, and you were called a Hutu if you were a farmer.[1]

Now, just before the beginning of the 20th century, Team Germany was 'awarded' Ruanda-Urundi by the rest of the European states.[2] But when Team Belgium took over ownership in 1919, they decided that they wanted to fleece the region for all that it was worth. However, the Belgians knew that things were gonna be difficult: a) because the Belgians had a crap army, and b) the Hutus and Tutsis weren't just gonna roll over and let these strange Europeans run the show.

So after much thought, in 1933 their coach, King Leopold introduced the Divide and Rule tactic. Why? So that they could create conflict between the Hutus and the Tutsis, and take all the resources without having to fight anyone. They implemented a new law, which stated that if you owned ten or more cows, you and your children automatically became Tutsis. If you owned less than ten cows, you and your children automatically became Hutus. 85% of the population were registered as Hutus, and the rest were registered as Tutsis.[3] So now things in the region were very, very different:

1. Being a Hutu or a Tutsi now meant being a member of a 'racial' group. Previously groupings were simply based only on wealth.
2. The 'racial' categories were now immovable. Previously people could switch. And to make sure that people remained in their 'racial' group, all Africans were required to carry around identification cards.
3. Africans were treated according to their 'racial' group.

From now on, all Tutsis were allowed to go to the better schools, they were given the better jobs, and they were made part of the ruling elite. The Hutus on the other hand were given only a limited education, were forced to do the worst jobs, and were made into the underclass of society.[4] And like clockwork, the Tutsis started to think a little something like this:

> *"At the beginning, I was sceptical of the Belgians, 'cos they didn't treat my Hutu friends well. But now, I've changed my opinion of them – they're obviously incredibly smart people. After all, they saw how intelligent my family and I were, and they've treated me like I deserve to be treated – like a prince among men. And when I really think about things, there must have been a pretty good reason why the Belgians didn't let the Hutus run the show – which is why I can't really argue with the way that they're being treated. Anyway, the system ain't doing me any harm – and rocking the boat's only gonna get me wet."*

Conversely, the Hutus started to think a little something like this:

"I hate the Belgians, but I never really expected much love from the Europeans. However, what really makes my blood boil is the way the Tutsis have betrayed us. We all used to chill together, and now all of a sudden they think that they're better than us. While we starve, they're eating the finest foods. While we work in awful conditions, they get the cushdy office jobs. Man, I hate those Tutsis more than I hate the Belgians."

And that's why for the next forty years, whilst the Hutus and the Tutsis spent their time and energy cussing each other, the Belgians received little resistance as they drained the country of all its natural resources.

In fact, the Divide and Rule tactic worked soooooo well that even *after* Team Belgium left in 1962, the mistrust and disagreements between the Hutus and Tutsis continued.

What you have to remember is that before Belgian involvement in the region, there had never been any racially-based massacres between the two groups…but all that was about to change… 'cos by the 1960s, the Hutus were itching to make the Tutsis pay for 40 years of humiliation.

When Team Ruanda-Urundi was split into Rwanda and Burundi, and Rwanda held elections for the first time, the 'Party for Hutu Emancipation', a party that was determined to take their revenge on the Tutsis, got the majority of the votes.[5] And so under the leadership of Kayibanda, the new Rwandan government conducted a series of brutal massacres against the Tutsis, and drove many out of the country and into neighbouring Burundi and Uganda.[6]

Kayibanda was replaced by Habiyarimana in 1973 but nothing changed for the Tutsis. For the next 21 years he continued to massacre them and refused Tutsi refugees the chance to come back home. As a result, many Tutsis, angry that they couldn't get justice in Rwanda, set up the RPF (Rwandan Patriotic Front) and, with help from the Ugandan government, invaded Rwanda in 1990.[7] With RPF gains being made and growing international pressure to give Tutsis more rights, Habiyarimana was forced to sign the Arusha Accord in 1993, in which he agreed to allow the return of Tutsi refugees, merge the RPF with the National Army, and allow free and democratic elections under the supervision of the United Nations.[8]

The Hutus were now mega pissed. As they saw it, the Tutsis sold them out when the Belgians were in town, and now these same 'cockroaches' were getting Team CANDY to help them run the show once again. They were having none of it and, in 1993, they began preparing for something *really* special.

When Habiyarimana's plane was shot down on 6 April 1994, the Hutu extremists got all the excuses they needed to carry out one of the worst genocides in human history. Within 90 days, at least one million people were brutally massacred with machetes.[9] From the foetus being ripped out of the bellies of pregnant Tutsi women,[10] to men's genitals being hacked off – this was the daddy of all atrocities.

As well as the genocide there were the vicious rapes committed against the Tutsi women. The Interahamwe (Hutu militia) would set up military checkpoints to identify Tutsi women, rape them, kill them, and leave their corpses naked with their legs spread apart – some even raped the corpses of women that they had just killed. In many cases, the rapes were followed by sexual mutilation of the vagina and pelvic area with machetes, knives, sticks, boiling water, and acid.[11] This is what happened to a woman called Perpetue:

"I was in the church building when the Interahamwe came and told us that [we were] to be burnt. They took a lot of people outside to kill them. One Interahamwe...took me to another building...and raped me...There were other women being raped there at the same time, maybe ten women and seven young girls. The next day...one of them [Interahamwe] sharpened the [stick] end...of a hoe. They held open my legs and pushed the stick into me. I was screaming. They did it three times until I was bleeding everywhere. Then they told me to leave. I tried to stand up, but I kept falling down. Finally I crawled outside. I was naked crawling on the ground covered in blood."

Perpetue stayed hiding in the bush for about one week until she found two men with a bicycle who were willing to take her to Gisenyi in the north-west part of the country. Unfortunately, when she arrived in Gisenyi, she was recognised by an Interahamwe from her home area. He immediately notified the other militia that she was Tutsi and she was taken to a mass grave:

"I was told to give my clothes to them. The mass grave was for women and girls...and it was being organized by a woman they called Donatha. She had a long knife and cut me immediately behind the knee. One Interahamwe saw me and took me aside along with four other women...he

raped me. I cried out because I was still wounded from before and he was opening all the wounds again. He beat me for crying and gagged my mouth. He told me that I was forbidden to cry because Tutsi had no rights. After the rape, I was left alone and naked. I crawled on all fours for two days in the bush. When I urinated, it came out like blood. Black, coagulated blood kept coming out of my vagina."[12]

Bernadette was 33 years old when the fighting began. During the genocide, 50 Interahamwe came to her house armed with machetes, knives and hoes. She was raped by six Interahamwe men, one after another, as she watched them kill her husband and all her sons. When they finished with her they threw her, her baby, and her three daughters into a river. "My children all drowned, but I floated back to the riverside. I tried to go toward Runda commune [but] was found by another group of Interahamwe. They also raped me. After the war, I found out that I was pregnant. But I had an abortion…no, not really an abortion. The baby just came out dead."[13]

Thousands of women and young girls were brutally raped, maimed both physically and psychologically in exactly the same way and even worse. When Tutsi women had children as a result of these rapes, many committed infanticide or abandoned their children.[14]

As the RPF began to move into Rwanda, they defeated the Hutu government. Fearing retribution, some two million Hutus fled into neighbouring Congo and Tanzania,[15] and this led to a refugee crisis, unprecedented in its scale. Around 50,000 predominantly Hutu refugees died from disease, hunger, and a lack of water.[16]

That's true Divide and Rule. **And it's the Candyman's same Divide and Rule tactic that's screwing up the British Black community at the moment.**

When I hear team members cuss others for being too dark – that's Divide and Rule. When I hear that K-Town boys stabbed Tiny Alien 'cos he was part of OC – that's Divide and Rule. When I hear that the 15 year old Somali boy, Kayser Osman, was murdered by Black people – that's Divide and Rule…and it's pure 'niggativity'.

I keep saying to the lads: "Since all of the petty beefs that Black people have with each other have been created by the Candyman, it makes us look kinda dumb." I know that some of our team have come out recently and said that they're "British first, and Black second'. And I know that in interviews, some of our players have even said things like: "I'm Congolese first, African second, and Black third"…but they need to hear me out…I'm not saying that Black people don't have differences – be they cultural, linguistic, facial, geographical or historical – but for the purposes of surviving in this world, we have to recognise that our Blackness is what defines us on Planet Earth.

'Cos in case the Black team hadn't noticed, Team CANDY doesn't give a s*** who they are – as long as they can trace their history back to the 'Dark Continent'. They-Are-Black…and that means that they're gonna be housed in the nastiest areas, given the lowest-paid jobs, and made to go to the worst schools. So whether they're West African or West Indian, Ghanaian or Guyanese, Mixed White/Black or Mixed Black/White – it don't make no difference.

It's kinda like this: if someone breaks into your house and tries to steal your sister's TV, you're gonna stop the thieves, right? Even if you had an argument with your sister the day before, you're still gonna stop the thieves, right? The reason: 'cos regardless of what happened between you and your sister, the bond that you have with her is stronger than anything in this world – 'cos you're family. And when it comes to dealing with other people, your relatives come first.

But if the thief knows that you're the type of person who'll let people steal things from your sister when you're angry with her, it means that your house is vulnerable to outsiders – which makes you more likely to be robbed.

And that's the type of mentality I'm trying to get through to our team. The more we bicker internally, the more we get exploited. But the more unity we show, the more power we hold in British society. It's that simple.

Geoff Shreeves: Can you be more specific about your team's problems…

Patrice: Take our GOALKEEPER for example. He's a real 110 percenter, but ever since he's started playing for Team BLK, he's been as sick as a parrot. I'm the first to admit that it's very difficult for him. He's the newest addition to our squad, having arrived in the early 90s when his previous side, Somalia imploded. Every training session, I try to boost his self-confidence, but the only way he's gonna keep clean sheets is when the rest of Team BLK start acting like he's a member of Team BLK. **'Cos for some reason, some Black people think that it's ok to cuss Somali people.**

Yea I know they speak a different language, I know they hang together, and I know that they're culturally different from West Africans or West Indians – but I feel embarrassed when I see members of our team cuss them – 'cos while Team BLK b****es and moans about racism from White people, they're guilty of racism that's just as vicious.

Some people like to believe that it's not that serious, but try telling that to the parents of Abdul Kadir Maye, stabbed to death in East London, or the family of Abdirizak Hamza, who was knifed six times in the heart and liver in North London – all by Black people. What this shows is that there are some really dumb Black people on my team. And they're dumb 'cos i) **they fail to realise that they got their anti-Somali attitude from the Candyman.**

You see, in case some Black people hadn't noticed, the Candyman declared war on Somalis loooong ago. And why did the Candyman do this…? The Answer: To save their own skin.

It's like this. As you know, the Candyman make it their mission to stay rich, and they do this by making sure there's enough people in the working class to do the jobs that are necessary to keep them rich. But this creates a problem, 'cos from time to time the working class get fed up with working for wages below the rate of inflation. And when they get fed up, they start voting for politicians who argue for better employment rights, they take industrial action, or they might even start rioting. Basically, they make life uncomfortable for the Candyman. Consequently, the Candyman tries to find a way of taking the heat off them, and tries finding a way of redirecting the working class negative sentiments. This normally comes in the form of an ethnic group, usually one that doesn't hold any political power, doesn't own any national TV stations, and one that doesn't own any national newspapers. That way, they don't have a voice to fight back.

With the Somalis (apparently) being relatively new to Britain, it made them an easy target – and as a result the Candyman moved into overdrive, making them Public Scapegoat Number One.

That's why ever since 1997, the government has introduced four pieces of major legislation on immigration to target Asians, Africans, West Indians – and of course the Somalis: The Special Immigration Appeals Commission Act 1997, the Immigration and Asylum Act 1999, the Nationality, Immigration and Asylum Act 2002, and the 2006 Immigration Asylum and Nationality Act…all of which have helped to restrict the employability and benefits for settlers in the

UK,[17] and all of which have given 'British' people the impression that their poverty is a result of 'the invasion' of Somali asylum seekers.

So that's why in the news, if it's not tales of 'Somali benefit fraudsters' in *The Sun* newspaper, it's accounts of their 'weird' Islamic practices in the *Daily Mail*. From *Panorama* programmes about 'Al-Qaeda Recruiting Somalis As Terrorists',[18] to films like *Black Hawk Down* characterising Somalis as primitive beasts,[19] the Candyman has worked damn hard to make us feel like Somalis are part of the reason why crime has increased in our communities.

And that's why some Black people started to think: "Boy, I got no job, I live in a disgusting estate, I got a criminal record and now all of a sudden I see these Somali people living in areas nicer than mine. I see them setting up businesses, driving cars, doing well in school and it pisses me off! So the next time I see a Somali kid, I'm gonna give him a piece of my mind.

In layman's terms, the Candyman has duped a feeble-minded minority of Black people into believing that their Somali brethren are the architects of their poverty – deflecting all the attention away from the Candyman's exploitative behaviour. Consequently, the NSPCC (National Society for the Prevention of Cruelty to Children) stated that Somalis have become the most victimised community in Britain. 'Cos from Bristol to Strathclyde, the Somali community have themselves reported an increase in racist attacks against them (from both White and Black people).

But this anti-Somali minority of Black people are also dumb **'cos ii) they fail to understand that Somali people are a pretty formidable people.**

Yes that's right, people would be surprised to know that there's more to Somali history than asylum seeking and khat. If they googled 'Somalia' instead of going on MSN or updating their Facebook profile picture, they might come across the American Invasion of 1991, in which the Somali people defeated the world's superpower.

Back in the early 1990s, Somalia experienced a bitter civil war after Siad Barre's government was toppled – and by August 1992, the UN reported that over 300,000 people had died as a consequence of the conflict and ensuing famine. Whilst most of the world saw a tragedy unfold before their eyes, the US administration saw an opportunity.

You see, ever since the end of the Cold War in 1989, the US was looking to implement its New World Order. And so from Bosnia to Iraq, from Haiti to Panama, George Bush I, and Bill Clinton did exactly that. The Americans quickly cooked up an excuse for entering Somalia: "to provide a secure environment for humanitarian relief operations" and named its mission, Operation Restore Hope![20]

Then, in December 1992, under the flag of the UN, they promptly stormed into the country, shooting thousands of Somalis and causing untold grief. But faster than you can say "Ho Chi Minh", the Somalis got kinda pissed off, and struck back by killing 24 Pakistani 'peacekeeping' soldiers in June 1993.[21]

The USA/UN claimed a guy called Mohammed Farah Aideed was responsible for this 'unprovoked atrocity' and proceeded to do what the USA does best. They nuked, they shot, they abused and they stole. However, when they started to tear up the Somali capital Mogadishu, and bombed a meeting between the Somali clan members, it was the final straw for the people of Somalia.

In the next few days, four Western journalists were beaten to death, four US military police were killed by a land mine, and two weeks later, six more US soldiers were wounded. The USA was sccccrrrreeeewwwwwwing and promptly deployed 400 elite Delta Force troops.[22] Hell bent on getting Aideed, on 3 October 1993, the Yanks raided the Olympic Hotel in Mogadishu.

After a 17-hour battle, 18 US soldiers were killed and 84 were wounded. It was the longest, most bloody battle that US troops had been involved in since the Vietnam War. It was at this point that President Clinton realised that he could never beat the Somalis. And so on October 7th he withdrew US troops from Somalia, and the hunt for Aideed was abandoned.[23]

And that's not the only reason why Somalis are such a proud people. If someone in our team bothered to pick up a book and read about Somali history, they might come across a freedom fighter called Sayyid Mohammad Abdullah Hassan who, along with the Dulbahante tribe, fought one of the longest and bloodiest anti-imperialist resistance wars against the British in Africa. Despite the better equipped and more heavily financed British army, he refused to sign a Protectorate Treaty and submit to British rule, which is why for over two decades his relentless and well organised warriors led a guerrilla war against them. As a brilliant orator, and with a very strong following of Islamic Fundamentalist dervishes, from the beginning of the 20th Century 'til his death in 1920, he managed to hold off the British Army.

And while we're on the subject of the British, I wonder if many Black people know that Somalis are one of the oldest African communities in Britain? When Britain 'ruled' the seas Somalis took a lot of jobs in the Royal Navy – fighting in the First and Second World War – which is why they've had communities in the port cities of Cardiff, Liverpool, Hull, South Shields and London for over a century now.[24] But does anyone in Team BLK take notice of this? Nah, they keep cussing and abusing them. Basically doing exactly what the Candyman tells them to do – forever weakening the position of Black people in Britain.

When it comes to our DEFENCE I'm the first to admit that, as individuals, they've got great engines, they're solid and they're brilliant ball winners. But whenever I put them on the same pitch together they play like they've been coached by Kevin Keegan, surrendering goals left, right and centre, and it's all because **for some unknown reason the Caribbean and the African lads don't get on with each other.** I know that some of the time they're only guys having a laugh, but if I'm honest, much of it comes across as ignorance.

So let me put some things straight. To those West Indians who look down on Africans understand this: taking the mick out of African names makes you look like a muppet, bearing in mind that it wasn't too long ago that your family had names like Yakubu or Anichebe, and the *only* reason why you've got 'White' names is 'cos you were forced to take the name of your slave master.

Taking the mick out of an African accent makes you look like a doughnut – bearing in mind that it wasn't too long ago that you spoke like that back on the slave plantation – and the only reason why you have the accent you do is 'cos you were stripped of your language and forced to speak the tongue of the people who made you work like a dog.

Taking the mick out of Africa as a continent makes you look like a plum – bearing in mind that you're actually cussing yourself – and simply shows the world that you've got zero knowledge about where you're really from.

'Cos despite what you saw Tarzan do, Africa wasn't quite the backwater that the Candyman likes to portray on TV. In fact, it was far more developed and powerful than you might think. Back in the

14th century, places like the West African empire of Mali were bigger than Western Europe, and Mali was one of the richest and most powerful states in the world.[25] Universities like Sankore, based in Timbuktu, developed the knowledge we have today in subjects like medicine, mathematics and astronomy.[26]

As Malcolm X once said: "In hating Africa and in hating the Africans, we ended up hating ourselves, without even realizing it. Because you can't hate the roots of a tree and not hate the tree. You can't hate your origin and not end up hating yourself. You can't hate Africa and not hate yourself."[27]

And to those Africans who look down on West Indians understand this: If it wasn't for West Indians, Black people, and for that matter all other 'minority' groups, would never have *any* of the opportunities that they have in Britain right now.

It was West Indians who were the first people to open the doors for non-White people to get into the media. From Lenny Henry, to Trevor MacDonald, from Moira Stewart to Norman Beaton. It was West Indians who were the first people to break into British sport. From footballers like John Barnes, Mark Chamberlain, Luther Blisset, Clyde Best, Cyrille Regis and Viv Anderson, to athletes like Linford Christie and Tessa Sanderson.

And perhaps most importantly, it was West Indians who were the first people to represent the interests of *all* cultural minorities in politics. Trevor Phillips was the Chair of the Commission for Racial Equality, and Bill Morris was the first non-White leader of a Trade Union.

So basically, when it comes to Blackness, Africa created it and the West Indies decorated it. And since it's clear that the Candyman doesn't give a s*** whether you speak Igbo or patois, we really need to stop beefing with each other.

Take some members of the police for example. Since 1978, over 174 Black and ethnic minorities have died in police custody[28] and since the year 2000 over 37 Black people have died in 'suspicious circumstances', either whilst being arrested or in police custody.[29] And I can guarantee that all those coppers involved didn't care whether the person they were beating on was as African as Samuel Eto'o, or as Caribbean as Thierry Henry – all they cared about was the colour of their skin.

From Michael Powell's death after being restrained by police officers in Birmingham in 2003, to Frank Ogboru's suspicious death at the hands of the police in 2006,[30] it's clear that the division between the West Indian lads and the African lads only hurts themselves, clearly leaving our defence wide open.

Now in the MIDFIELD, we've got four players who read the game brilliantly. **But the light-skinned players and the dark-skinned players just keep cussing each other about the way they look.**

Geoff I'm telling you, we got a midfield that's more obsessed with colour than an interior designer! I got this one mixed-parentage lad who plays on the right. All day he gets told: you've got no right to play for Team BLK 'cos you're not fully Black; 'cos you're a Half-Breed; you're a Mongrel; you're a Quadroon; you're an Octoroon; you're Half-Caste; you're Coloured.

But I got a message for all those Black people who think that mixed-parentage people aren't Black. If that's the way you think, don't ever be trying to claim the following people as Black in the future:

Adam Clayton Powell (Civil Rights Leader)
Alesha Dixon (RnB Singer from Mis-teeq)
Alicia Keys (RnB Singer)
Allen and Albert Hughes (Film directors of Films such as *Menace II Society* and *Dead Presidents*)
Amerie (RnB Singer)
Andre Petion (Haitian President for Life in 1807)
Arthur Wharton (Britain's first professional non-White footballer)
Ashley Cole (Premiership and England Footballer)
Billie Holiday (Singer)
Bizzie Bone (Bone-Thugs-N-Harmony Rapper)
Blu Cantrell (RnB Singer)
Bob Marley (Reggae Singer)
Booker T Washington (Black Activist)
Colin Kazim-Richards (Turkish International Footballer)
Colin Powell (American Politician)
Chilli (RnB Singer from TLC)
Christina Milian (RnB Singer)
Craig David (RnB Singer)
Daley Thompson (Double Olympic Decathlon Winner)
David Haye (Heavyweight Boxer)

David James (England International Goalkeeper)

Dorothy Dandridge (Actress)

Faith Evans (RnB Singer with *Bad Boy* Records and Wife of Late Rapper The Notorious B.I.G)

Frantz Fanon (Writer)

Frederick Douglass (Black Activist during the American Civil War)

Halle Berry (Actress and Oscar Winner)

Henrik Larssen (Swedish Footballer)

Jason Robinson (England Rugby Captain and 2003 World Cup Winner)

Jeremy Guscott (Former England Rugby International and 1991 World Cup Finalist)

John Carew (Premiership Striker and Norwegian International Footballer)

Kanya King (Founder of the MOBOs)

Kelis (RnB Singer)

Kelly Holmes (2004 Olympic 800m and 1500m Champion)

Kieron Dyer (England Footballer)

Langston Hughes (American Poet)

Lenny Kravitz (Pop Singer)

Leona Lewis (Pop Singer)

Lewis Hamilton (Formula One Driver)

Mario Van Peebles (Actor in Films such as *Ali* and *New Jack City*, Director of Films such as *Panther*)

Mary Seacole (Nurse during the Crimean War and best selling Author)

Ms Dynamite (RnB Singer)

Mya (RnB Singer)

Neneh Cherry (Pop Singer)

Oona King (Former Labour MP)

Paul Boateng (Labour Politician)

Paul Gilroy (Writer and Academic)

Paul McGrath (Former Irish International Footballer and Former PFA Player of the Year)

Rio Ferdinand (Premiership Footballer)

Rosario Dawson (Film Actress who starred in *Sin City*)

Ruud Gullit (Former Dutch International Footballer and 1988 European Championships winner)

Sade (Soul Singer)

Samantha Mumba (Pop Singer)

Shirley Bassey (Pop Singer featuring on several *James Bond* soundtracks)
Shola Ama (RnB Singer)
Stacey Dash (Actress in Films such as *Clueless*)
Tatyana Ali (*Fresh Prince of Bel Air* Actress and RnB Singer)
Thandie Newton (Actress)
Tiger Woods (World Number One Golfer)
Traci Bingham (Actress and *Baywatch* Crew member)
WEB DuBois (American Civil Rights Leader)
Zadie Smith (Author)
...most Brazilian footballers...
...Malcolm X (who was also one quarter White).
...oh, and don't forget Barack Obama, whose mother was very much White!

The interesting thing is, it's estimated that on average, most African Americans have between 17-18% White ancestry. (In other words, out of the 128 ancestors that they've had over the last two centuries, 106 were Black, and 22 were European.)[31] And a recent study has suggested that 25% of *all* Afro-Caribbean people have a recent White ancestor.[32] So the chances are that those same Black people who wanna cuss mixed people are probably mixed themselves!

Anyway, that aside, the point is, some Black people fail to realise that it don't matter whether you look like Theo Walcott or Didier Drogba – you're gonna get treated exactly the same by the Candyman. The reason? Because in Britain and in much of the USA there still exists the 'One-Drop Rule'.

Geoff Shreeves: And what is the One-Drop Rule?

Patrice: It's the belief that if you have one African ancestor, you're Black. It was developed by British slave masters who needed a solution to all the raping that they were doing. Basically, they couldn't keep their hands off Black slaves which meant that there was a whole generation of mixed-parentage children on the plantations. Now this raised a number of serious issues:
a) Were they slaves or not?
b) Should they live in the slave master's house, or in the slave quarters?
c) Should these children be classified as Black or White or mixed?

The solution was to make all the mixed-parentage slaves legally classified as Black and this was 'cos:

i) The slave masters' wives weren't too happy about the fact their husbands had played away, and certainly weren't keen on raising a child that wasn't theirs.

ii) If a 'half-Black kid' got the same rights as a White kid, then it kinda jeopardised the whole philosophy of slavery and racism – 'cos how can you justify racism on racial grounds if the very definition of 'Black' is in question?!

Essentially, making them Black meant that they could continue their abusive treatment of Black people. From then on, the One-Drop Rule became tacitly accepted in British and American society.

However, fascists in the USA started to get a little worried that some light-skinned Black people might try to 'pass' as White. So in 1910, Tennessee passed a law enforcing the One-Drop Rule. This law was adopted by Louisiana, Texas, Arkansas, Mississippi, North Carolina, Virginia, Alabama, Georgia and Oklahoma.[33] Florida, Indiana, Kentucky, Maryland, Missouri, Nebraska, North Dakota and Utah also changed their laws so that it was in effect a One-Drop Rule.[34]

From now on, everyone who was previously mixed, half-caste, mulatto etc, now became Black. Although the US Supreme Court reversed the One-Drop Rule in 1967, to this day, British and American people still implicitly acknowledge the rule. Why? Because the Candyman can't risk those White people who don't give a s*** about racism accepting that the colour lines are blurred. 'Cos if White people can't tell the difference between White and Black people, the Candyman might realise that it's increasingly harder to blame Black people for there being such awful public services. After all, if it's harder to define who's actually Black, then you got no natural scapegoat.

And if this happens, then working-class White people might start directing their anger where it should've been directed in the first place – at the Candyman.

That's why the British government has consistently stigmatised mixed-parentage people as a dirty, mongrel, sub-group of Black people which has led to:

• More than a quarter of mixed-race people aged between 16 and 24 having no qualifications as compared with one in eight White British of the same age.[35]

- Mixed-parentage pupils facing exclusion rates equal to that of Black pupils.
- Mixed-parentage people, in England and Wales, being more likely than those from other cultural groups to be victims of crime.[36]

So as you can see, all this 'who's-Blacker-than-who' bulls*** is a waste of time. We all get treated the same anyway.

On the flipside, however, **there are a lot of light-skinned Black people, mixed or not, who think that they're better than dark-skinned Black people** – simply because they're lighter!

I hear light-skinned Black people cuss Black people by cracking jokes like: "You're so Black your mum loses you in the cinema" and "You're so Black you have to wear white gloves to hail a night bus."

I listen to light-skinned Black people cuss other Black people by saying: "Your hair's pickier than the landscape of Asia" or "You got thicker lips than an Orang-utan."

Man, these people just don't understand that to succeed in a game of football, you need *skill* co-ordination, not *colour* co-ordination.

You see, for anyone with Black heritage who uses these cusses, for anyone who thinks that having dark skin is a source of amusement – they got a screw loose… 'cos somewhere deep down inside, they really don't like being Black.

After all, if they *did* like being Black, they wouldn't find Black features funny now would they? And considering the amount of racism that they've probably had to endure from White people for being part-Black, it's kinda odd cussing other Black people for being Black…it's almost like they haven't realised that They-Are-Actually-Black. IDIOTS.

Whilst I totally disagree with it, I kinda sympathise with Black people who impale themselves, 'cos after all, if your own people tell you that it's better to be light, it's kinda hard to turn a blind eye to it.

Sure, the Candyman's done his bit to make Black people feel inadequate about their skin tone, but we Black people have certainly taken that baton and run with it. Some of us have made it our life's mission to convince everyone that the colour Black is the worst, most disgusting, most repulsive colour imaginable.[37]

So if you ever wondered why you see WAGs with weave, with horse hair extensions, with blonde highlights, or with blue eye contacts – understand that it's 'niggative' Black people who make them feel like their Black features are not beautiful enough.

If you ever wondered why you see Black women using Skin Bleaching products like Fair and Lovely, Medik8 White Balance or Arbutin Skin Whitening – it's because 'niggative' Black people make them hate their complexion.

It's 'niggative' Black people who put lighter-skinned people like Vanessa Williams, Shemar Moore and Halle Berry up on a pedestal. And it's 'niggative' Black people who make Beyoncé and Lil Kim wanna look lighter with every trip to the salon.

The thing is, I find this whole 'light skin' obsession so strange, 'cos if you're aware of the awful history of light-skinned Black people, we probably wouldn't desire them so much.

Think about it. Those light-skinned Black people are lighter skinned precisely *because* their ancestors have been brutally and viciously raped by slave masters. The resulting children, forced into slavery, would have had an awful experience – perhaps worse than other slaves – because their own fathers would have subjected them to slavery! As a mixed-parentage slave once commented:

> *"Even his own child, by a Black woman or a mulatto, when the child is called a quadroon, and is very often as White as any English child, is frequently sold to degradation. There are thousands upon thousands of mulattoes and quadroons, all children of slaveholders, in a state of slavery. Slavery is bad enough for the Black, but it is worse, if worse can be, for the mulatto or the quadroon to be subjected to the utmost degradation and hardship, and to know that it is their own fathers who are treating them as brutes."*[38]

The point is, most light-skinned Black people are a symbol of rape, of concubinage, of White dominance, and of the ultimate violation of Blackness. That's why it is sooooooooo embarrassing when I hear us b**** about skin tone; 'cos it makes that through ball straight down the middle so much easier for Team CANDY to play.

Then, we come to our lone STRIKER. He's probably the most talked about footballer of his generation, he's got an educated left foot, he's a natural finisher and he's got a great touch for such a big man. But right now I feel like giving him the hair-dryer treatment. Just 'cos he plays better and gets paid more than other Black players, he thinks that he's beyond being Black. But I've seen his type before. 'Cos **there are some Black people who, when they've made their Pz, think that they're better than all other Black people.**

They look around their workplace, and suddenly think, "I'm the only Black person in my office."[39] Then, when they get home, they look around their area, and they suddenly think, "I'm the only Black person in this neighbourhood!" And what can happen if this person's not careful, is that they start to say to themselves:

"I made it out of the Ghetto through hard work, through blood, sweat and tears. I went to University during the day, and stacked shelves in Tescos in the evenings. I worked damn hard to be where I am today. And what I don't understand is – why can't more Black people be like me? Why can't more Black people be more like the White people that I work with? I get vexed with Black people – always going to prison, f***ing up their exams, f***ing up their lives. I don't wanna know nothing about Blackness for the rest of my days because all I ever see from Black people is 'niggativity'."

But this is a common schoolboy error. These Black people aren't thinking hard enough.

One. It's true, the Black community needs to step up its Game, but that ain't to say that the Game that they're playing is an easy one. From the housing estates, to the inner city schooling, to the jobs that they're denied – not to mention the ignorant 'niggative' fools that some of them are surrounded by – there are lots and lots of young Black people who're desperate to do something positive with their lives.

Two. Black people aren't all f***ing their lives up: it's only a minority of them who are acting 'niggative'.

Three. Any Black person that believes that every Black person is 'niggative' is 'niggative' themselves.

Four. As Malcolm X once said, "do you know what they call a Black person with a college degree in New York...? Nigger!"[40] In other words, no matter how much money a Black person has, no matter what qualifications they have, they will always be B-L-A-C-K.

If anyone remembers OJ Simpson, the Black American Footballer who went to trial for allegedly bumping off his White ex-wife and her White boyfriend in 1994, they might recall that before he was arrested for murder, OJ was the Whitest Black man on the planet. If there was a prize for 'the trying-to-fit-into-White-society award', OJ would have been the Multiple World Champion. He played golf all the time, he hung around with White people all the time, he moved to a rich White area of L.A. called Brentwood, he married a White woman, and he continued to date White women after he got divorced. This is a man who tried harder than any other Black man on this planet to be accepted by White people. But a fat lot of good that did him.[41] 'Cos the day his White ex-wife was stabbed to death, OJ Simpson changed from The Most Loved Black Man in White America to more Black than Louis Farrakhan. All those years of talking and smiling to old White men who missed the 'lynching' days, all those days trying to make White women feel comfortable leaving their handbags around him were undone in an instant. Because when a White woman was brutally murdered, White America got back to doing what it does best – criminalising Black folk.

What I'm saying is that in the Candyman's eyes, "there's no such thing as an upper-class [Black person]…because he catches the same hell as the other class Negro".[42] Sadly though, our centre-forward hasn't quite realised this yet – and he loves Team CANDY soooooo much that he finds it hard to score against them.

Geoff I'm telling you, things are so bad in the first team, sometimes I wish I could just use our YOUTH TEAM instead. But in many ways, they're even worse! They've got a high tempo style of play and good footballing brains – but trust me, the Youth Team got more divisions than La Liga, and more beef than a Sunday roast.

For example, **we got Jamaicans who think they're better than Trinis**, simply because their island is bigger. I've never heard anything so stupid. Don't they get it: they were dumped on the island. They had no choice where they went, and wherever they went they were raped, beaten, abused, and forced to live a life of utter and complete misery. It's kinda like people in Broadmoor prison cussing people in Wormwood Scrubs saying, "we got a better prison than you". Don't they realise that it doesn't matter what prison they're in: the fact remains that They – Are – In – Prison! As an old Jamaican guy once said to me, "Jamaica is an island, but is not I land". They were all kidnapped from the same place – they just got dropped on different bits of rock.

Then we got Nigerians who think that they're better than Ghanaians, simply because they used to have a better football team, or because their countries have had some political issues in the past or because…man, I don't even know why.

All I know is that they're only in different 'nations' 'cos the British and the French decided to draw national lines where they wanted to, which went right through cultural groups, languages and villages.

And when all is said and done, a) they're in England now, and b) both their countries are being exploited for the same reason, at the same time, and by the same crooked people (the World Bank, USA etc etc). So I keep asking myself why they don't squash their ridiculous geographical battle and start fighting the fight that really needs to be fought.

But possibly the stupidest beef that we got in the Youth Team is between different postcodes – **people from certain areas hating on people from other areas.**

My question is this: when we got so many other problems, like the fact that Black people are five times more likely to be arrested than White people,[43] or that Black people are six times more likely to be sent to prison than Whites and more likely to be imprisoned for a first offence,[44] why the f*** are we fighting with each other over something as trivial and as pointless as 'different endz'. It might have escaped our attention, but the estates in Angel Town are pretty much the same as those in Stockwell. And the poverty experienced by Black people in Lozells is pretty much the same as it is in Aston. And the gap between the rich and the poor is pretty much the same in Moss Side as it is in Rusholme. Basically what I'm saying is that in case they hadn't noticed, the Candyman, the person who really f***s their life up, doesn't give a s*** where you're from. As long as you're Black you're good and ready to be exploited.

So **for the second half, I want my players to wear their hearts on their sleeves**. I want them to salute the supporters when they arrive on the pitch. I want them to kiss their shirt when they score. As I told the boys, it's a game of two halves, and we've been through more relegation battles than Harry Redknapp so it ain't over yet.

Er...sorry about that Geoff, I kinda went off on one there. The fact remains, we've got a point to prove, and three to win. So I hope when you interview me in 45mins time, I'm singing a different tune.

Geoff Shreeves: Thanks for your time Patrice.

> "They divided both to conquer each..."
> *Frederick Douglass*

NOTES

1. *Rwanda Development Gateway* http://www.rwandagateway.org/article.php3?id_article =114 (accessed 22 June 2008).
2. *History World: History of Rwanda.*http://www.historyworld.net/wrldhis/PlainText Histories.asp?historyid=ad24 (accessed 22 June 2008).
3. *ibid.*
4. *ibid.*
5. *ibid.*
6. *ibid.*
7. *ibid.*
8. *ibid.*
9. *ibid.*
10. *ibid.*
11. *Human Rights Watch: Shattered Lives,*(1996). http://www.hrw.org/reports/1996/ Rwanda.htm (accessed 22 June 2008).
12. *ibid.*
13. *ibid.*
14. *ibid.*
15. *ibid.*
16. *ibid.*
17. *North West Asylum Seekers Defence Group – Britain's Racist Immigration controls.* http://www.asylum-seekers-defence.org.uk/wiki/index.php?title=Britain%27s_ racist_immigration_controls (accessed 22 June 2008).
18. Lusher, Adam, *Islamists Use Raid To Stir Up UK Somalis, (Sunday Telegraph* 14/01/2007). http://www.telegraph.co.uk/news/main.jhtml?xml=/news/2007/ 01/14/wsoma14.xml (accessed 22 June 2008).
19. Sexton III, Brian, *What's wrong with 'Black Hawk Down'?* 03/2002. http://socialistworker.org/2002-1/395/395_08_BrendanSexton.shtml (accessed 22 June 2008).
20. *The United Nations and the Situation in Somalia,* (United Nations Department of Public Information Reference Paper 01/051994).
21. Snyder, R, *Operation Restore Hope/Battle of Mogadishu,* August 2001.novaonline.nvcc.edu/eli/evans/his135/Events/Somalia93/Somalia93.ht ml (accessed 22 June 2008).
22. *ibid.*
23. *ibid.*
24. *Port Cities,* http://www.portcities.org.uk/london/server.php?show=ConNarrative. 109&chapterId=2309 (accessed 22 June 2008).
25. *British History: Abolition of the Slave Trade 1807.* http://www.bbc.co.uk/history/british/

abolition/africa_article_03.shtml (accessed 22 June 2008).

26. *ibid.*

27. X, Malcolm transcribed and edited by Ali, Noaman, *After the Bombing / Speech at Ford Auditorium*, 14/02/1965.

28. *Black Deaths in Custody*, (Institute of Race Relations 2004). www.irr.org.uk/2002/november/ak000006.html (accessed 22 June 2008).

29. Frank, Ogboru, *Another Death in Police Custody*, (07/10/2006 *Socialist Worker Online*). www.socialistworker.co.uk/article.php?article_id=9869 (accessed 22 June 2008).

30. *ibid.*

31. Sailer, Steve, *Race Now, Part 2: How White Are Blacks? How Black Are Whites?*, 08/05/2002, http://www.isteve.com/2002_How_White_Are_Blacks.htm (accessed 22 June 2008)

32. *Motherland: A Genetic Journey* (BBC Documentary, 2003). This also stated that 25% of Afro-Caribbean people have a European ancestor in the paternal (Y chromosome) line of descent.

33. Patterson, Orlando, *The New Black Nativism*, Time: 44, (19/02/2007).

34. *ibid.*

35. Frith, Maxine, *Britain Today: A Nation Still Failing its Ethnic Minorities* http://findarticles.com/p/articles/mi_qn4158/is_20030508/ai_n12694331?tag=artBody;col1 (accessed 22 June 2008).

36. *Ethnicity and Identity: Victims of Crime*, (National Statistics Online). http://www.statistics.gov.uk/cci/nugget.asp?id=467 (accessed 22 June 2008).

37. X, Malcolm transcribed and edited by Ali, Noaman, *After the Bombing / Speech at Ford Auditorium*, 14/02/1965.

38. Fredric Francis, *Fifty Years of Slavery*, (1863). www.spartacus.schoolnet.co.uk/USASfredric.htm (accessed 22 June 2008).

39. X, Malcolm transcribed and edited by Ali, Noaman, *After the Bombing / Speech at Ford Auditorium*, 14/02/1965.

40. *ibid.*

41. Moore, Michael, *Downsize This*, (Pan Books 2002), Pg. 225.

42. X, Malcolm transcribed and edited by Ali, Noaman, *After the Bombing / Speech at Ford Auditorium*, 14/02/1965.

43. *The Criminal Justice System*, (Institute of Race Relations 2004). http://www.irr.org.uk/2002/november/ak000004.html (accessed 22 June 2008).

44. *ibid.*

CHAPTER FOUR
House Negroes (Hip-Hop Rmx)

**"I dedicate this to the one dimension-al,
no imagination..."**[1] *The Roots*

THE PHANTOM OF THE BLUEPRINT

Gumiya: Who the f*** is this? Bothering me at 5.46 in the morning, kicking in my door!

Phantom: It's only been a little over a decade and already you don't recognise me?!

Gumiya: Oh my word? It's you! What the hell are you doing here? You really did fake your death!

Phantom: Don't be stupid! How could I fake my death! Me – I'm deader than the Sega Master System.

Gumiya: But if you really did die, then what on earth are you doing in my bedroom!?

Phantom: I've come to help you.

Gumiya: Help me? From what?

Phantom: From yourself.

Gumiya: Trust me, I don't need help from no-one. I'm a successful Black man in a successful Black industry. I can get into clubs for free, I get invited onto 'urban' radio chat shows, I drive an Alfa Romeo, I got girls all over me every time I step out my house – my life is better than anything I could ever imagine! So let's not waste time talking about me. Let's talk about you! I haven't seen you in ages. We need to catch up! What you up to? How you been? How comes you're looking like Treach carrying that rusty, cumbersome chain around with you?

Phantom: This is what happens when you've lived the life that I lived. This is my punishment for voluntary enslavement on Earth.

Gumiya: Enslavement? I don't understand...? Oh...you must mean prison.

Phantom: I was in prison, but it wasn't the four walls of a penitentiary that enslaved me. It was the way I lived that made me a slave.

Gumiya: You? A slave?! What you talking about? Are you mad? You were anything but a slave. You got shot five times and survived. You introduced the porno music video to the MTV generation. The anger that you expressed in your battle tracks hyped people all over the world and your rivalry with the East coast gave us Black kids something to get excited about. You were the first rapper to have a double CD. You were probably the first man to have a number one album in the charts whilst you were in prison[2] and your sales to date have reached 36 million.[3] You were a Black role model and a Hip-Hop icon.

Phantom: You're wrong. I had all the talent, I had all the ideas, I had all the positive intentions – but I soldout – and as a result, I obliterated the progress that many brothers and sisters struggled to achieve. I let myself get pimped.

Gumiya: Pimped? Nah, you and me, *we're* the pimps.

Phantom: It all started off so cool. Sure, I wasn't earning millions from record sales, but I was making a living, and I was making music that got to the heart of the issues that Black people faced – police brutality, single mothers, absent fathers...but then I let the system get the better of me, and I let the Candyman run my life. I made music that separated the Black community, not unified them. I did things that embraced the Black stereotype, not dismantled it. And I've come here to warn you that you're making the same mistakes that I made.

Gumiya: But I ain't made no mistakes. I'm making Pz. I'm the American Dream. And the British one too!

84

Phantom: Bredrin, to Black people you're the American nightmare – and the British one. Just like a 112 tune, you've been remixed. The Candyman has turned you into a star-spangled slave, a union-jacked nigger, and the mother of all house Negroes.

Gumiya: A house-who?

Phantom: A house Negro: A subservient Black man who has voluntarily chosen to fit into the stereotyped, inferior, second-rate image given to you by the Candyman.[4]

Gumiya: Say what?

Phantom: Let me tell you a story. Back in the day, during slavery, there were two types of Black people: those who worked in the slave master's field and those who worked in the slave master's house.[5]

The field Negroes were in the majority. They lived in the slave quarters, they worked the hardest, they were whipped daily, and they ate food that was fit only for a dog. Needless to say, the field Negroes hated their master.

The house Negroes were in the minority. They lived in the basement in the slave master's house, they worked hard, but they were treated better, and they ate the food that the slave master left. The house Negroes loved their slave master. They loved their slave master more than they loved themselves.

If the slave master said, "We got a good house here", the house Negro would say, "Yeah boss, we got a good house here". Whenever the slave master said "we", he said "we". If the master got sick, the house Negro would say, 'What's the matter, boss, we sick?" We sick! He identified himself with his master, more than his master identified with himself.

And if the field Negro came to the house Negro and said, "Let's run away, let's escape, let's separate", the house Negro would look at him and say, "Man, you crazy. What you mean, separate? Where is there a better house than this? Where can I wear better clothes than this? Where can I eat better food than this?" That was the house Negro.

You my friend are fashioned from this **Blueprint**. You are fashioned from this 'niggativity'. You are a house Negro.

Gumiya: Whoa! Calm down fam. Me? A house Negro? You know I ain't no house Negro. I keep it real. I'm 100% ghetto. I'm a field nigga through and through.

Phantom: Listen to me very carefully. From now 'til 6 in the morning, you shall be visited by three phantoms ...
... *The Phantom of the Takeover.*
... *The Phantom of Big Pimpin'.*
... *And The Phantom of Prose Combat.*

Each one has something different to show you.

Gumiya: But why do they have to see *me*?! If I'm so bad don't you think that Black people would have told me that already?

Phantom: It doesn't work like that. Imagine you're in the middle of the desert, the sun is beating hard down on you, and you're dying of thirst. Now imagine that someone offers you a glass of foul, dirty, unclean water. What would you do?

Gumiya: I would drink the water of course. I have no choice.

Phantom: But now imagine that this same person offers you two glasses of water. The same foul, dirty, unclean water and a glass of pure, clear, clean water. Which would you choose?

Gumiya: I would choose the pure water of course!

Phantom: Well, right now, there are very few prominent, positive Black people in the public eye to look up to (Abdul Kareem Jabbar retired a long time ago)! So what happens is that because you're one of the few Black people who regularly features on magazine covers, who is repeatedly interviewed on the radio and who frequently appears on TV channels, many Black people feel they have a close affinity with you.

So when you get criticised by the *Daily Mail*, and the *BBC*, and the *Conservative Party*, and *TalkSport Radio*, and virtually every other mouthpiece of the Candyman, their reaction is to defend you. Especially, since the *Daily Mail*, the *BBC*, the *Conservative Party*, and *TalkSport Radio* are the same people who have helped to criminalise the Black community for generations. That's why no-one Black says s*** to you. But today, you will learn the truth about yourself. You will learn that what you do is much bigger than Hip-Hop.

Gumiya: Can't I see the phantoms all at once and get it over and done with? I got things to do…
…Phantom…?
…Phantom…!?
…Hello…??
…Are you still there…?!

THE PHANTOM OF THE TAKEOVER

"There are Negroes who will never fight for freedom. There are Negroes who will seek profit for themselves alone from the struggle. There are even some Negroes who will co-operate with their oppressors. These facts should distress no one. Every minority and every people has its share of opportunists, profiteers, free-loaders and escapists."[6]
Rev. Dr Martin Luther King, Jr.

Phantom: I couldn't believe how lucky I was when they told me that I had to haunt you. Let me just take this opportunity to tell you that the production on your last album was sik! I can't tell you how much the boys and I think of your musical ability. But enough of that – let's get down to business.

Gumiya: Are you the Phantom of the Takeover?

Phantom: Indeed I am.

Gumiya: So what's your story…?

Phantom: In a nutshell, I'm here to show you how blind you've been. I'm here to show you how subservient you are. I'm here to show you **how the Candyman runs the Hip-Hop industry.**

Gumiya: You've come to tell me all that!? Man, leave me alone. You listen to my tunes, you heard my Grime stuff from 'way back when'. You know that everything I talk about is raw and from the streets. I don't try to impress anyone and I especially don't try to impress White people.

Phantom: Trust me. You know nothing about yourself or the music industry. The next few minutes will change this. From the outset, what you need to understand about the Candyman is that they *hate* it when Black people start doing things that empower their communities. It just eats them up inside.

Gumiya: Why's that?

Phantom: Because when Black people act as a unit, no-one can stop them from being everything that they want to be. That's partly why people in the Hindu community do so well economically in Britain today. They look out for each other. When they go shopping, they buy from people who look just like them. When a child is born in their family, every member of their family is ready to support its development. And if anyone has a problem with one of them, then they have to deal with the whole community, because they don't ever let anyone come into their neighbourhood and f*** it up! If Black people were allied with each other in this way, the Candyman would have a serious problem.

Gumiya: A problem? Like what?

Phantom: Well, for starters, who are they gonna be able to shift the blame onto when the media slams the government for the latest rise in crime figures? Who's gonna want to work the s***ty jobs that the middle classes don't wanna do? How are they going to be able to guarantee that their kids will take the executive positions in those city firms?

You see, **when Black people continue to f*** each other up, it makes the Candyman happy.** It means that Black people pose no threat to their wealth and power and it means Black people can be exploited ad infinitum.

Gumiya: Oh, Ok. I'm with you so far.

Phantom: Remember the rise of the Black Panthers in the USA during the late 1960s and 1970s?

Gumiya: Oh yea. I remember watching the movie with Mario Van Peebles.

Phantom: Well remember how it disappeared faster than Kaiser Souze? The government just couldn't handle the fact that the Black Panthers started to get Black people to call each other 'brother' and 'sister' like they meant it! But what they really couldn't handle was the fact that people like Huey P Newton, Bobby Seale, George Jackson, Angela Davis, Bobby Hutton, Eldridge Cleaver and Fred Hampton were inspiring young Black people to question the f***ed up system that they lived in and got them to take ownership over their communities.

The Black Panthers began to kick the drug dealers out of the ghettos and actually started building some *real* community spirit: setting up a 'survival programme' for Black people living in poverty, providing things like free breakfasts for children, and encouraging Black people to defend themselves against police brutality. Man was it a kick in the teeth for the US government, which depended on Black criminality more than Hollywood depends on plastic surgery.

So for a drastic problem the Candyman required a drastic solution, and their solution was to traffic crack cocaine into the Black ghettos. The way they saw it, it was simple:

Black Revolutionary Who Is Depressed By Perpetual Racism **PLUS** Crack A Drug That Provides Intense (Short Term) Pleasure **EQUALS** No More Talk Of Blackness! Bring On Talk Of Guns, Gangs and Prostitution

And that's exactly what happened! During the early 1980s, all over America, the CIA started a drug epidemic that decimated the Black community. Who had time to care about 'Black' when Crack was in town!

Gumiya: That can't be true. That's just a whole heap of conspiracy talk. The US government would never be able to get away with that.

Phantom: Don't just take my word for it. The next time you're on the internet, google 'Gary Webb'. He was the investigative journalist who, in 1996, exposed ex-US President Ronald Reagan's attempts to finance his war in Nicaragua, whilst simultaneously flooding the ghettos with Crack to keep Black folk occupied. It can all be found in his book, *Dark Alliance – the CIA, the Contras, and the Crack Cocaine Explosion*, which he dedicated to the people, "most of them poor and Black", who "paid an enormous price" for the CIA's drug dealings.[7]

Gumiya: I...I can't believe it.

Phantom: Ask Larry Davis, the man who was forced from the age of 16 to sell Crack to Black people by the NYPD, and who later exposed the New York Police Department's involvement with drug dealing. If you get the time, watch the documentary *The Larry Davis Story* by StreetGangs. It explains everything.

Gumiya: Whoa! That's the sickest thing I've heard since DMX's *Flesh of my flesh* album.

Phantom: Now hear this. Right now the Candyman is trying to f*** up Hip-Hop, and whether you like it or not, your type of Gun-Hoe music is an invaluable tool in keeping the Black population of the UK and elsewhere in the world at war with each other – leaving the Candyman free to plunder and pillage.

Gumiya: Wait, wait, wait...let's go back a bit. 'Gung-ho'? You mean my music is enthusiastic and dedicated!? How nice of you to say!

Phantom: No. 'Gun-Hoe'. It's all about Guns and Hoes.

Gumiya: Gun-Hoe huh...I never heard that before. That's an interesting name...

Phantom: You see, when Hip-Hop came along, the Candyman were screwing. Early on when DJ Kool Herc and the Sugar Hill Gang were doing their 'thang', Uncle Blanco didn't really pay Hip-Hop no mind. The Candyman thought that this was just a fad. That it would wash away within a few years. I mean, a Black art form dominating the world – Paleeeeease! But when it took off they were pissed.

'Cos the thing about Hip-Hop is that it started to have a positive effect on Black people. It encouraged unity, community awareness, a greater focus on education, and in many cases, a growing popularity in Islam and Black empowerment.[8] Yep, you heard me, it encouraged that scary phrase 'Black Empowerment'! People like Afrikka Bambaata, a major gangster in New York City during the 1970s was so inspired by Hip-Hop that he swapped the gun for the mic and began to make tunes about 'peace, love and unity'.

You had people like KRS-One encouraging warfare through

music and words, not through physical violence, and you had people like Ice T releasing tunes like *Killers* talking about "work[ing] together for peace"![9] Even tunes like Sir Mix-A-Lot's *Baby Got Back* were political, and you have to bear in mind that its opening line was "I like big butts and I cannot lie". Now it takes hard work to make *that* political! And to top it off, you had Public Enemy making uncompromisingly anti-establishmentarian records that even some young White people liked!

They must have been distressed when they saw Black working-class kids from the Bronx body popping in a way that looked like they were made out of elastic, using spray paints in a manner that art college graduates could only dream of, creating their own music by using two turntables in ways that seemed impractical, and innovating the English language like they were Professors of Literature.

Something had to be done. And that's why when Hip-Hop blew up in the 1980s, the Candyman did what the Candyman have always done when they don't like something Black people are doing: they f***ed it up. They came up with a plan for exploitation called **GTA (Grand Theft Artform): The Rap Management Game.** This was their **Takeover**.

Their plan was simple. To create and promote the most 'niggative', hateful, f***ed up, dirty, violent, over-sexual, idiotic Black rap stars you and I could possibly imagine and to play their music to as many Black and White kids as was humanly possible. If you thought COINTELPRO was dead – think again!

Initially they would take a poor Black person from the ghetto, willing to do literally anything to get paid. Then they would give them a contract with plenty of zeros in it, a sports car, and some platinum rims. Finally they would tell them to rap about buying iced jewellery, killing Black people, and having sex all the time.

The Conclusion? Black people, already starved for role models, see these Candy-rappers on every music channel and begin to idolise them thinking that this bulls*** lifestyle is the way to live. And hey presto, you have a generation of young Black people who think that 'f***ing hoes' and 'gangsterism' is more reputable than a degree from LSE.[10]

Gumiya: Wait a moment. Hold up one second. Since when did the Candyman (or whatever you call him) take over the Hip-Hop industry? I say and think how I want my tunes. I run things.

Phantom: Nah, you think you run things. You're kinda like someone working behind the till in a petrol station thinking that they're the Chief Exec of BP. But I know how it is for you and the rest of the Hip-Hop buying public – sitting in front of Channel U – seeing all these Black people on the screen, and naturally assuming that Black music was run by Black people. After all, they're the ones who write the songs, produce the tunes, play the instruments, perform in the videos, and get the awards. But just 'cos the person pulling the strings is in the dark, it don't mean that the person *is* dark.

Whilst the rest of your fans think that they're listening to some tunes straight from the street, (thinking that Lil' Kim really is the 'Queen' B), the reality is that White people run the whole game. The Godfathers of Hip-Hop are pale, light, fair and White.

Let me pull that up because I can see that you don't believe me. **The person crackering [sic] the whip in Hip-Hop and RnB is White**. And when I'm talking about White, I'm not just talking about 'normal' White. I'm not talking about the White person who lives on a council estate in Kidbrooke or the White person working as a sales assistant in PC World, Merseyside. I'm not talking about regular White people. I'm talking about super-rich White people, silver spoon White people, trust fund White people, Ivy League White people. Yep that's right, I'm talking about the Candyman.

It's the Candyman's boot that's up your arse when it's time for you to devise a video, or to sign an endorsement contract, or to write some lyrics. It's the Candyman's laser pointer that's flashing at his PowerPoint presentation when your album covers are designed, when he fixes your dress sense and when he determines your character. These are people who cannot ever, ever claim to be street or working class, or Black in any way.

These are White people like Edgar Bronfman, the CEO of Warner Music. Check out his background. He was born into an über-wealthy family which owned the large company Seagram which distilled and distributed large quantities of Alcohol in Canada, and also had dealings in Oil and Gas. When Edgar was a nipper, his family sent him to school at The Collegiate in New York City, costing a mere $27,100 per year,[11] and whose other notable attendees have been John F Kennedy, and the former NYC Deputy Mayor. It was here that he began to take an interest in the arts, so his parents kindly built a new theatre at the school which they humbly named after themselves. During his summer holidays, his daddy, already well connected at MGM film studios, would fix him up with jobs shadowing producers on major Hollywood film sets. Edgar didn't fancy Uni much – 'cos why bother with Uni when your parents are minted. So he tried to launch a career as a songwriter, but that didn't pan out too well. Then, in 1982, he asked mummy and daddy for a job, and they made him the Managing Director of Seagram Europe – just like that! By 1994, his family decided to promote him to CEO of Seagram. His first decision was to diversify Seagram into music and entertainment and he bought large shares in Warner.

This man now controls around a quarter of all the Black artists to hit the record stores. This man dictates what they say, what they rhyme about, and how they look. This is the man who runs the lives of Black 'role models' like Trick Daddy and P Diddy. So understand this: Dre, Timbaland and Swizz Beatz ain't controlling s***.

Let me introduce you to the real CutMasters of the Hip-Hop world, and since they're the real 'Gs', I think it's only right that they should be addressed by 'G' titles. Please welcome Rolf 'Slick' Schmidt-Holtz, Doug 'the Mack' Morris, Guy 'Super' Hands and Edgar 'the Beast' Bronfman Jr: The CEOs of Sony BMG Entertainment, Universal, EMI, and Warner Music Group respectively. These are the men that control 85% of the music industry,[12] and manage the majority of the world's most recognisable Hip-Hop labels and artists. All of them White. mLami. Branco. Albus. Blanc. Blanke. umLungu or however you want to say it. None of them Black. All of them loaded.

Gumiya: Ok I take your point. So the Candyman runs the industry. But does that mean that the Hip-Hop industry is f***ed?

Phantom: Well it does if you're Black. The reason? **The Candyman only likes to sign and promote certain types of rappers** – and they're not the types of rappers who like to quote the 'Ten Point Programme' on the regular. They're pretty easy to identify:
- Black people who haven't worked out that killing Black men, and raping Black women is f***ed up.
- Black people who haven't worked out that bling/Gun-Hoe lyrics are as constructive to the Black community as Japanese concentration camps were to Allied POWs.
- And Black people who haven't got the grey cells to work out what the record exec's plan is really about.

Gumiya: Come on man. This 'GTA' plan that you're talking about – you can't seriously believe that it even exists?

Phantom: Bredrin, the plan exists and it's in full effect. Like a conveyor belt young Black men and women are signed up, provided with their lyrical range, and promoted like Apple promotes the iPod. It's played out better than an episode of *Mission Impossible*. From Mobb Deep, to Lil' Jon and the Eastside Boyz, from Too Short to Biggie – and believe me, it pains me to say that about him – they're all products of the same system.

And that's why the record industry must have wet themselves when they discovered and signed 50 Cent. If there was anyone who could be a more f***ed up role model for Black people, this man was it. The Candyman must have prayed for centuries to be given the ultimate Coon: the Yoda of the house Negroes; the undisputed heavyweight champion of 'I-HATE-BLACK-PEOPLE' niggers. And in the late 1990s, the Candyman got their man.

Gumiya: Yea I'm not really feeling 50 right now.

Phantom: I'm kinda bored of him too, but it ain't his musical ability that's the problem. It's the whole 'fiddy' package that you should be worrying about.

Let's look at him in depth **starting with his stage name** '50 Cent', which he, Curtis James Jackson III, stole from the Brooklyn born Kelvin Martin, a member of the notorious drug dealing crew the 'Supreme Team'. Kelvin murdered over 30 people and robbed several others, including local officials, a number of former friends, drug dealers and the rap group Whodini. As with everyone who lives that life his luck didn't last long, and in 1987 at the age of 23, he was shot dead. Curtis James Jackson III felt that assuming the persona of a multiple murdering, drug-dealing lunatic was the perfect way to introduce himself to the musical world. **Moving on to his lyrics**:

The Gun
"If there's beef, cock it and dump it, the drama really means nothin,
To me I'll ride by and blow ya brains out (brains out)
There's no time to cock it, no way you can stop it
When niggas run up on you wit them thangs out (thangs out)
I do what I gotta do I don't care if I get caught

The DA can play this motherf***in tape in court
I'll kill you. I ain't playin, hear what I'm sayin, homie I ain't playin".[13]

The Hoe
"Man, b****es come and go, every nigga pimpin' know…
B**** choose with me, I'll have you stripping in the street
Put my other hoes down, you get your ass beat
Now Nik my bottom b****, she always come up with my bread
The last nigga she was with put stitches in her head
Get your Hoe out of pocket, I'll put a charge on a b****
Cause I need 4 TVs and AMGs for the six
Hoe make a pimp rich, I ain't paying b****
Catch a date, suck a d***, shiii*, Trick".[14]

Yep that's about 99% of his lyrics accounted for. 50 Cent kinda finds it natural to open his mouth and spit lyrics as if he just finished reading *American History X* (and I ain't talking about the film, I'm talking about the David McKenna book). Everything about his words are hostile, aggressive and all about f***ing Black people up.

Moving on to his persona, his claim to fame is about one thing: being shot nine times. I can't even count how many times he goes on about it. Even on his website it says: "that's not a dimple on 50 Cent's face, that's a bullet wound!"[15] Well done 50, we're all proud of your gun gash. And lastly, let's look at his politics. On a television appeal for victims of the New Orleans floods in 2005 Kanye West blasted:

> *"I hate the way they portray us in the media. You see a Black family, it says, 'They're looting'. You see a White family, it says, 'They're looking for food'. We already realise a lot of people that could help are at war right now, fighting another war – and they've given them permission to go down and shoot us… George Bush doesn't care about Black people"!*

50 Cent, offended by Kanye's comments replied: "What Kanye West was saying, I don't know where that came from. The New Orleans disaster was meant to happen. It was an act of God."[16]

Bearing in mind that 80% of New Orleans's poor people are Black,[17] think about this. Nearly a year after the hurricane:
- Only half of all public transportation routes were open and only about one-fifth of buses were operating in the city.[18]

- Roughly eight out of ten child-care centres remained closed, and those that were functioning are spread out and disproportionately in White areas of town.[19]
- Finally, although Black people were only a little more than two-thirds of the population at the time of the flooding, they represented almost 75% of all persons displaced.[20]
- Oh, and before I forget, Charity Hospital – the free system utilised by the city's poorest residents, of whom 85% before the storm were Black – to this date remains far below pre-storm capacity.[21]

An act of God eh? Can anyone tell me how 50 Cent differs from the muscular, stupid, White-loving, Black buck? The strong, criminal minded, dim-witted, sex crazed, I-want-Whitey-to-like-me, nigger? Now let me ask you this. Who has been the most hyped Black musician over the last few years?

Gumiya: I'd say 50 without a doubt. I see posters of this guy everywhere. From his films, to the dolls of himself. I even saw him hanging out with Bart Simpson. I'm sure he's got a video game out too!

Phantom: Yep, *Bullet-Proof*, a game which was created by our old friend Mr Bronfman Jr. A game surely to boost the aspirations of those role-model starved ghetto youths – not! I mean this is a guy who, even after his first album sold $10million copies, is still getting involved in gun battles with fellow rappers Jayceon 'Game' Taylor and Ja Rule. Negro please!

If Black people had any kind of a choice, do you honestly think that they would put 50 Dense on every magazine cover (including *GQ*)? If you were looking for someone negative for Black kids to imitate, wouldn't you blaze him all over the TV too? He is about as Black as Alan Partridge, and has as much understanding of Blackness as a shower curtain. If he even dreams that he is Black, he'd better apologise to us all.

Gumiya: Wait, so you're saying that the TV stations are in on it as well? You think they play his s*** regularly on purpose?

Phantom: It ain't just the record labels that are in on GTA – the Candyman pulled everyone of his gang members into the Rap Management Game – including the music television companies and the radio stations. Think about it. What types of rappers receive the greatest amount of air and screen time?

Gumiya: Well er…peeps like myself I suppose.

Phantom: And who are these stations run by?

Gumiya: I dunno?

Phantom: Let me help you out there. Choice FM, run by rich White people at Capital FM – which explains why they sacked Geoff Schumann in 2004. Apparently Black people don't like talking about issues – they just wanna groove.

BBC 1 Xtra, run by the rich and very White Ian Parkinson. The man who recently, in response to complaints about the overwhelming use of the word nigger targeted at young audiences, claimed that "the overwhelming majority of the audience" did not interpret the use of the n word as racist.[22] Nice.

Channel U, run by Video Interactive Television, which is run by the rich, White male, Paul Dixon. The same station which has made its name playing 'porno' music videos after dark…and so on and so forth. From Popworld to Kiss to MTV…

Gumiya: Hold-up, you can't be telling me that MTV are racist. They have a music channel *dedicated* to Black music.

Phantom: Are you talking about *MTV Base*?

Gumiya: Yea. And they have *MTV cribs*, and *Pimp my ride*, and all other kinds of things supporting Hip-Hop. MTV has been Hip-Hop's greatest ally ever since 'Yo! MTV Raps' first appeared in the late 1980s.

Phantom: Boy you're naïve. **MTV's relationship with Hip-Hop is like HIV's relationship with the human body**. Let me explain something to you. Back in the early days MTV *refused* to play Black music, with the emphasis on Black. Sure, if you were Black and you released a couple of 'White guitar rock' tunes as Tina Turner did once or twice, you might just be able to get your face on their channel, but artists like the multi-million selling Prince had problems 'cos he wasn't playing that kind of music too often.[23]

Rick James, one of the biggest artists during the early 1980s, rarely had his videos played, despite the fact that his 1982 album *Street Songs*, had sold three million copies and featured the tunes *Give It To Me Baby* and *Super Freak*. I don't know about you, but I can't see how anyone wouldn't want to play *Super Freak*.[24]

Even the King of Pop, the pioneer of the modern music video, Michael Jackson, had to struggle to get – wait for it – *Billie Jean* played on MTV! Allegedly, it was only when his record label CBS threatened to pull all their artists' videos from the channel that MTV eventually decided to change their tune. I'm sorry, the pun was too tempting not to use.[25]

Things were so messed up for Black musicians that when Herbie Hancock released his classic track, *Rock It*, he opted not to appear in the video or have any Black people featured in it simply because he figured that with dark-skinned people on the screen, it probably wouldn't be shown.

Gumiya: But they've changed now so why are you talking about the past. They made a mistake, and now they've rectified that mistake.

Phantom: Blood, MTV only decided to start playing RnB and Hip-Hop because a rival music channel, Video Music Box (VMB) [remember them?!] were playing Black music regularly and were getting very popular as a result.

Gumiya: So why was VMB playing Black music?

Phantom: Because VMB was a station that gave the viewer *all* the power. The premise was that people phoned up and chose the music videos that they wanted to see. Stations like this are normal now, but back then this was the first of its kind. In the 80s, Black music was over-popular (when hasn't it been), and lots and lots of people, Black and White, were requesting the station to play lots and lots of Black music and lots and lots of Black and White people were tuning in as a result. MTV panicked and in 1988 they launched the show *Yo! MTV Raps*.[26]

However, MTV, being controlled by the Candyman, had their own set of standards for the Hip-Hop videos that they played. After all, they were reading from the universal GTA manual, the same one that every other member of the Candyman was reading from – and they followed it step by step. So they decided to play, as they do today, the bling bling, big Buick, big booty, big breasted, big berretta videos. They fundamentally rebranded Hip-Hop as an aggressive, materialistic, misogynistic art form, totally obliterating its origin and hopefully (the Candyman thought), Black kids all over the Western hemisphere would identify Blackness with the 'niggativity' that they saw on their screens.

That's why **on the B-side, execs, TV stations and media outlets** from back in the day to now, **work overtime to resist socially-conscious Black rappers from getting rotation,** 'cos that kind of Hip-Hop doesn't fit into the GTA gameplan. After all, an intelligent, pro-Black rapper getting Black people feeling good about themselves, wanting to make money the legit way, walking around doing things to impact positively on the Black community, can only alter the balance of power for these aged, rich White folk. Why d'you think we don't see Dead Prez anywhere? There are plenty of rappers who have alternative messages, or who don't talk about things like 'your wifey's creaming her panties picturing me'[27] in every tune. But they don't get airplay because it is not what the Candyman wants you to hear.

Sure, I'm not saying that a few conscious/semi-conscious rappers and singers haven't broken through – Immortal Technique, Jurassic 5, Lupe Fiasco, Pharoahe Monch, the Fugees. And I'm not saying that Ms Dynamite or Spearhead don't get played once in a while – but they certainly don't receive the type of attention that Chamillionaire and the rest of the Gun-Hoe crew get. TV executives only prefer Black people who can rhyme 'nigga' and 'trigga'.

Would it surprise you to know that Interscope Records had at one point Common, Talib Kweli and Mos Def on their books – possibly the most talented and well known trio of 'conscious/semi-conscious' rappers around? But for some reason, they didn't get anywhere near the same promotion that the Gorilla Unit[28] got. You could say maybe it had something to do with their talent, but you know I'd be lying. The reason? Because the Chairman of Interscope Geffen A&M Records, Jimmy Iovine doesn't seem to want to endorse a Black man talking about anything constructive on his label. And just in case you didn't guess it already, Jimmy Iovine is White.

Gumiya: Man it can't be as bad as all that.

Phantom: I'm afraid it is. Generally it works like this. Whenever an anti-police/anti-establishment record is due to be released, either the record companies step in to tone its message down, or it gets forced off the shelves. Don't just take my word for it, do your own research:

- Talk to artists like Paris Smith or Da Lench Mob about what life was like as a rapper back in the 1990s. They will tell you that they were told point blank by record labels/music channels that their videos would not be played unless they deleted scenes which depicted aggressiveness towards the boys in blue.

- Read about Ice T and his tune *Cop Killer* produced in 1992 that got him sacked from his record label after he refused to withdraw it from his album.[29]

- Watch the Tupac video, *Trapped*, in which he had to delete a scene at the end that showed him shooting a police officer.[30]

- Study the Wu-tang Clan's career success. Even they are not exempt from the media's 'Black-out' of socio-economic issues in Hip-Hop. Their first groundbreaking, largely 'fight-music' album got massive airplay on radio/TV stations, and got nominated copious times for MTV awards. This media response was sharply contrasted with the release of their second album, which focused largely on female exploitation and social degradation. It was nominated for no MTV awards, and videos off the album rarely appeared on music television channels.

- But Dead Prez is the ultimate example of political Black musicians who have been royally 'rogered' by the Candyman. Check what happened when they released their first album entitled *Let's Get Free*. Firstly, their album cover was rejected by 'Loud' records because it showed Black soldiers with guns and their label thought that it was too extreme. Secondly, their record label severely under-promoted the album because they weren't keen on its general theme – the f***ed up and racist side to the American government. And thirdly, their video, *They Schools* was rarely played on channels like MTV primarily because music television stations didn't like the fact that it showed Black children being held in nooses in their classrooms – symbolic of the American school system. The truth hurts huh! That's how the GTA plan works.

Gumiya: Wait a minute…the original Phantom mentioned to me something about being a house Negro?

Phantom: Oh yea, I almost forgot my conclusion. My bad. **Uncle Blanco has fixed things so well** so that not only does he run the Hip-Hop industry, and not only does he get to promote negative Black artists, **he also gets paid**. And man does he get paid squillions.

Gumiya: But Black people are making a lot of money from the Hip-Hop industry at the moment. I can prove it to you.

Phantom: You don't have to prove it to me. I know bare people who are getting paid from the Hip-Hop industry. Even though I never really liked the guy's music, P Diddy, the CEO of Bad Boy Entertainment is estimated to be worth more than $400 million with over ten musical acts on his record label, several movie and television projects and a sizeable stake in his clothing line, 'Sean John'. And then you have Russell Simmons, the CEO of Rush Communications who is worth more than $200 million with Def Jam Records, Phat Farm clothing and Rush advertising agency.[31]

But get this, whilst rappers are getting paid, none get anywhere near the amount that the record executives are getting.

Gumiya: That can't be true. I'm minted – I must be – I'm all over the music TV stations at the moment. There is no way that my record executives are earning anywhere near what I make.

Phantom: Fam, trust me on this one, you're wrong. Here's a crash course into the economics of the record industry. Most rap artists, indeed most music artists, make approximately 10% from every unit sale.[32] That means that for every £15 CD sale, you take home a meagre £1.50. But that money ain't yours – you have to pay your dues first. So check out this example of how much a Record Label divided up the $1.625 million profits of a band from record sales of 250,000:
— *Manufacturing, packaging and distribution:*
   $2.20 per record which totals $550,000.
— *Promotion, studio time, video production, travel costs, administration etc etc*
   $250,000.
— *Lawyer, agent, manager, producer and previous label costs:*
   $262,500.

The Record Company thoughtfully helped themselves to $710,000, which left the band with well under $100k each.[33] Sounds like I'm joking right? Sounds like this is an isolated case huh? This is the reality. Rappers in comparison with their executives earn a similar ratio to Macky D sales assistants and a McDonald's executive. Whilst you think you're getting paid, the reality is that you're getting plaid.

You see, as far as I know there are only a few rappers that run things different. Master P for example, decided that he was gonna be one of the few field Negroes in the industry. When he signed to his record distributor, he made sure he controlled *all* publishing rights and got his distributors to pay him 80% of all sales revenue from his record label.[34] He also bucked the trend of paying pathetic percentages for an artist's work. But since Master P is a rarity, the rest of the game runs like this:

— *The Hip-Hop industry is the slave plantation.*
— *The mix-master record exec is the slave master.*
— *And the rapper is the house Negro – remixed.*

They are treated better than most Black people, they live in better houses, they dress in clothes that the Candyman wears, and they love their record execs more than they love themselves – but they're still slaves.

THE PHANTOM OF BIG PIMPIN'

When the tree cutter came into the forest with his axe, one tree said to the other tree, "don't worry, we're ok, the handle is one of us"[35]
Unknown

Gumiya: Don't tell me – you're the next Phantom huh?

Phantom: You guessed right.

Gumiya: And what have you come to tell me? That I'm too violent, that you find my lyrics offensive? Whatever it is, save it. Your last ghost-buddy has already covered it. It's simple. I have a talent. I utilise that talent. Now get off my back.

Phantom: I'm not here to argue about your talent. I'm gonna show you **how you help certain people justify their negative behaviour towards Black people.**

Gumiya: What behaviour?

Phantom: Do you know anything about your history…Black history, or the history and relationship of Black and White people on this planet?

Gumiya: Um, I know that it's something to do with October. Does that count?

Phantom: Er not really. I suppose that's why I never saw you at the last Roger Sylvester demonstration.

Gumiya: Roger Sylv-who?

Phantom: Don't worry about it. But without going into the entire history, there are two types of White people on this earth. The White people who like racism, and those White people who don't like racism. Those who like racism – often distinctive because they're part of the Candyman Cru – usually pursue Hannibal Lecter-like attitudes towards Black people, chiefly because they can gain some sort of financial reward for it. Unfortunately for you, these kinds of White people have run the show for a long time, and that's why things like the maangamizi in Tasmania happened.

Gumiya: The 'what' in 'where'??

Phantom: The 'maangamizi'. It's a Kiswahili word that means annihilation.

Gumiya: Oh ok…and Tasmania?

Phantom: Ain't you ever heard of Tasmania?

Gumiya: Tasmania????? Oh Tasmania! As in the Tasmanian Devil! Is that what you're talking about?

Phantom: Well the 'Tasmanian Devil' bit is real, but it ain't no fictional cartoon character. Tasmania is an island off the coast of Australia where a little while ago, the entire Black population (yes that's right entire population) was wiped out: 10,000 people.[36]

You see, for a little over 35,000 years, the Aborigines were living at one with nature, in equilibrium with their environment.[37] Then when the British landed in 1803, everything changed. Their number one aim was to take land – asap! Land equals power. And power equals the ability to make money. And the only thing standing in their way from making money was a 'pesky dark-skinned' group of people who had lived on the island for thousands of years. So they did what any God-fearing Candyman would do – they slaughtered the lot of them.

Tactics for 'hunting' Tasmanians included riding out on horseback to shoot them, burning them alive, and setting out steel traps to catch them. The whites would cut off the penis and testicles of aboriginal men to watch them run a few yards before dying, and then feed the remains to their dogs.[38]

White people thought nothing of hunting Black people for sport, casually shooting, spearing or clubbing the men to death, tying them to trees and using them for target practice. Black women were kidnapped, chained, tortured and exploited as sexual slaves and Black infants were roasted alive.

Gumiya: But what about crimes against humanity and punishments for the people who did this?

Phantom: Well nobody really cared much about Black humanity. After all, Abos weren't even really considered humans anyway.

Gumiya: But there must have been some punishment?

Phantom: Well, now you mention it, a White man was once flogged for exhibiting the ears and other body parts of a Black boy that he had mutilated alive. Another White man was punished for cutting off the little finger of an Aborigine and using it as a tobacco stopper. Oh, and a White man was once given twenty-five lashes for tying "Tasmanian women to logs and burning them with firebrands, [and] forcing a woman to wear the head of her freshly murdered husband on a string around her neck",[39] because when he wanted to rape her she refused. Not a single White person, however, was ever charged for the murder of a Tasmanian Aborigine.

Gumiya: Boy, it sounds like something out of *Silence of the Lambs*, *A Nightmare on Elm Street*, *Scream*, *Hellraiser*, and *Cape Fear* – put together!

Phantom: Nah, trust me, this was much worse. With the declaration of martial law in November 1828, White people were actually at fault if they *didn't* kill a Black person in Tasmania. It was tenderly named, 'Black catching', and you could be rewarded with five pounds for each adult Aborigine, and two pounds for each child. Although some Black people offered resistance, their wooden clubs and sharpened sticks were no match against the firepower and savagery exercised by the White people against them. After the majority of the Black people had been wiped out, the rest were rounded up and placed in concentration camps. (Now where have you heard of concentration camps before? You didn't think that the Nazis first came up with the idea of concentration camps did you?)

On 7 May 1876, Truganini, the last full-blooded Black person in Tasmania, died at 73 years of age. A White mob had stabbed her mother to death, kidnapped her sister, and drowned her intended husband in her presence while she was raped.[40]

Gumiya: Man, White people are evil!

Phantom: It might seem that way but it's not quite as simple as all that. Like I said before, there are two types of White people.

Gumiya: No way. There ain't no White people who care about Black people – apart from my record execs.

Phantom: Well let's see now, there were things like the Female Society for Birmingham formed in 1825 that established a network of women's anti-slavery groups all over the UK. There were people like John Brown who was executed for leading a raid on an Armoury, which was attempting to lead a slave insurrection all over the American South. There were people like Edmund Dene Morel, John Harris and the Congo Reform Association who fought vehemently to bring an end to King Leopold's brutal rule over the people of Congo during the early 20th Century.

Then you had the American Jewish community that supported the Civil Rights Movement, as well as the Communist Party USA that supported equal rights for Black people. And one can't forget the White Panthers and people like Marlon Brando and Jane Fonda who supported the Black Panthers. In fact if you go to any Anti-Nazi League demonstration today, the majority of the people there will be White.

Gumiya: Fine, fine don't bore me to death with facts.

Phantom: Now because there are **White people who don't like racism and who have worked hard to reverse the hegemony of the Candyman**, the Candyman has needed to keep finding ways to make righteous White people feel more comfortable with its vampire-like attitude towards the Black population: from convincing people that God agreed with slavery, to falsifying scientific experiments to show that Black people were semi-human. But they quickly realised that **the best way to make White people consent to the abusive treatment of Black people was through entertainment** i.e. films, music etc. After all, it's far more interesting letting Jim Davidson, John Wayne, or Vivian Leigh teach them that Black people are ugly, crazy, base creatures than letting a crusty biology teacher do it.

For example, when Hurricane Katrina struck in New Orleans in 2005 and Bush and Cheney wanted to exclude Black people from their relief operation, they turned to the 'entertainment' industry to convince people that 'niggers' didn't deserve any assistance.

You see, whilst Black people were being refused transportation out of the city, being turned away from sheltered accommodation, being stopped from leaving flooded areas, Bush and Cheney badly needed a way to justify their blatantly racist attitude. The solution? To get their media chums to report on the news that Black people in New Orleans were behaving like Orks from *Lord of the Rings*. That they had begun to form into roving street gangs who were going round raping and murdering White people. That Black people were looting shops for designer clothes, wide screen TVs, gold chains and $140 trainers. In an instant, lots and lots of White people in America accepted the horrific treatment of Black people in New Orleans.

That's right, the 'Entertainment' answer has been used in the West for generations – and was probably **first used with the creation of the Minstrels way back in the 1800s.**[41] The Minstrel was the American Candyman's version of 'the Black man'. He was a character that was played in a variety of shows and theatre performances that would chronicle the behaviour of Black people. In other words, it was their way of validating their f***ed up attitude towards Black people.

Probably the most famous example of the Minstrel act was 'Amos 'n' Andy', the story of two Black bumbling fools who move from the deep south to Chicago. Played by two White men with boot polish on their faces, in every show they would talk about how much they wanted to have sex with White women, how desperate they were to fit into White society, and how much they loved their old slave plantation/slave master.[42] The Candyman even made up songs for Minstrels that cemented the idea that Black people wished that they could return to slavery. They would bust lyrics like:

"There's where I laboured so hard for old Massa,
Day after day in the field of yellow corn;
No place on earth do I love more sincerely
Than old Virginny, the state where I was born.

...Massa and missis have long since gone before me,
Soon we will meet on that bright and golden shore.
There we'll be happy and free from all sorrow,
There's where we'll meet and we'll never part no more."[43]

As you can expect, from the mid-1800s to the early 1980s, White people adored the Minstrel shows. Even the great Ronald Reagan, the dear old man that he was, entertained a Minstrel performance at his Presidential inauguration in 1981 – bless. With the success of the Minstrel performances, three things happened:

1. Seeing Black people act thicker than Katie 'Jordan' Price and miss slavery like England miss penalties made White people believe that their government's genocidal behaviour was beneficial for both White and Black people.
2. It confirmed the prejudices that White people held of Black people, that Black people were thick and lazy. This meant that they could sleep easy at night, safe in the knowledge that they were right all along – Black people should be treated like idiots.
3. Normal White people who usually sat on the fence began to feel like Black people probably deserved everything they got.

But after about 170 years of the minstrels, some White people began to feel just a little uncomfortable with the idea of White people dressed like weirdos, behaving like Dumb and Dumber and claiming that they were acting Black. So **just like Nokia updates phones, the Candyman updated their design** and came up with their version of the Sirocco. Why not get Black people to play the Minstrel role instead! The good thing about a Black Minstrel as opposed to a White Minstrel is that:

- They're authentically Black, so it's easier for the Candyman to say, "look, this is what all Black people are like"…and…
- No matter how dim-witted they act, they can't be accused of being racist, because after all, they're Black!

Gumiya: I understand what you're saying, but who on earth would voluntarily be a Black Minstrel?

Phantom: Well the thing is, most Minstrels don't even mean to be Minstrels. In fact, people whose general actions are far from those of Minstrels, often get 'Minstreled' by accident!

Gumiya: You've lost me. What are you trying to say?

Phantom: Ok. Let's talk about things in layman's terms. Let's look at Hollywood and the acting industry.

Gumiya: Cool. I can relate to that celeb lifestyle.

Phantom: An actor acts. They might play a good character, or they might play a bad character. Sometimes they might play someone who's gay and sometimes they might play someone who's psychotic. In one film they might play someone who's charming or in another film they might play someone who's nasty. That's the nature of acting.

Gumiya: Ok I'm with you so far.

Phantom: Well the Candyman in Hollywood makes sure that he rewards any Black actor who plays a character that re-affirms the Black stereotype. The Minstrel/house Negro/Black buck/Mammy/tragic Mulatto stereotype. And the Oscars are a good example of this.

Gumiya: With people like who?

Phantom: Mr Denzel Washington.

Gumiya: Denzel?!!! Whoa, whoa, whoa. You gotta be joking! You can't start on Denzel!?

Phantom: Let's get things straight here. I'm not in any way saying that

Denzel is a Minstrel. What I'm saying is that because Denzel is an actor, it's natural that he's gonna play some pretty diverse characters. And the Candyman, knowing that Denzel is a very well-respected member of the Black community, waited and waited until he played a character that they thought could identify best with their f***ed up version of Black people – and then gave him an award for it.

Gumiya: How d'you mean?

Phantom: Well for years, one of America's finest actors just couldn't seem to get his hands on that 'Academy Award for Best Actor in a Leading Role' when he was playing positive Black people. But once he took the role of a drug dealing, drug taking, thieving, abusive, hateful, raping, materialistic, murdering, amoral, corrupt cop – bingo, he gets the gong. Let's look at this in greater depth (see diagram on page 110)

There's Whoopi Goldberg who won a 'Best Supporting Actress' Award in 1990 for her character in *Ghost* who plays a Black woman with an attitude who bitches about everything and acts like she's got a chip on her shoulder.

Then there is Cuba Gooding Junior's 'Best Supporting Actor' gong for *Jerry Maguire* in 1996, playing…well…a Black man with an attitude who bitches about everything and acts like he's got a chip on his shoulder.

Another example is Halle Berry's Academy Award for 'Best Actress in a Leading Role' in 2002, the first Black woman to do so in the history of the Academy. But what did she win it for? A woman in a lunatic asylum who spends half the film gagging to have sex with a White man (called Billy-Bob of all names!).

Gumiya: Oh yea, and you even got Three 6 Mafia's Oscar winning tune in 2006, *It's Hard Out Here For A Pimp*.

Phantom: Exactly! But whilst these types of unofficial/unconscious Minstrels are effective, it only works properly if a Minstrel puts their heart and soul into being the Black stereotype. And having a part-time Black minstrel only brings in part-time dividends. This is where the **Big Pimpin'** began.

One of **the first full-time House Negresses**/Minstrels/ stereotypes was a young lady called **Josephine Baker**.[44] With a

Film	Character	Character's Situation	Character's Attitude	Oscar?
The Hurricane	*Rubin 'Hurricane' Carter*	*Imprisoned for a crime he didn't commit*	*To free himself mentally from imprisonment*	*Nope*
Malcolm X	*Malcolm X*	*Black Nationalist*	*Aim of creating Black unity and Black self-empowerment*	*Never*
John Q	*John Quincy Archibald*	*Holds up a hospital until they perform a life-saving operation on his son*	*Willing to do anything to save his child's life*	*No Way*
Training Day	*Alonzo*	*Corrupt Police Officer*	**The Black stereotype!**	*Damn Right*

bottom that shook quicker than a washing machine, Josephine perfected the art of becoming the White man's fantasy.

Back in the 1920s and 1930s, middle and upper-class White men would pack into theatres and watch this 'strange' and 'exotic' young woman parade around in the tiniest clothes possible. And when I say the tiniest clothes possible, I'm talking about a skirt made of bananas, and not a lot else.

The whole idea behind this sluttish image was to confirm to White men that Black women were ready and waiting to sexually satisfy the Candyman by any means necessary. It's kinda similar to the way that Lil' Kim struts up and down in her dresses, or how Khia busts around in a thong for her tune, "my neck, my back, my p***y and my crack"!

Gumiya: But can't you see that Lil' Kim is different, she don't do it for White audiences?

Phantom: Check the stats my friend. More White people buy Hip-Hop and RnB tunes than Black people these days. A few years ago the *Boston*

Globe reported that 70% of Hip-Hop bought in the States is purchased by White people.[45] In order to be the biggest selling RnB/rap star these days, you have to cater for the White market not the Black market. Don't be fooled into believing that video girls like Esther Baxter and singers like Cassie and Rihanna are doing it for the 'brothers' anymore.

Gumiya: But didn't Josephine pave the way for Black women to get recognised as stage actresses, just as Lil' Kim has helped turn Black women into sex icons again?

Phantom: I think what you mean is that Josephine Baker, just like Lil' Kim, paved the way for Black women to get recognised for being 'naaaaasty girls' who want to do whatever White men want them to do (shaking it like a Polaroid picture). The only thing that she *did* do for Black women was sustain the notion that Black women were the White man's toy, a notion that has been played with for a looooooooooong time here in the Western Hemisphere...being raped copious times a night by the slave master in the 18th century...converted into being the White land owner's concubine in the 19th century...converted into being prostituted by White men during the 20th century. Josephine was maintaining that violated, worthless status.

She did redeem herself years later by working for the French Resistance against the Nazis during World War Two,[46] but prior to this, the lady was the prototype booty shaking, trashy, exploited, Black whore/tragic Mulatto stereotype.

The Daddy of all house Negroes, however, was an entertainer called **Stepin Fetchit**. One might say he was the *original* 50 Cent; the shoe shining, gibberish talking, act-a-fool nigger. I'm not trying to take anything away from Cam'ron, or Jamal 'Shyne' Barrow – they're all house Negro stars in their own right – but this guy was the Del Boy of Black entertainment.

During the 1930s, Stepin [the originator] Fetchit was *the* major US attraction on the silver screen, and became one of the most popular entertainers with White, American mainstream audiences.

Now you gotta understand that back in those days, Black people rarely appeared on the TV. After all, this was at a time in America when segregation was alive and well, and on average two or three Black people were brutally lynched every week.[47] Yet during this period, Stepin [King of Bling] Fetchit owned 12 automobiles, had 16 servants and was one of the first Black millionaires in America.

Born in Florida in 1902, his real name was Lincoln Theodore Monroe Andrew Perry. Whilst writing for the Black newspaper, *The Chicago Defender*, he created a Black character called, 'The Laziest Man In the World' and began performing this character as part of a two-man vaudeville act. He claimed that he got his stage name, 'Stepin Fetchit' from a race horse. Yeah Whatever! The truth – quite obviously – is that his name was a contraction of 'step and fetch it' – a name to remind all White people of the aspirations of Black people in America.

Perry diversified his act over the years and he created the Coon character – the Black man who is lazy, arrogant, slow-witted, dumb, inferior, dirty, filthy, jive-talkin' and desperate to find a way to make money from doing nothing.

As you can imagine, he was a hit with White audiences! They just loved seeing a Black man act up to the stereotype that they held of Black people! At last it made them feel like everything they had always been saying about Black people was true, and that their homicidal treatment of Black people was the only way that humanity could successfully survive. And the beauty about 'Step' was that this wasn't simply a White person playing a Black character; this was an *authentic* Black man acting in a way that made White people feel truly superior again.

Through lavish overspending on blinging materialistic crap (like some Black entertainers we know today) he was a charity case by the 1960s. He died on 19 November 1985. However, his thick-witted characters are still remembered today. The other day on an American, ultra-conservative Christian website, a White man posted the following:

> *"We know that Uncle Tom won't beat us up, but somewhere in the back of our minds, we wonder if he might not steal the silverware. That's why I think you should…ask…the Black community to embrace Steppin Fetchit. Think about it. Steppin Fetchit, or at least the characters he played, is the perfect Black man for the current times. Nobody fears him because he completely marginalizes Black people as economic and political threats."*[48]

Well done, Step. Your legacy lives on.

Gumiya: Wow! Stepin Fetchit sounds like a strange kinda guy!

Phantom: Now as the saying goes, if it ain't broke – don't fix it. So consequently, the same system has since been used for many Black people.

Gumiya: But me and my peeps ain't nothing like Stepin Fetchit. And we certainly ain't house Negroes.

Phantom: You think not? Let's look at the traits that make you a key player for the Candyman's 'house Negro Allstar Team'. **Personality Trait 'A': Act more animal than King Kong**. The Candyman needs a Black person who acts like a Baboon. That way he can convince the White public that you're natural born criminals who deserve the foul treatment that you receive such as:
a) being imprisoned – even if you haven't committed the crime that you're convicted for like Winston Silcott in 1987
b) being suffocated at your house by Immigration police like Joy Gardener in 1993
c) being murdered in police custody like Christopher Alder in 1998
d) and being shot dead by the 'feds' without committing an offence like Azelle Rodney in 2005.

And with lyrics from Ludacris like, "[I'm] a full fledged killer, part time MC, full time drug dealer"[49] and "wait till you see my d**k 'eh bitch, I'm a beat that p***y up"[50] from the Yin Yang Twins – it becomes very easy for the Candyman to use you to pedal the image that Black people are more beastly than Godzilla. Along with the glorification of murder and sexual exploitation, you guys go a long way to creating and fostering negative opinions in the minds of many White people who never even come into contact with Black people in their lifetimes.

Additionally, just like Step, you give yourselves stupid names to help White people remind themselves that you love crime. Names like Bling Blaow, Pimp-C, Ricky Ross (named after the notorious drug dealer) and C-Murder (who briefly changed his name to C-Miller after he actually got charged with murder in 2002!) to name but a few.

Even record labels have stupid names, like the label Murder Inc Records (now changed to Inc Records after its CEO was arrested pending an investigation into his relationship with Kenneth 'Supreme' McGriff and major drug-dealing murderer). Murder Inc was originally the name that Lucky Luciano gave to the assassination arm of the Mafia back in the 1930s.

Even your name, 'Gumiya', is something that you need to think about very carefully. Perhaps the stupidest rap name though has to be Tony 'Yayo'. Yayo being the slang for Cocaine. Someone needs to sit Tony down and whisper a couple of things in his ear:

In Britain, the number of Crack Cocaine offences has risen,[51] whilst the number of Londoners addicted to Crack is estimated at 50,000.[52]

In places like Washington State, USA, where Black people are less than 1% of the population, 91% of all Crack Cocaine prosecutions are brought against Black people.[53] Nationally, Black people constitute more than 80% of those sentenced under the harsh federal law stating that a mandatory 5 years must be served for possession of Crack – despite the fact that 66% of Crack Cocaine users in the USA are White or Hispanic.[54] Needless to say, it ain't that clever glorifying Coke, especially when you're Black or more specifically, a Black American.

But the most important part of acting animal is to resemble the behaviour of a rutting Rhino, and that's why certain rappers make sure they spell out their opinions of Black 'Hoes'. And that includes Jim Jones (who named himself after the mass murderer) talking about a "fly b**** up in the coup"[55] and the veteran lyrical misogynist Jermaine Dupri talking about being "a pimp with mine every time, I don't give a f*** who she is, B**** you can go, Get another cause they love us niggas in the fast life".[56]

And if White people still don't get the message, you've always got Trina and other female rappers showing us that it's not just a 'man' thing. With lines like, "Now can I ride you like a soldier, and do you like your woman's 'sposed ya? Cause it's my party tonight, I'm tryin to cum befo' it's ovah", or, "So put your pimp cups and shake this booty to the ground, Keep me moanin makin funny sounds"[57] – sexual desperation is firmly perceived as a 'Black thing'.

Personality Trait 'B': Maintain an inane love for White people. A brilliant way of convincing White people that they are superior to Black people is to get 'blinging', Gun-Hoe rappers to act like they're desperate to be White, desperate to live White, and desperate to look White in a way that makes Frank Bruno look like H Rap Brown. That's why they get rappers like you to show their adoration for everything and anything that's White. One of the best ways to do this is to sign rappers who give themselves names of famous White people or famous White companies. From 'Gucci man', to 'Royce the 5'9', to 'Noreaga' (named after Noriega, former President and former drug runner in Panama. I know he might be mestizo somewhere down the line but he certainly looks White!). It's all about aiming for Whiteness that even Dulux can't match.

But the cherry on the pie is when rappers give themselves the names of White people who hate Black people like the Mafia, and other assorted crims. Remember in *Goodfellas* when Henry Hill's wife was getting worried about him getting caught by the police and he replies:

> *"Nobody goes to jail unless...they make themselves get caught. They don't have things organised...You know who goes to jail? 'Nigger-stick-up-men' that's who. You know why, because they fall asleep in the getaway car..."*[58]

Well it weren't fiction. It genuinely was the way these irrepressible Italian criminals felt about Black people. They did, and many still do, hate you. It's a fact that the Mafia, starting with Lucky Luciano (amongst others), was responsible for bringing Cocaine and other narcotic goodies into the Black ghettos.[59] And remember the line from *The Godfather Part I* when the crime families are talking about introducing drugs into their business and Don Zaluchi says:

> *"I don't want it near schools. I don't want it sold to children! In my city, we'd keep the traffic [of drugs] to the Dark People, the Coloureds. They're animals anyway, so let them lose their souls."* [60]

So let's get this straight – the same people that you want to emulate are the same people who think you're niggers and are presently responsible for the destruction and terrorisation of your communities through the drugs trade and have become millionaires through your misery. (Let's not forget that while NYC Don Italiano is chilling in his Jacuzzi at his $8 million palace in the Hamptons, Black people comprise 58% of those in state prisons for drug-related offences in the USA.)[61]

From Irv 'Gotti', to Daz 'Dillinger', from 'Capone' to 'Luciano' to a whole heap of people scrambling to call themselves 'Corleone' and 'Gambino', this insane obsession goes on and on. You guys have exhausted just about every Italian Gangsta name. And even that's not enough for you people. You move on to taking samples out of Gangsta films.

Now I'm not saying that I don't like what you've done with the scores from *Scarface*, and Jay-Z's *I'm re-loaded* skit was a classic. But it's just kinda weird how you make role models out of people who think that your skin colour makes you – to use a word used by the fictional hoodlum Tony Montana – a 'cockroach'.[62]

It's kinda like a group of Hasidic Jews singing Zemirot (Jewish Hymns) and calling themselves 'The Heinrich Himmlers'. It would be kinda weird wouldn't it? In fact, it's a bit 'Bunny Boilerish' if you get what I mean – begging to name yourself after someone who disrespects you.[63]

Gumiya: I never thought about that.

Phantom: **Personality Trait 'C': Maintain an inane love for White/non-Black things/shiny bling things.** A fantabulous way of assuring White people that Black people loooooooooove them is to get rappers to make endless tunes about White products. No house Negro would be complete without such an attribute. As Lil Wayne explains in the *Shine* remix:

> *"Let the diamonds and the jewellery light s*** up*
> *Each piece of jewellery I own, I ice it up*
> *You don't wanna put your vehicle next to us*
> *'Cause all of our vehicles, we dress 'em up*
> *With television, Dreamcast, DVDs*
> *Nice sounds, buttons...*"[64]

Gumiya: Are Dreamcasts White?

Phantom: Well it weren't created by 'the brothers' was it? It's kinda funny because you don't like to advertise Black unity, but you loooooooooove to advertise White businesses. You mention White when they sell you something shiny, but you only mention Black when you shoot them up. Burberry, Alize and everything else is talked about like it's the Holy Bible in your Hip-Hop tunes and you love it so much, you do it for free.

From Jay-Z's Iceberg fetish, to Lil' Kim's Donna Karen fixation, it's a greater love match than that between the middle classes and organic vegetables.

Ok, so Nike did offer Nelly a cash deal for all his talk of Air Force

Ones. But regardless of Nelly's talent, there is no doubt that when he started bragging about his 110s, he was doing it for the love! From the 'Prince of Bling', Chingy wearing $200,000 of jewellery at his shows,[65] to Young Buck yapping about "the Murcielago, lemme show you how it rolls, I got a Bentley that I only drove one time",[66] it's non-stop White product placement.

The now world-famous 'Jacob the Jeweller' has made millions because rappers just can't stop saying his name. Faith Evans, the late BIG, our friend 50 Cent, P Diddy and B2K and too many others to mention feel the need to utter Jacob's name so that they can advertise his stuff for them.[67] All this combined helps to convey an image of Black people who want nothing more than skin as pale as Morticia Addams.

Personality Trait 'D': Big up the ghetto 24/7. Just as the Minstrels used to lament about the plantations like it was as comfortable as a night in the Waldorf Astoria, you do what the Candyman desires – you try with all your heart to portray the image that Black people want to live in ghettos.

The Candyman can then tell everyone about the shockingly low expectations of Black folk, and how they want to live in crime-ridden squalor for eternity. And when White people believe this, they don't feel guilty about not doing anything to alter Black poverty anymore.

And that's why they get chumps like you to talk about the Ghetto like it's the Hanging Gardens of Babylon, like it's where all Black people wanna be.

People like Mobb Deep chat about "these my parts, you outta town out here...We don't give a f***, flip for any ol' reason, Just for the fun have your b*** ass leakin",[68] and Eightball and Thorough on about, "We true gangstaz, equipped with the guns and drugs, mean mugs, actin bad just because, That's how it does and ya damn sure gon' respect it".[69]

It all helps White people truly believe that Black people love poor housing, and love crime-ridden communities. And as easy as A-B-C (and D), we have the Minstrels of our age.

Gumiya: You got it all wrong. We brought 'Black' into the public sphere. Hip-Hop brings White people closer to Black people because through the lyrics, they can get an understanding of what it's like to *be* Black.

Phantom: You doughnut! Just because I've seen *Carlito's Way* umpteen times, it doesn't mean that I have an understanding of Puerto Rican people, Puerto Rican culture or that I'm fluent in Spanish. You know why? Because Hollywood's depiction of New York, Puerto Rican Gangsters in the 1970s is a very narrow part of the Puerto Rican existence on this planet. So a White person listening to Chamillionaire's *Ridin* is not necessarily getting an understanding of Blackness; in fact, far from it.

Gumiya: But at least it gives them a *little* insight into the Black community.

Phantom: Let's get serious for a moment and stop making silly excuses. What is there about the present state of MTV-censured Hip-Hop that is a representation of the Black community?

Gumiya: Er…

Phantom: Is it the half-naked Black women energetically rotating their bottoms as money is pushed into their bras? Is it the talk of hollow-tipped bullets and the ten crack commandments? Or wait, is it that bit when Nelly slips that credit card down that Black woman's butt crack? Is that the moment at which the world is brought that little bit closer to Black people?

Gumiya: Well…er…

Phantom: Let me tell you what White people get out of the commercial Hip-Hop that you espouse. In between the appreciation they may have of the Black art of Hip-Hop, they probably take away the following:
- That Black men are sex-crazed individuals who want nothing better than to put their ding-a-ling into a woman's gism prism.
- That Black men (second only to sex) loooooooooove guns!
- That Black women are sex objects desperate to get f***ed.
- That Black people are criminally minded and 'smoke weed everyday'.
- And that a Black person's dream is to spend all their money on a mansion, a set of sports cars, a swimming pool and as much jewellery as they can place around their well-greased bodies.

Yes! That's what White people understand 'Black' to be at the moment. And here's a newsflash, that doesn't do anything positive for you. There's a lot of Hip-Hop out there that sends alternative messages, messages about the richness of Black culture and the depth of Black history. But let's be clear about this, the present stuff on Channel U/Kiss FM rotation isn't doing that.

Unless you get Mos Def and Co. to run things, all you get is hyper-capitalistic nonsense. And I don't know about what you think, but from what I can see, that is a very, very small part of what exists in the Black community today.

I don't hear many MTV/Candy-sponsored rappers assuming the personality of the young, college student working in Burger King to pay for his education? Or a Black carpenter? Or a Black person who attends Mosque every Friday or Church every Sunday? Or a father who works during the day and studies in the night? Or the single mum who works three jobs?

Gumiya: I take your point, but at least we made 'Black' cool.

Phantom: And what does that do for Black people? Does it give them jobs, improve their housing, or give them better schools? You see, middle-class White kids might like Black Hip-Hop, but it don't mean they care about Black people.

'Black' serves a purpose for them between the ages of 10 to 29, and maybe 'til 35 if you really push it. Because, to them, 'Black' is a fad. 'Black' provides street cred when they need it. Every Hip-Hop album purchase/San Andreas-style video game for them is like a visit to the safari: it's 'cool' to experience, it's a little dangerous, it makes them feel a little grimy, but you can be damn sure that a) they never ever want to live the ghetto life and b) they never ever want to be robbed at gun point.

Once these White kids get their degree, everything changes. When they get a job as a lawyer, or a financial analyst, and hang out with their tennis/rugby-playing chums drinking lattes, they'll have the same impression of Black people as their parents did: that they're all sex-crazed, money-obsessed, lazy, ghetto-loving fiends. Hence, the Candyman will have achieved his aim; maintaining the status quo by keeping Black people down, and keeping the White middle-class fighting the Candyman's cause for them. You paid the cost to be the boss. Thank you Gumiya for being Pimped.

THE PHANTOM OF PROSE COMBAT

"Wise men speak because they have something to say;
fools because they have to say something".[70]
Plato

Gumiya: I can't take any more of this. When are you gonna let me go?
I can't deal with another one of you...you...ghosts talking me to
death!

Phantom: Don't worry. I am the last of your visitations.

Gumiya: Listen, I had no idea what I was doing before. It wasn't my
fault. I've seen what I've done wrong. I get your point. I'm really sorry.
I understand things now. Can't you just let me go? Pleeeease!

Phantom: Stop whinging and let's get through this... **I am going to
show you the effect you have on the lives of young Black
People.**

Gumiya: Ok ok. But before you start your soliloquy, just tell me one
thing: why have I had to go through all this! I mean, why am I so
important? Why are rappers so important? Why not go haunt David
Lammy or Trevor Phillips or that weird one who Channel Four kept
commissioning to make all those 'Black' documentaries...

Phantom: Darkus Howe?

Gumiya: Yea Darkus Howe! I mean, why does everyone always ask *us*
to be so damn socially conscious. We're musicians, not politicians!

Phantom: Like your old friend told you, Black people have so few famous
role models outside of the music industry. With perhaps the exception
of sport, Black musicians have been, are, and will always be some of
the most prominent people in the 'Black British' community. From
Jazz, to Reggae, from Rock n Roll to House, music has been one of the
few areas in which Black people have been given a little appreciation
from the White media. Today Black musicians are some of the richest,
most photographed, most hyped Black people in the Western world.
And with Hip-Hop being one of the most powerful mediums in the

Black community today, whether you guys like it or not, you have a huge amount of influence over the way young Black people think. I mean let's face it, more people are interested in D-Block's new album than in what I'm saying right now. And no matter how hard I'm trying to make this flow, it ain't got nothing on Swizz Beatz production!

Gumiya: You see, this is where I get a little confused. All you Phantoms have been telling me that *I'm* responsible for the way Black people act, but I disagree. I might have a teeeeeeeny tiny influence on Black people, but I don't have *that* much of an influence.

Phantom: Well in actual fact…

Gumiya: I mean, strip clubs and the objectific…obectific…the cussing of women started long before Lil' Wayne came to town, Cypress Hill didn't create Marijuana, and I don't ever remember reading that NWA were the originators of Capitalism.

Phantom: …Ok but…

Gumiya: If you're gonna blame us, then don't forget to blame Vin Diesel, Tom Cruise, and the rest of those 'shoot-em up' actors that get Pz to fire off those rocket launchers on the big screen.

Phantom: Hey, calm down a little…I'm not saying that you're responsible for what *all* black people do, and neither am I saying that you have the power to make *all* black people do what you want…but you *do* have an influence. Let me tell you a very short story…

Gumiya: Man, do all of you guys have to wax lyrical and tell stories all the time… Deep down I think you guys just like the sound of your own voices.

Phantom: Can you be quiet and let me get on with my story! You probably don't remember, but back in the day, there was this cognac that only old men drank. It was the type of drink that you might buy your granddad for Christmas – but something that no-one who thought of themselves as 'cool' would ever drink. This drink was called Courvoisier. But then, in 2002, Pharrell Williams teamed up with Busta Rhymes to release the tune *Pass the Courvoisier*.[71] All of a sudden, a drink that not many people knew about (particularly young, Black British people) became the drink that every Hip-Hop/RnB/Garage playing bar and club wanted to stock. The sales of the parent company for Courvoisier, Allied Domecq, increased by 20% in a matter of months as people everywhere began to desperately waste their hard earned money on a glass of brown water that people didn't even like the taste of.[72] All it took was for a couple of well-respected members of the Black Hip-Hop community to make a tune bragging about the stuff – and bob's your uncle – it becomes the flavour of the month.

And it ain't just the image of Courvoisier that Hip-Hop has had a hand in. Today, when you hear people in the UK greeting each other by the phrase, "What up", or calling the police 'the Feds' – you know that it came from a rap tune that someone in the UK was listening to. 'Baller', 'Hater', 'Holla', 'Murk', 'Playa', 'Ruckus', 'Scrub', 'Wifey' and 'Whip' are words straight out of the Hip-Hop/RnB world – and words that have become commonplace in everyday UK street vernacular.

If you bothered to listen to music from other countries, you'd realise that people all over the world, from Germany to Tanzania, from France to Peru, are making their own kinds of very successful rap music – all because they respect and appreciate the Black Hip-Hop art form. From the baseball cap, to jeans hung low, from the over-use of the word nigger, to the battle-talk used in Grime lyrics, it'd be foolish to argue that your tunes don't influence the way young Black people think, act and talk.

Consequently, when you and other well-known and massively-promoted Black people release 'I-HATE-BLACK-PEOPLE' tunes, it f***s Black people up.

Gumiya: But we don't make 'I-HATE-BLACK-PEOPLE' tunes.

Phantom: Ok ... so when Clipse glorify the drug trade with lines like:

"17 a brick, yeah, go and tell 'em that
I got the wamp wamp when I move it its still damp
Mildew-ish when I heat it, it turn bluish
It cools to a tight wad, the Pyrex is Jewish
I get paper, it seems I get foolish".[73]

...they were just joking? And when Big Tuck (signed to our old friend Bronfman's Universal Records) talks about:

"I'ma skirt around the club till I see this nigga here
I'ma rush the b**** nigga hit his head with a beer
I ain't playin' neither, I ain't playin' neither
I'ma swing till there's blood on my wife beater".[74]

...he was just playing, right...?

Gumiya: Er...I'm not really sure anymore.

Phantom: You guys make this music because (and I don't know how else I can say it) you and the Gun-Hoe crew hate Black people.

Gumiya: We what?

Phantom: You hate being Black. You hate your eyes, your features, your skin – you hate your Black self.

Gumiya: Are you crazy? How can I...how can we – hate ourselves?

Phantom: Well gimme a moment and I'll show you. Close your eyes for a moment and imagine that I'm White.

Gumiya: But you are White. You're a ghost!

Phantom: Well imagine that I'm a White police officer who released a tune with lyrics like this:

"I shot the Whitey in his head
then stabbed his Barbie in her bed
as she moaned with delight
succumbed without a fight
I killed her too
Stupid flat ass fool...
when oink, oink...
went the sound of the Met
surrounded I was
by the stench of those hogs
blam, blam I killed
those honkeys from Trident
blam, blam I killed

123

a Whitey for fun
blam, blam I killed
another paedo homosexual
blam, blam I killed
them all those cracker scum".[75]

Gumiya: If a White police officer wrote lyrics like that, I'd say that either all his dogs weren't barking, or that he had some serious, serious issues with himself. I mean, he's talking about 'cracker scum', and 'honkeys' – I always thought those were terms of abuse towards White people. And then he's busting lines about 'paedos'...lots of Black people tell me how all the paedos who get thrown in the slammer are White people – not Black, not Asian, not Chinese...as if being a kiddy fiddler is something that only happens to White men! So this rapper is cussing himself! In fact, now I come to think of it, if this person really *was* White, it's almost like he doesn't realise that he *is* White – 'cos he's saying some nasty things about White people.

Phantom: Do you see the correlation?

Gumiya: ...kind of...

Phantom: **So that's why us Phantoms are utterly perplexed by your lyrics.** You sound more like a Combat-18 speech than a rhyme straight from the streets... and speaking of Combat-18, check these lyrics out:

"Niggers just hit this side of town
Watch my property values go down
Bang, bang, watch them die
Watch those niggers drop like flies".[76]

Gumiya: Hey, I like the flow – who wrote that? Lil Scrappy, Prodigy, Kurupt or Juvenile?

Phantom: Now that's what I call funny!

Gumiya: What do you mean funny? Funny how?

Phantom: It's funny because those lyrics are taken from a song written by a group of British, White neo-Nazis called Beserkr. It's funny because there's a scary similarity between these lyrics – the lyrics of this fascist band, and the lyrics of Black rappers like you. It's funny because, if I didn't know that you were Black, how could I not assume that you hated black people?!

Gumiya: But...but...but I don't hate myself. You just have to understand that I've grown up in a pretty f***ed up situation. Me...I...we come from some pretty nasty places. We never had any positive role models in our lives, and so you have to understand that our lyrics are a reflection of what we watched on the TV and saw from outside of our windows. As Big Tray Dee of Three 6 Mafia said:

> *"I'm with everything positive that has to do with the advancement of my people, but we didn't go to college and get no degree to rap...We speak from experience...Me, personally, I did 13 years behind bars. I don't know step...1, 2 and 3 to get us out of the condition we're in".*[77]

Phantom: Stop making excuses for yourself. It ain't like I don't understand where you're coming from. Your upbringing might explain your lyrics, but it doesn't condone them. I'm sure you've heard of James Brown.

Gumiya: Of course I have ... he's the Godfather of Soul. I attended his funeral.

Phantom: This man was born in 1933 during the American Great Depression, the worst economic crisis in American history. As you can imagine, the Great Depression was much worse for a Black person, and much, much, much worse for a Black person living in the deep south. And I'm not talking about the ordinary south, I'm talking about Augusta 'Apartheid' Georgia, possibly one of the most racist parts of the USA at the time. Now since his father left home when he was just four years old, he found himself staying in a variety of relatives' houses, in different parts of town, and even living in a brothel at one point. Desperate to earn money, he bunked school and had to help out the rest of his family pick cotton and shine shoes in the local town.[78]

Well since that kind of employment ain't gonna put much food on the table, he started to get involved in crime, and at the age of 16, he was sent to a detention centre for armed robbery. This is a man who experienced hardships harder than the hardest hardships today – and he still managed to write songs like *Money Won't Change You*, *It's a Man's Man's Man's World* and *Say It Loud I'm Black And I'm Proud* – pretty much setting Malcolm X's manifesto to music. So please don't use your upbringing as an excuse for your lyrics.

But that aside, the problem is, when you talk about "pistol whipping niggers", and "sliding and dividing b****es", you kinda make it ok for other Black people to hate Black people. You see, what happens is that young Black people (especially in the UK) think: "I listen to Y2K everyday, and I see Black people all over TMF every night, thinking, talking and acting the same way, and I assume that this is simply the normal way for Black people to act. It must be normal to call women Hoes. It must be standard to act thuggish. It must be natural to keep a gun to protect myself from 'niggas'. After all, the richest, best dressed, most attractive Black people I know do those things!"

Now don't get me wrong. I'm not saying that you single-handedly turn Black people into Velociraptors or Michael Myers, but you definitely help to keep the expectations of Black people lower than a Dirty South Baseline.

Gumiya: But White people listen to Gun-Hoe tunes too, one of the Phantoms said so themselves!

Phantom: …but when White people go home and they switch on the telly, they've got plenty of people who look like them doing a variety of different and positive things. Who have Black kids got? Ainsley Harriott?!?!?!

Gumiya: I'm hearing you, but I still don't buy all of what you're saying. I can't be the only reason why Black kids are screwing up so badly.

Phantom: True-say. Even if your lyrics were positive – I'm not saying that Black people would be as happy as George Formby with a Ukulele in his hand. But even Rocky Balboa can work out that things might be a little better for the Black kids on the street if you guys started making tunes about the positive things associated with Blackness (not how easy it is to shift kilos of Coke, and how much you wanna jack a 'nigga's' phone).

Gumiya: Ok ok, I take your point. But if what we're saying is so bad, why aren't the parents stopping their kids from listening to it? I mean, we only make the music, we don't determine who listens to it!

Phantom: If you're from the streets – like you mention all the time – then you should know that the situation with Black parents is kinda messy at the moment. In the USA, only 36% of Black children are living in households with two parents, compared with 74% of White children and 64% of Hispanic children.[79] In the UK, over 45% of Black families are headed by a single parent.[80] That's why many young Black people are not getting the support from parents.

Gumiya: But rappers like us do *some* positive things for the Black community. Remember in 2005 when the Governor of California at the time, Arnold Schwarzenegger sent Stanley Williams AKA 'Tookie' to the death chamber?

Phantom: Oh yea. He'd been on death row for murdering two people back in '79. He was one of the original Crip gang members...

Gumiya: Yep, and whilst he was in prison he had turned his life around trying to steer young people away from the gang culture.[81] So plenty of us rappers came out against his execution. Daz Dillinger released a statement saying: "I, Daz Dillinger, urge the Black community and Hip-Hop community to stand up for Big Tookie. God puts opportunities in our midst to test us and challenge us to see if we are willing to risk it all to do what's right. I am willing to do what is right and I am asking the Hip-Hop community and the Black community: Are You"?[82] And Snoop said: "We're not just gonna sit around and let y'all kill niggas like it's the thing to do...We're gonna stand up and say something."[83] That proves that 'Gun-Hoe' rappers *do* try to galvanise the black community.

Phantom: Man you've been listening to too much RnB.

Gumiya: But I was never into Jodeci.

Phantom: You fool ... I'm talking about **R**eagan '**n**' **B**ush. Life doesn't work like that:
   a) You can't spend your life affiliating with gangs, killers and drug

dealers – the very same people who kill more Black people than Cancer – and then beg Black people to come together to save the life of a Black man. All Snoop and Daz go on about in their tunes are their links with 'niggative' street criminals, saying things like he's a 'Dogg Pound Gangsta, Criiiiiiiiip'.[84]

b) You can't spend a decade writing Gun-Hoe lyrics – and then suddenly talk about inspiring the Black community. I remember them saying things like: "...you niggaz better back back or get clapped, I ain't trippin', got the clip in smokin' bomb while I'm whippin' and you know I'm steady crippin' steady grippin' on that nina trigger finger"[85] ...and..."Run Nigga, Run Nigga (Plow)...I wouldn't be the nigga that I am If I didn't pop niggas in their mouth".[86]

c) You can't make tunes specifically designed to separate the Black community, and then ask for community cohesion. Both artists made tunes in tandem, cussing the East coast. In their video for 'New York, New York' they enacted a scene in which they toppled buildings in Manhattan.[87]

Bottom Line: Both of them are grade-A 'niggative' rappers coming straight from the Candyman franchise. So for you to say that Black people should respect their meagre offering, is like trying to get me to praise Hitler for being a vegetarian (which in actual fact he was). One minor gesture doesn't make up for a lifetime of stupidity and slavery.

Gumiya: ...but...but...we need to make some money. If we made music that was political – who would buy it?

Phantom: Don't be fooled by the Candyman. I know he tells you that you have to bust lines about "spanking that booty" in order to sell records, but come on...you can't be that gullible...? Give Black people more credit than that. Stevie Wonder, Aretha Franklin, Bob Marley, Nina Simone and Marvin Gaye didn't have to beg for pennies. Black people (and White people) will buy your music as long as it sounds good.

Gumiya: I suppose you're right.

Phantom: I know I'm right. And besides, I kinda get the feeling at the moment that Black people are looking for something different, something more educational and something more inspirational in the music that they listen to. The Krumping dance-thing in LA is in direct opposition to the whole 'bling' bulls*** that's been pushed into our faces.

In the Caribbean, Machel Montano, now the world's biggest Soca artist, is a musician who writes songs about putting an end to foolish violence and uplifting women's self-esteem. And in 2005, when Dave Chappelle chose the artists that he wanted to perform at his Block Party, he said that he only wanted artists that were saying things that were relevant to Black people's condition. Indeed, the fact that artists like Dead Prez still have careers despite the assault from TV/record execs should show you that Black people are looking for something outside of the Gun-Hoe bracket.

Gumiya: Yea, I kinda felt a little disappointed that Chappelle never invited me to that Block Party.

Phantom: So why not try to say something different when you next step into the studio?

Gumiya: If I'm honest, the main reason why I keep spitting 'niggativity' on wax is 'cos I feel like I have no choice. It seems like any Black man who gets up and talks about Black things for the benefit of Black people gets f***ed. When the over-talented actor/singer Paul Robeson visited the Soviet Union, spoke out against Franco during the Spanish Civil War, and demanded an end to lynching, he was pretty much outcast by the theatrical world and he was banned from leaving the USA.[88]

Then you got Sista Souljah, the very talented and inspirational artist whose two videos from her 1992 album, *360 Degree of Power* were banned by MTV and this helped her album sales plummet. Then her media career pretty much went out the window when she was reported saying, "If Black people kill Black people every day, why not have a week and kill White people?"[89] The interview failed to print the context of her comments and make clear that she meant it in a ret…in a rot…

Phantom: …in a 'rhetorical' way?

Gumiya: Yea, that's right, in a rhetorical way. And then you have Ras

Kass, the man who made that classic tune called, *The Nature of the Threat* in the 90s, the tune that taught me so, so much about Black history. Boy that tune opened my mind to so much stuff. Anyway, his record company weren't really feeling the material that he was putting out (what a surprise!) and as a result of a contractual dispute he wasn't allowed to release anything for ages.

Phantom: I'm impressed! You do know something about your industry.

Gumiya: I have my moments…

Phantom: Look, I gotta go soon, so let me be straight with you. A wise old man once said, "out of suffering comes great art". I ain't gonna lie, you produce incredible art … even if you chat s*** 95% of the time. I could never tell you that I didn't want to buy Juelz Santana's *What's The Game Been Missing*, even if the majority of his tunes seem to be about selling Crack.…and I will always rate Lil Jon for the tune that he did with Usher and Ludacris…what was it called…?

Gumiya: …*Lovers and Friends*…!

Phantom: That's the one…Yea. That tune is decent. I could never tell you that I didn't put that tune on my MP3 (yep even Phantoms got MP3s). And even though I know that Raekwon's *Cuban Linx* album was about some pretty grimy subjects, for me it's still one of the best Hip-Hop albums to date. And then there's that lyric, "for every rhyme I write, it's 25 to life"…

Gumiya: …from Mobb Deep huh?!

Phantom: I've been watching that *Shook Ones* video on YouTube for weeks now! I can't get it outta my head.
    And that's why we came to you. You guys are some of the most talented people on this earth and, as a result, it's you that holds the destiny of the Black community in your hands. Now I know that it's unfair to pile so much responsibility on to you – that's why I'm not asking for you to be a raptivist or a monk (we can't all be Anthony B). I'm just asking you not to be 'niggative'. You could be like Nas, MC Dynamite, Styles P, Kano, La Brigade, Sizzla, Black Twang, Jeru The Damaja and a whole host of other artists – dropping a socially-

conscious tune into your album now and then, or a political verse into your new release, just to let people know that you ain't the mouthpiece of some crinkled, geriatric White guy who wished all Black people were still living in slave quarters.

Or you could simply be like Roots Manuva, Papoose, Pharaoh Monch, Supernatural and Lupe Fiasco – people who are concerned chiefly with displaying their verbal proficiency – but who make it clear in their lyrics that they are about the Hip-Hop Art, and not being a White exec's biaatch. Just like the way the word 'Urban' now replaces 'Black' as a musical definition, you, your rapper friends, and the rest of the Black community are being played better than a gaming expert plays ISS Pro.

So the question is: are you going to let these punks continue to ride your arse like a Grand National winner from one place to another, collecting the winnings whilst continuing to f*** you and your peoples? Or do you want to re-claim Hip-Hop for yourself and the rest of the Black community?

Gumiya: I'd like to think that I could be the latter…

Phantom: If you need inspiration, remember what life was like for you growing up. Ask yourself what would have motivated you to become all that you could be, and remember that what you do is bigger than Hip-Hop. You ain't just producing tunes, you're producing the aspirations of the next generation of Black people on this planet. You're free to go. **Peace out**.

> "Come on baby light my fire.
> Everything you drop is so tired
> Music is supposed to inspire
> So how come you ain't getting no higher?"[90]
> *Lauren Hill*

NOTES

1. The Roots featuring Raphael Saadiq, *What They Do*, (Geffen Records 1996).
2. British Film Institute 2006, (8/08/2006). http://www.bfi.org.uk/about/media/releases/2006/2006-08-08-tupac-shakur.pdf (accessed 22 May 2008).
3. Rap, Robert, *News Network*, (23/08/2006). http://www.rapnewsdirect.com/0-

202-259395-00.html?tag=artistnav (accessed 22 May 2008).

4. The Random House Dictionary of the English Language, Second Edition 1987.

5. Paraphrased from Malcolm X, *Message to the Grass Roots*, (10/11/1963). http://www.spartacus.schoolnet.co.uk/USASdomestic.htm (accessed 22 May 2008).

6. Noel, Peter, *Call and Response Targeting Silent Rappers: A Street Fight for Justice or Hip Hop McCarthyism?*, (5-11/2000). http://www.villagevoice.com/news/0027,noel, 16183,1.html (accessed 22 May 2008).

7. Goodman, Alan, *Remembering Gary Webb*, Revolutionary Worker No.1263 (26th December 2004) rwor.org (accessed 22 May 2008).

8. *Source* Magazine, (04/2006).

9. Ice T, *Killers*, (Electrobeat 1984).

10. "Just as the Slave master of that day used Tom, the house Negro, to keep the field Negroes in check, the same old Slave master today has Negroes who are nothing but modern Uncle Toms, twentieth-century Uncle Toms, to keep you and me in check, to keep us under control, keep us passive and peaceful and non-violent. That's Tom making you non-violent. It's like when you go to the dentist, and the man's going to take your tooth. You're going to fight him when he starts pulling. So he squirts some stuff in your jaw called Novocain, to make you think they're not doing anything to you. So you sit there and because you've got all of that Novocain in your jaw, you suffer peacefully. Blood running down your jaw, and you don't know what's happening. Because someone has taught you to suffer peacefully." Malcolm X, *Message to the Grass Roots*, (10/11/1963). http://www.thespeechsite.com/famous/MalcolmX-2.htm (accessed 22 May 2008).

11. Collegiate School. www.collegiateschool.org (accessed 22 May 2008).

12. Henry, Conan, Personal communication, (28/08/2006).

13. 50 Cent, *Heat*, (Aftermath/Shady 2003).

14. 50 Cent, *P.I.M.P,* (Aftermath/Shady 2003).

15. *50 Cent Slams Kanye's 'Bush is Racist' Comment*, (01/11/2005). http://contactmusic.com/new/xmlfeed.nsf/mndwebpages/50%20cent%20slams%20kanyes%20bush%20is%20racist%20comment (accessed 22 May 2008).

16. *50 Cent disagrees with Kanye West on Bush*, (02/11/2005).http://www.ctv.ca/servlet/ArticleNews/story/CTVNews/20051102/50cent_kanye_bush_051102/20051102? hub=Entertainment (accessed 22 May 2008).

17. Whorter, John, *White do-gooders did for Black America*, (The *Sunday Times* 11/09/2005). http://www.timesonline.co.uk/article/0,,2089-1774271,00.html (accessed 22 May 2008).

18. Brookings Institution, 2006

19. Agenda For Children (New Orleans), data provided to GNOCDC, 06/2006

20. Congressional Research Service, (CRS) Report for Congress, *Hurricane Katrina:*

Social-Demographic Characteristics of Impacted Areas, November 4, 2005; also, U.S. Census Bureau, *2004 American Community Survey*.

21. Wise, Tim, *Erazeing Historical Revisionism and the Denial of the Obvious*, (Civilrights.org, 25/06/2006). http://209.85.129.104/search?q=cache:cdeukj KE3_gJ :www.northwestern.edu/mcc/diversifyinu.html+facts+statistics+racism +new+orleans+katrina+Black+people&hl=en&gl=uk&ct=clnk&cd=9 (accessed 22 May 2008).

22. BBC investigated by police over racist n word broadcasts, (28/12/2006). www.ligali.org/article.php?id=597 (accessed 22 May 2008).

23. McGrath, Tom, *MTV: The Making of a Revolution*, (Philadelphia: Running Press, 1996).

24. *ibid.*

25. *ibid.*

26. *ibid.*

27. Oxide and Neutrino, *Rap Dis*, (East/West 2002)

28. Ford, Tracey, *Mr. Kweli Honours Ms. Hill: Rapper pays musical tribute to Fugee on new CD*, (2006), http://www.rollingstone.com/artists/mosdef/articles/story/8835077/ mr_kweli_honors_ms_hill (accessed 22 May 2008).

29. Cloonan, Martin, *Popular music and censorship in Britain: An overview*, (Routledge 1995)

30. Alridge, Derrick P, *From Civil Rights to Hip Hop: Toward a Nexus of Ideas*. http:// www.questia.com/PM.qst;jsessionid=FtkWSGQGnrJZHfQr2crSyggvkppJn519g DQ27nW2LQfNGLr2VKN3!48714160?a=o&d=5011984879 (accessed 22 May 2008).

31. LaFranco, Robert, *The 2004 Rock Rich List. The Stones top the annual list of music's biggest moneymakers*, (2004). http://www.rollingstone.com/artists/theeagles /articles/story/5939025/the_2004_rock_rich_list (accessed 22 May 2008).

32. *Should I buy this?*, (29/06/2005). arts.guardian.co.uk/features/story/0,11710,151 7058,00.html

33. Albini, Steve, *The Problem With Music*, negativland.com/albini.html (accessed 22 May 2008).

34. Muhammed, Cedric, *Taking Care of Business: Hip Hop artists day it's time to take control of billion dollar music industry*, (Online Music and Hip Hop Slaves, Blackelectorate.com 12/12/2001).

35. Lowe, James B, *The American Directory of Certified Uncle Toms*, (Chicago: Lushena, 2002).

36. *Tasmanian Aboriginal People and History*. http://www.aboriginalartonline.com/regions /tasmania.php Right now, there are no full Black Tasmanians left at all.

37. Rashidi, Runoko, The Destruction of the Tasmanian Aborigines in *The Global African Community Black War*. http://www.cwo.com/~lucumi/tasmania.html (accessed 22 May 2008).

38. *ibid.*

39. *ibid.*

40. *ibid.*

41. Of course this was not the only way to sort the problem, but it certainly helped

42. *Amos and Andy Television Radio Show.* http://www.amosandy.com/ (accessed 22 May 2008).

43. *Carry Me Back to Old Virginny James Bland*, 1878. http://www.musicanet.org/robO kopp/usa/virginny.htm (accessed 22 May 2008).

44. http://www.things.org/music/al_stewart/history/josephine_baker.html

45. *Hip-Hop Setting the Bear in First Black Artists Hold Billboard's Top 10* (04/10/2003 *The Boston Globe*) http://www.hsan.org/content/main.aspx?pageid=21 (accessed 22 May 2008).

46. Jules-Rosette, Bennetta, *Josephine Baker in Art and Life: the Icon and the Image* (University of Illinois, 2007)

47. O'Mailey, Michael, *A Blood Red Record: the 1890s and American Apartheid*, www.ferris.edu/news/jimcrow/links/misclink/1890s/ (accessed 22 May 2008).

48. Gen JC Christian, *Traditional Jim Crow Values*, (17/03/2005). http://patriotboy. blogspot.com/2005_03_13_patriotboy_archive.html (accessed 22 May 2008).

49. Ludacris, *Get the f*** back*, (Ral 2001).

50. Yin Yang Twins, *The Whisper Song*, (TVT 2005).

51. Morris, Nigel *Cocaine Offences Rise 16%*, (07/12/2005). http://news.independent. co.uk/uk/this_britain/article331619.ece (accessed 22 May 2008).

52. Meikle, James, *50,000 Londoners Addicted to Crack, says Study*, (20/09/2005). www.guardian.co.uk/uk_news/story/0,,1573750,00.html (accessed 22 May 2008).

53. caselaw.lp.findlaw.com/scripts/getcase.pl?navby=search&case=/data2/circs/9th /9430313.html (accessed 28 June 2008).

54. 15/10/2006 creativedestruction.wordpress.com/2006/11/15/crack-cocaine- sentencing-systematic-racism-at-work/ (accessed 22 May 2008).

55. Jim Jones, *J.I.M.M.Y*, (East Mountain Music 2004).

56. Jermaine Dupri, *Money, Power and Hoes*, (So So Def 2001).

57. Trina, *It's Your B-Day*, (Atlantic Records 2005).

58. *Goodfellas*, (Warner Bros Pictures 1990).

59. *The Godfather*, (Paramount Pictures 1972).

60. Lusane, Clarence, *Pipe Dream Blues: Racism and the War Drugs*, (1991 South End Press, Boston, Mass), Pg.39.

61. Beck, Allen J., PhD, and Paige M. Harrison, US Dept. of Justice, Bureau of Justice Statistics, Washington, DC 08/2001) Pg.11, Table 16. http://209.85.129.104 /search?q=cache:W9PTTqU8SLQJ:www.drugwarfacts.org/racepris.htm+Black +drug+addicts+african+american+statistics+58%25&hl=en&gl=uk&ct=clnk&

cd=1 (accessed 22 May 2008).

62. *Scarface*, (Universal Pictures 1983)

63. "When they see this man's house on fire, you don't hear the little Negroes talking about 'our government is in trouble.' They say, "The government is in trouble." Imagine a Negro: "Our government"! I even heard one say "our astronauts." They won't even let him near the plant – and 'our astronauts"! 'Our Navy" – that's a Negro that is out of his mind, a Negro that is out of his mind". Malcolm X, *Message to the Grass Roots*, (10/11/1963).

64. Lil Wayne, *Shine' remix*, (Cash Money 2004).

65. *Chingy: Fucknut or Superstar?*, (May 2005 *Craccum* Magazine). http://72.14.221.104 /search?q=cache:opJDyvxvgKYJ:www.craccum.com/2005/05chingy.htm+chingy +behind+the+bling&hl=en&gl=uk&ct=clnk&cd=3 (accessed 22 May 2008).

66. Lil Scrappy featuring Young Buck, *Money In The Bank*, (Reprise 2006).

67. The funny thing is that although Black people made this guy famous, I can only find White models on his website. Strange huh?

68. Mobb Deep feat Lil Jon, *Real Gangstaz*, (Loud Records 2006).

69. Eightball, *Don't 4Get*, (8 Ways Entertainment 2001).

70. http://www.silverstones.com/thebat/CoOkies%20for%20Bat.txt (accessed 22 May 2008).

71. Hein, Kenneth, *Cognac is in the House*, (22/09/2003). http://www.newmediastrategies .net/buzz_brandweek2.html (accessed 22 May 2008).

72. *ibid.*

73. Clipse, *Wamp, Wamp What It Do?*, (Jive Records 2006).

74. Big Tuck, *Tussle*, (T-Town Music 2004).

75. Media News Ofcom won't intervene to halt N word usage by BBC Westwood (18/10/2005). http://www.ligali.org/article.php?id=440 (accessed 22 May 2008).

76. http://www.splcenter.org/intel/intelreport/article.jsp?aid=452 (accessed 22 May 2008).

77. *Source* Magazine, (02/2005).

78. Freeman, Scott, *James Brown: Soul Brother No. 1, 1933-2006*, (01/10/2007).http:// atlanta.creativeloafing.com/gyrobase/Content?oid=oid%3A181542 (accessed 22 May 2008).

79. Hunts, Holly, *Family Works and Demographics.* http://www.montana.edu/hhunts/ courses/437/Lectures/Family%20and%20Work%20Demographics.ppt (accessed 22 May 2008).

80. *Focus on Families* (National Statistics 06/2005) http://www.statistics.gov.uk/downloads /theme_compendia/fof2005/families.pdf (accessed 22 May 2008)

81. Tookie's Corner. www.tookie.com (accessed 22 May 2008).

82. *Source* Magazine, (02/2005).

83. *ibid.*

84. Daz Dillinger, *DPG Fo' Life*, (So So Def 2006).

85. Daz Dillinger, *All I Need*, (So So Def 2006).

86. Snoop Dogg, *Vato*, (Geffen Records 2006).

87. Tha Dogg Pound, *New York, New York*, (Death Row 1995).

88. http://www.spartacus.schoolnet.co.uk/USArobeson.htm (accessed 22 May 2008).

89. *Washington Post*, (13/05/1992).

90. Lauren Hill, *Superstar*, (Ruffhouse 1998).

CHAPTER FIVE
How To Look Black In Five Days

"In the Arctic, where the indigenous people sometimes might hunt a wolf, they'll take a double edge blade and they'll put blood on the blade and melt the ice and stick the handle in the ice so only the blade is protruding. And a wolf who smells the blood and wants to eat will come and lick the blade trying to eat. And what happens is when the wolf licks the blade he cuts his tongue and he bleeds and he thinks he's really having a good meal and he drinks, and he licks and licks and of course he's drinking his own blood and he kills himself."[1] *Omali Yeshiteta*

Kahina[2]: Ok, so welcome back from the break. In the first part of the show, Candace and I showed you how simple it was to change your cluttered room into a spacious, tidy environment, fit for all your modern needs.

Candace[3]: In this, the most exciting part of the show, we will, in just 5 days, give the Lucky Winner of Last Week's Competition the most exciting Black 'Look' for the 21st century. That's right, YOU have won the **Essential Black Makeover.**

Kahina: Now in response to that 'Black' issue of the Italian Vogue recently, we've received thousands of emails asking us how you can achieve the true Black Look.

Candace: And this is because you've noticed, as have we, that there are a lot of Black people who are looking more Freak! than Chic!

Kahina: I'm talking about those people who gold up the front row of their teeth, but still live off benefits …I'm talking about those people who rent limousines for their Saturday night out on the tiles, whilst they spend their college classes listening to their MP3s and cussing off their teachers. I'm talking about all those people who whinge about 'the White man', whilst buying their lunch from McDonalds instead of Maureen's West Indian Restaurant situated next door. You see, looking like you've been fed, dressed, and educated by advertising consultants, marketing specialists, publishing gurus and television execs is not a good look.

Candace: Especially since the last time that I checked, those advertising consultants, those marketing specialists, those publishing gurus and those television execs were, well…they were all Candymen!

Kahina: That's why over the next five days, our lucky winner and the viewers will be treated to the secrets behind the look that everyone wants to imitate: the Dapper Look; the Black Look; the look that brings money, power and self-respect! Let The Makeover Commence!

DAY 1: THE FASHION VICTIM
'Understanding The Game' Is The New Black

"The goal for the corporations is to make as much money as possible and to maximise market share. So the people have to be turned into mindless consumers of goods that they don't want. The corporations therefore develop what are called 'Creative Wants' and impose on people what's called a Philosophy of Futility. They focus them on the insignificant things of life, like fashionable consumption. The ideal for the corporations is to have individuals who are totally disassociated from one another, whose sense of value is simply, 'how many created wants can I satisfy?' There are huge industries, public relations industries, advertising and so on, which are designed from infancy to mould people into this desired pattern."[4] *Noam Chomsky* (paraphrased)

Candace: So what's the first thing we need to do with our lucky winner?

Kahina: We need to fix up the sunglasses of course!

Candace: That's right! Style always, always, always starts with the eyes. **Change One** is gonna be about throwing away your old pair of Christian Dior 'pimp tints', and **Change Two** is replacing them with a pair of hydrophobic, anti-reflective, 3-D, trifocal spectacles…the types of shades that let you really see what's going on.[5]

Kahina: When I saw you (our lucky winner) come into the studio with those mirror shades on, I knew that you were in desperate need of help. If I'm brutally honest, you'd be better off wearing a sign on your head that said, 'I-don't-know-what-the-f***-I'm-doing'.

Candace: Or even better, a sign saying 'I-don't-know-s***-and-I-ain't-ever-gonna-be-s***'! The reason? Because at present you're dropping the 'ignorant' look, not the Black Look.

Kahina: You see, the BIG problem with the pair of spekkies that you're wearing is that you bought them from someone who doesn't want you to see what's going on. They're the types of spekkies that distract you from seeing reality. They're the types of spekkies that have you focused on the new series of *Wife Swap*, the latest celebrity fashion disaster in *Heat* magazine and your horoscope in *The Sun* newspaper, instead of the things that you really need to be seeing – such as the World Title Bout that is presently going on for control of your mind.

Candace: **And in this World Title Bout**, there are two fighters. **Fighter A is You and anyone like you**. The Black working class, the Black people who don't own any advertising firms, the Black people who don't own any Fortune 500 companies, the Black people who don't own any media outlets. Basically all those Black people who don't have any real political or economic power. **Fighter A's Aim**: To hold on to as much of their hard-earned cash as is possible.

Fighter B is The Corporation, or as you probably know them, **the Candyman**. They're the people who run multimillion-pound companies, who trade resources by the shipload, who make deals with the presidents and prime ministers of nations – basically all those people who own the means of production. **Fighter B's Aim**: To perpetually scam you, Fighter A, of your money – all day and all night.

Whether it be their leadership, their hairspray, their ideology, or their computer software, the Candyman is dedicated to making you buy something, something that you either don't need, that you have never heard of, that you don't understand, or that they raped, maimed and killed someone to bring to you.

The Venue. This Title Bout is contested in the landscape in which you live: the roads, the skies, the buildings, the fields, the playgrounds and the offices.

We have adverts on wall paintings, billboards, printed leaflets, web banners, web pop-ups. We have adverts wrapped around buses, trains, trams, street furniture, cars, bus shelters, taxis, airships, roof mounts, underground platforms and even apples in supermarkets. We have adverts on the radio, at the movies, on television, in magazines, in newspapers, at sports events, on stickers, on the opening sections on DVDs, on the back of ticket events, and even on the back of receipts. We have covert advertising in films, music videos, during football matches and computer games. We also have unsolicited advertising through emails, fax machines, letter boxes, telephones, text messages and too many more to mention.

A report by the Chartered Institute of Marketing claimed that the average consumer is exposed to around 1,500 advertising messages every single day.[6] That's over one a minute.

Kahina: Consequently **The Scorecard** looks as shameful as an Audley Harrison fight. You are being massacred. Right now in the UK, the richest 1% of the population have increased their share of the national income from around 6% to 13% in just 20 years and the wealthiest 10% of the population now own more than half the country's wealth up from 47% to 54% over the past 10 years.[7] Whilst for the rest:

- The average household debt in the UK is approximately £9,223 (excluding mortgages). It increases by £12.10 every day[8]
- The UK's personal debt is now increasing by £1million every five minutes.[9]

Because whilst you and the rest of the working class live in a dreamworld, believing that your principal function in life is to go to work to get paid and then to go shopping, in reality you have been screwed in a more spectacular fashion than in *Debbie Does Dallas*. And in order to screw you, the superfly guys with the bags of dough need to screw the third world in order to produce the merchandise that it needs to flog to you. So right now on our planet:

- The 400 highest income earners in the USA make as much money in a year as the entire population of 20 African nations – more than 300 million people.[10]
- The GDP (Gross Domestic Product) of the poorest 48 nations (i.e. a quarter of the world's countries) is less than the wealth of the world's three richest people combined.[11]

Now, the reason why they're getting richer, and you're getting poorer is because the Candyman is a trained expert at the 'Consumer Jedi Mind Trick'. The 'Consumer Jedi Mind Trick' works by fusing commodity consumption with self-worth that equates to a desire to part with cash.

Candace: In other words, they get you to believe that what you own defines who you are. And so you become 'I-think-my-possessions-define-me-better-than-my-brain-defines-me' human beings.

Kahina: And that's why in every advert, they focus on telling you how much better your life would be if you bought their product. So take something simple like a Giorgio Armani fragrance advert. They always have some square-jawed man with a ripped body doing something very chilled or 'artified' in a dreamy, spacious, comfortable-looking apartment, being caressed by a thin, leggy model who looks like she is more attracted to him than the magnets are attracted to my fridge.

And you start to think: If the TV can show a person living this type of lifestyle then this lifestyle must exist! And if this lifestyle exists then I want this lifestyle. 'Cos I want to be groped by a delectable model! And I wanna live in a wicked apartment! And I wanna look buff goddamit! But now I feel discontented with my life, because I'm thinking that I should have so much more. But if buying this fragrance can make women want to f*** me, if buying this bottle of liquid can make me feel like I'll be improving my life, if buying this glass of fragranced water means that I am getting closer to that advert's lifestyle, then I'll buy it!

So in the same way those Storm-Troopers were duped by Obi-Wan, we are duped into believing that we need to buy material things in a never ending pilgrimage to find value in ourselves.[12]

From magazines that like to tell you how much Nicole Kidman's Balenciaga Oscar dress would cost, to the endless coverage of celebs and their five million pound Amalfi Coast villas, we all think that spending is the only way to be happy, that spending is the only way to feel normal.

You see, if adverts told you that you were already happy, wonderful people you wouldn't need their products. So that's why every advert tells you that you're a nobody, and that by possessing their product, it makes you a somebody.

Candace: If you don't have that new Poco Pink Mac Lacquer Lip Gloss, you're gonna need to stay away from the club scene 'cos everyone will laugh at your crusty mouth. And if you don't have the latest leg wax from Parissa, people will laugh at you and say, hey, that's the woman who looks like she just stepped off the *Planet of the Apes* film set. If you don't have that new La Vendi refining facial cleanser, no man will ever want come near you again – ever – and you'll die unmarried and alone. Beneath the logos, beneath the slogans, every commercial tells you that you're not just buying merchandise, but the gateway to a different life.

Nike posters don't say "Just Do It", they say, "Your words can't define you but your trainers can". Coca-Cola adverts don't say, "The Real Thing", they say, "regardless of what you've achieved, without Coca-Cola, you don't know what life is." L'Oreal TV commercials don't say, "Because I'm Worth It", they say, "Self-expression is not about how you act – how you look says more about who you are"!

Kahina: And just in case whilst you're rinsing your plastic, you manage to see through your Candy-manufactured glasses, and have a panic attack about how much Wedge you're blowing, the Candyman dedicates every other day to putting you at ease with your spending sprees.

Candace: …telling you not to worry about what you spend today …'cos tomorrow you might get lucky. That's why they commission endless TV programmes about how to get rich, or how to get famous, or how to get both – overnight and quick. From *Who Wants To Be A Millionaire* to *The National Lottery*, from *X-Factor* to *Big Brother*, it's all about convincing people that poverty can be reversed – with ease! That way, Carli-Jane and Le-Anne, who work at the Greasy Spoon Caf' in Gateshead, don't have to worry about how much they spend on their dress for their Saturday night out on the 'toon', because there's always the chance that they could be spotted by the Chief Exec of Chanel (who will just happen to be in the Caf' one day) and give them a modelling contract – whereupon they will become the most photographed women in the world, marry Brad Pitt, adopt a Chinese baby – and be able to pay off their debts. Hence, last year, there were a record number of bankruptcy petitions issued by the courts.[13]

Now since Black people are some of the lowest paid and most under-qualified racial groups in Britain – and since you are Black – it makes you the fighter with the glass jaw in this Title Bout.

Kahina: That's why Day One has been all about finding you a better pair of specs.

Candace: So you can discard that ignorant look – it was so over anyway. And you can begin to fight this **Title Bout** like it was supposed to be played with you winning and knocking the Candyman the F*** Out! Now let's get to work on your new wardrobe...

DAY 2: HAUTE COUTURE
'High-Intelligence' Is The New Black

"You know the worst thing about niggers? Niggers love to not know. Nothing makes a nigger happier than not knowing the answer to your question. 'Hey man, what's the capital of Zaire'? 'I don't know that s***! I'm just keeping it real'. Yeah, you're keeping it real dumb. If you're afraid a nigger will break into your house, and you wanna save your money...You put the money in a book. Cause niggers don't read."[14] *Chris Rock*

Kahina: Now let's get a good look at the outfit. It's pretty bad isn't it Candace?

Candace: Quite frankly, it's awful. It's so sad when bad clothes happen to good people.[15] No wonder you ain't got no friends on Facebook. Ok, so at one point in our lives, I know that Kahina and I dressed like we were thicker than a prison wall wearing the Moschino Moschino Moschino Moschino Moschino Moschino Moschino Moschino Moschino Moschino tops, and pulling our Versace G-Strings up so high that it could be seen over our cream Iceberg Jeans. But sooner or later, once we'd got a sense of style we stopped making fashion *faux pas* and we started dressing in high fashion: Haute Couture. Garments that created a style that was our own, and not a style that some Candyman in Italy thought that we should wear. Haute Couture is exactly what we're gonna give to you.

Kahina: Today's **Change One** is all about throwing out that desire to look rich when you're not rich.

Candace: Yea that's right, we need to re-jig that age-old determination by some Black people to look like you got Pz, when in actual fact your bank balance looks like Robert Maxwell was running it.

Kahina: You see, your over-priced ensemble with the Ralph Lauren Polo Shirt and the Nautica sweater just doesn't work. And the reason is, because it just isn't you. The thing about Nautica and Ralph Lauren is that they're labels that have been exceptionally popular in the Black community for a number of years now, a fact which must be fairly surprising to the people who run these firms. After all, Ralph Lauren design clothes for the aristocratic Candy-Gang members who often participate in playing Polo...

Candace: ...the game where you ride on horses and carry sticks and chase balls...

Kahina: ...and Nautica is designed for aristocratic Candy-Gang members who consider themselves Yachting fanatics...

Candace: ...the pastime in which you buy boats costing anywhere from £200,000 to millions and millions...

Kahina: Now since you don't spend your Saturdays on luxury boats, or your Sundays in the saddle, if we weren't extremely perceptive fashion critics, we'd be scratching our heads, asking ourselves what on earth was going on.

Candace: But because we *are* extremely perceptive fashion critics, we know the real reason behind this choice of clothing. It's because you're trying, with all your heart, to prove to your friends and everyone else that you got more green than St Patrick. Now this would be cool if you *had* more green than St Patrick, but the reality, sadly, is that you don't. And that's why whenever you buy your Evisu jeans, your Burberry jackets, your Etienne-Ozeki man-bags, your Bapes trainers, your Louis Vuitton handbags, or your DKNY hoodie, you make sure that you buy one that has the label splashed all over it – after all, how else would people know that you have the cash to buy these garms!? 'Cos when people see the expensive designer labels...You – Feel – Like – You – Are – Somebody – Special!

Kahina: The origins of this malfunctioning ethos go 'way back when', and it went a little something like this. You want to be rich like everyone else, but you're living in a poor part of town with not much money, yet you still want people to think that you're rich when you're not. So you spend what little money you have on trying to look rich. From that brand new Nokia phone that you have with no credit, to that Asprey gold ring on your finger, from Fendi shirts to Mulberry accessories, you buy expensive label designer things from expensive shops that give you nice carrier bags to put your expensive items in, and you inevitably end up being poorer than you were in the first place.[16]

Candace: Essentially, you have a bank balance that's touching bottom more times than a regular at the Blue Oyster, and an even smaller chance of becoming rich.

Kahina: It's a backwards philosophy that makes no sense…

Candace: …like training for a marathon after you've run it, or like giving open-heart surgery and then going to medical school.

Kahina: So this is how we're going to make you over. Instead of trying to *look* rich you need to *be* rich. So **Change Two** is dressing cheaply.

A Question. Have you noticed that if you go to certain clubs frequented by wealthy people, they dress in the scruffiest clothes and not in the blingiest clothes? The answer: because they *are* bling. They don't need to tell people about it as well![17]

Another Question. Have you noticed that when rich people *do* buy expensive clothes, you don't often see them with the labels emblazoned all over them. The Reason. Because many wealthy people think that the 'advertise-my-clothes-label-while-I-wear-it' style is vulgar. They don't need to tell people they're rich 'cos they *are* rich.

One last Question.[18] Have you noticed that a lot of rich people remain rich. The reason: because they don't spend their wonga unnecessarily on clothes to make themselves look rich. They're more concerned with *being* rich. So they have trust funds set up for their kids, they put money in high interest bank accounts and hire accountants to help them cut tax corners. (If you thought rich people lost money during the Credit Crunch, think again.) They spend what they need to spend, and invest the rest.

As a fashion consultant, I know the importance of looking good, but the idea that you have to buy something that has been made by a wealthy member of the Candy-family to look good is not necessary.

Candace: That's right. Trust me, H&M, New Look, TK Maxx and Matalan are the stores you need to be hitting. It's all about putting your confidence in a thing called Logic:

a) The Logic that you can quite easily make yourself look good in clothes that cost under a tenner – having money left over to use wisely.

b) The Logic that one shouldn't worry about how rich you look when you ain't rich.

c) The Logic that getting cash is a process that takes patience and hard work.

d) The Logic that *being* rich is better than *looking* rich.

Kahina: Which brings us neatly to **Change Three: The Book Look**. The look that's designed to get you rich!

Candace: Let Kahina work backwards with you to get you to overstand the look we want you to go for.

Kahina: The end result is *you get rich*:

Stage Five: what gets you rich is a job that pays you lots of money.

Stage Four: in order to get a job that pays you lots of money you need to have the confidence and the attitude to apply for those jobs.

Stage Three: to have the confidence and the attitude to apply for those jobs you need to get the qualifications.

Stage Two: in order to get those qualifications, you need to make education your number one priority.

Stage One: to make education your number one priority, you need to get the **Book Look.**

The Book Look – the look for people of all ages – is about experiencing things that challenge you, like travelling outside of your area. **The Book Look** is about studying and understanding other cultures, religions, languages and learning how to interact with people who are different from you. **The Book Look** is about, most importantly, getting educated and qualified.

Candace: Trust me, I was ignorant once and I know that the Classroom

Experience versus the Diesel Jeans/Donna Karen Perfume experience is a pretty one-sided affair.

I mean after all, when we see the Black 'role-models' of our age brag about the *Label Look* like it's the shiznit, it's easy to understand why so many of us shun the Student of Knowledge style. Whenever we see the Footballer's bedrooms on *MTV Cribs*, we see the Huge Sony flat screen television, the massive bed, the walk-in wardrobe and the endless shoe racks. Whenever we see the rapper's living rooms in the Hip-Hop videos, we see the huge surround-sound speaker system, the freshest PlayStation, and the lavish furniture. But we never, ever, see any of these Black people – ever – with any books.

The Reason: 'Cos the Candyman *loooooooooves* to make television programmes attempting to convince Black people that rediscovering the **Book Look** is not in their interest. And when I say rediscover, I say this because we seem to forget that Black people used to flaunt the **Book Look** like Liberace used to flaunt glitter.

Lewis Latimer used to parade **The Book Look** when he was helping to improve the first electric light bulb so that it could be produced cheaply, making it affordable for all people.[19]

And Garrett Morgan, well he was to **The Book Look** what Angela Davis was to the Afro. He invented, among dozens of other things, the early Gas Mask and the Three Way Traffic Signal.[20]

Phillip Emeagwali was a devout follower of **The Book Look** when he helped with the thought process behind the multibillion-pound, generation-changing World Wide Web.[21] He helped develop the world's fastest computer when he was involved in the construction of the Connection Machine, an instrument which utilises 65,000 computers linked in parallel and can perform 3.1 billion calculations per second.

Mark Dean, a **Black Book Look** Guru, is the architect of the modern day computer. He is the man who developed the interior architecture that enables modern devices such as modems and printers to be connected to personal computers. In other words, because of Dr. Dean, the PC has become part of our daily lives. He recently led a design team to create the first 1-gigahertz processor chip, making computers faster and smaller. Presently he has over 30 patents pending.[22]

From the Pencil Sharpener to the Blood Bank, from the Fire Extinguisher to Instant Coffee, from the Refrigerator to the Clothes Dryer, from the Elevator to the Electric Lamp, Black people have been representing **The Book Look** for a very long time.

Now hear this; the Black affiliation with **The Book Look** has been a persistent problem for the Candyman. You see, whenever Black people use **The Book Look,** they begin to get better paid jobs, they begin to set up their own businesses, and eventually they don't have a need for the Candyman, because they're more successful and more powerful than the Candyman. As you can imagine, this is the Candyman's worst nightmare. And so the Candyman does what the Candyman does best – it f***s things up.

And so for years the Candyman has given the Black community the worst schools, they've refused them loans to set up their own businesses, they've denied them getting well paid jobs, and they've victimised and alienated their kids. Consequently, Black people have gradually forgotten about **The Book Look**, and the Candyman has been able to rely on scores of Black people f***ing their lives up, guaranteeing them and their Candy-children an easier path to a 'cushdy' lifestyle. But today, you're gonna bring back **The Book Look** like the Paris catwalk brought back platform heels.

Kahina: Now we're not unreasonable. We know that **The Book Look** is an acquired taste, but believe me when I say that no amount of clothes can make you look as good as a degree does. Those same geeks that you cussed for not wearing 'respectable' labels back in school, rocking the Dunlop Green Flash Plimsolls that made them look funnier than Dwight Yorke, are now raking in the cash while you're living paycheque to paycheque.

Trust me, **The Book Look** is the little black dress that every fashion collection should have.[23]

DAY 3: AVANT GARDE[24]
'Forward Thinking' Is The New Black

"Just maybe…if we didn't spend all our money on rims, we would have some [money] to invest. Black people…love rims. We will put shiny ass rims on any piece of s*** car in the world, we don't give a f***. A brother will put some rims on a toaster if you let him… 'They spinning nigger they spinning'!"[25] *Chris Rock*

Kahina: Ok now what on earth is that!?

Candace: It looks like a 5 double O drop-top to me Kahina!

Kahina: Well that most definitely has got to go!

Candace: I most certainly agree! The car fetish is *soooooooo* last season. From the shiny rims, to the shiny grills, to the shiny spoilers, to the wattage of the sound system, to the shape of the speakers, to the make of the CD changer…yada yada yada, you just *loooooooooove* the automobile.

Kahina: …but we're gonna change all this. 'Cos the new style, hot off the designer's sketchbook, is the Property Look. So **Change One** is eliminating the car obsession, and **Change Two** is initiating the house fixation. Because whilst you have always had the wickedest wheels on your estate, from the Bima to the Merc to your 4x4, it doesn't make the slightest bit of difference because **you-still-live-on-an estate!** Now don't get me wrong, living in a housing estate isn't necessarily a problem if you:

a) Live in one of those gated-community estates with private gyms, swimming pools and sports centres.
b) Live in one of the few estates that are designed for working-class people that are actually safe and pleasant to live in, like some of those Peabody estates, or those Coin Street estates by the Thames.
c) Have no choice but to live on an estate.

You might be a first generation settler in the UK who came here with nothing and had to live in council houses in order to find your feet, or you might not speak English well enough to get a job that pays you much money, or you just might be in a situation where you were born on an estate and your parents are working to move off the estate. BUT, that doesn't change the fact that a social housing estate is not what you want to be aiming for. And here's why…

Candace: **Because estates are generally not nice places!**

Kahina: That's right Candace. I know it sounds rather controversial, but there are around six million people living on council estates in Britain,[26] and for those that do it's no surprise that they are twice as likely to be victims of crime than if they lived in a private housing area. On average, one in three people who live on council estates has been the victim of a crime, two in five have been the victim of burglary, a third have been assaulted and a quarter have been robbed.[27]

Candace: Some people like to say: "but I need to stay close to the streets. I need to be close to my peoples. I need to live in the hood."

These people are mentalists. Personally, if it's a choice between **putting my family's well-being at risk whilst having an intimate 'knowledge of the streets' versus living a sheltered but crime-free life** I'd choose the sheltered but crime-free life. Call me Ms Unadventurous, but if your number one aim in life is to take care of your parents, to give your children the best start in life, and to live a peaceful existence, the stats show quite clearly that, regardless of how many times they repaint the walls on those crummy buildings, the estates in St. Ann's, Nottingham, the Aylesbury in Elephant, or Easterhouse in Glasgow are not the best places to do it.

Kahina: But the main reason why you should want to own your own house outside of an estate is **because you want control of your life**. The aim of every person (Black or not) living in this land should be to be as powerful as they can possibly be. Why? Because history has shown us that lack of power leads to exploitation – not things I'm sure that you want to experience (again)! You see, in a Capitalist society, money equals power. If you get some money, you can have some power because when you have cheddar, you can afford the top lawyers, the smartest accountants and receive the best investment advice. Hence, you are less likely to get imprisoned and more likely to make even *more* money.

But the problem is, there are some people who haven't worked this out yet, because they always believe whatever the Candyman tells them, and for the last 200 years they have let the Candyman tell them that Black people don't need Economic Power – that we need Political Power. And like mugs we bought it, which is why driving around in that 15k Saab, you look thicker than the big print version of the complete works of William Shakespeare.[28]

Over and over again, we hear the Candyman say: "Don't worry about financial power and making good investments, once this new Parliamentary Bill on equal opportunities is passed, it'll be OK. Once we prosecute that police officer for shooting your cousin, it'll be OK. Once you get a Black Cabinet Minister, it'll be OK. So you just keep focussed on buying those flashy cars on finance, and you let me, your trusty reliable Candy-friend worry about your power and equality in British society."

So whilst the Candyman, along with every other cultural group, open businesses, screw us over when we bank with them, make their children go to universities and become doctors and lawyers and buy their houses – you're blowing all your cash on a whip, living on an estate that resembles something out of a post-Apocalyptic movie, whilst waiting to see what David Lammy, Paul Boateng or Barack Obama can do for you.

It's so stupid, it's actually 'tupid! (You have to say it with a Jamaican accent for it to sound right!) It's 'tupid because since money equals power, understand that regardless of the current economic climate, it's houses that make you money not cars.

Now I'm not an accountant, in fact I only got a C for maths GCSE, but when you buy a car on finance you actually pay far more for the car than if you bought it outright. Let's say you wanna buy a brand new Audi TT with a one off payment – you're looking at paying 18 grand if you're lucky. Now let's say you wanna buy that same brand new Audi TT on finance. You're looking at paying £21k, since you're likely to pay around 6% interest, just for the privilege of showing the people outside CC nightclub what a lovely vehicle you drive. And if you miss your payments you could end up getting the car repossessed, in effect having 'rented' the car.

'Cos when you buy a car, unless it's an old classic or something very, very special, (and I'm talking about something as rare as a car once owned by Sir Walter Raleigh or something as ridiculous as that) it will almost certainly depreciate in value: rapidly. So, although whilst driving that Z4 you might get laid once in a while, you have no hope, ever, of recouping anywhere near the money that you spent on it. A Ford Mondeo, for example, loses £2,883 off its original value every 12 months whilst a Peugeot 106 reduces by £1,440[29] every 12 months.

Candace: Yep that's right, the average depreciation value for a car is around 15-20% in its first year, and 10% every year after.[30]

Kahina: So to put it bluntly – buying a car is NOT a sound financial investment.

Candace: But buying a house on the other hand is a totally different kind of financial investment.

Kahina: OK, now I know that things aren't perfect in the house market at the moment, what with the Credit Crunch and all that – but things are gonna change – and it doesn't take Sir Isaac Newton to work out that buying a house rather than a brand spanking new car is a more likely way to make your money work for you. Let's use an example to make this concrete for you. Imagine that Timi the Till Assistant at Tescos from Tooting earns one grand a month, and saves £200 per month from this grand. After saving for four years he now has £9600 – a nice tidy sum. He now has two choices:

1. **He can buy a very nice car**. He can drive around in his nice car and people will think he's rich when they see his nice car. But the spare parts for his new car are naturally very expensive, it's also expensive to fill up his huge 2 litre tank with petrol (which as you know ain't cheap), and even more expensive to service the car – so he's rinsing all of his money on the damn thing. His car will be worth a third of its original amount in about three or four years. So when he sells the thing, he is left with pocket change and no savings. *And* he still lives in a grimy flat!

2. **He can use his savings to put a deposit on a flat in a nicer area**. Every penny he puts into savings from now on goes onto his mortgage which means that he's investing in his investment. And even if the value of the flat doesn't increase, he can rent out one room of his flat and use that extra cash to buy a modest 'run-around' car. The moral of the story: **Cars Take Money – Houses Make Money!**

And before I forget. On a side note it's 'tupid buying a flash car instead of a house because what you've never considered is that you can't do anything with a car, except drive the damn thing.

Things You Can Do In A Car:
Go places – so long as there's parking
Listen to music – while going places
Have uncomfortable sex
Er…go more places…
Things You Can Do In A House:
Sleep
Listen to music
Have comfortable sex
Give your family somewhere to live
Rent a room to make more money
Study
Watch TV

Play XBox
Cook
Wash clothes
Have a party (have you ever had a car party? – didn't think so!)
Have a bath/shower *Etc. etc. etc.*

You could get all the perks of a house in a car if you wanted, but that means moving into a caravan – not a very sexy option. That's why even Marc Jacobs could not have dreamt up a better style than the **Property Look**. In short, the house is the *benchmark* for looking hip. The sports car on the other hand is what's called the *skid mark* for looking hip. It's the 'Loser for Life option'; the 'fair play' award; the 'also-ran' gift; the thanks-for-taking-part-consolation prize. From today, the flash car comes out of the wardrobe, and the house goes in. (When you have the house, the nice car goes back into the wardrobe.)

DAY 4: THE MUST-HAVE ACCESSORY
'Being Old & Living Large' Is The New Black

"There is no fate worse than debt." *Unknown*

Candace: Whoa! Now you're looking smoother than Torvill and Dean, and fresher than a Tic Tac.

Kahina: But when I look at the collage that we've put together for our winner, I get the feeling that something is missing…

Candace: I know what's missing – it's that all-important accessory! Now I know that our winner's favourite accessory has always been that bottle of Alize and a five-draw, but anyone who hasn't been brainwashed by the Candyman can see that it doesn't complement *any* part of what the Black Look represents. So today, **Change One** is taking away the ghetto passion for Spirits and Sensi.

Kahina: I know how it is for you, that whole 'I'm-so-flash-cos-I-gotta-joint-behind-my-ear' look, that 'I-feel-like-I'm-important-because-I-have-a-bottle-of-champagne-in-my-hand' style – it makes you feel like you can say to the world: I Am A Badman! But it just doesn't suit you at all and here's why:

153

a) **Cannabis messes you up!** (And I'm Not Talking About Getting You Lean.) Regardless of what people may say about how wonderful cannabis is – they have about as much truth in them as the Da Vinci Code – they're all 'urban' myths. What you have to understand is that the biggest importers and distributors of marijuana in Britain and America are not Black and usually tend to be men who are much paler than you, like David Wyler the man recently imprisoned by the police who made over £600,000 from selling cannabis all over the UK.

Candace: So the next time you tell yourself that smoking blunts are 'good for you', ask yourself who first told you that, and why they might wanna make Black people believe it?

Kahina: Ain't that the truth C. Furthermore, the stuff that's in cannabis smoke contains things that damage your lungs, badly affect your physical health and fitness and, if smoked over a long period of time, is likely to cause cancer, lung disease and chronic bronchitis. Cannabis gives you short-term memory loss, affects your attention span, and seriously affects your ability to process complex information. In other words, don't expect to pass exams, hold down a well-paid job, or have any kind of motivation to do things when you choose to smoke the stuff, particularly from a young age.

It also increases the risk of your developing mental health problems. If you already have a history of mental illness (such as schizophrenia or depression), smoking cannabis is likely to bring it on stronger! And if you're smoking skunk, which can be laced with anything from cocaine to...well...anything, then the effects are...well...who knows???

b) **Alcohol is more dangerous than you think**. It's worth remembering historically that alcohol has always been used as a tool for the Candyman in his quest for power and land. I know that alcohol might seem sweet to you but, for the last 250 years, it has comprehensively destroyed and permanently ghettoised more colonised communities around the world than Crack. From the Aboriginal slums in Redfern, Australia, to the impoverished Maori communities in Auckland, New Zealand to the townships in Soweto, South Africa, to the filthy outskirts of Nairobi in Kenya, alcohol came, it saw, and it conquered.

Probably the most tragic example of this has been the demise of the Native Americans. When the Europeans landed in the 'New World' in 1620, they naturally needed food and materials, and more importantly land. But not just little bits of land: they wanted it all. Amongst the 'old school' forms of land appropriation such as violence and genocide, they stumbled upon an interesting way of getting all that they wanted without having to waste time and energy on bullets and wars. It was called Alcohol.

Now because these 'injuns' had little or no experience with alcohol before the Europeans came to the Americas, they had no time to socially adjust to the 'juice'. The European traders knew this, and made an extra special effort to turn them all into alcoholics. Because once the Native Americans were desperate for the drink, they began to sell anything they owned for a bottle of the good stuff, from Buffalo robes to their wives, including the very thing the Europeans wanted: their land.[31] And that's when things turned really bad. Pretty soon the European immigrants started to enhance their 'special brew' with strychnine, a poison, to make them go crazy.[32] Eventually, the Native Americans lost Everything! And today:

- Alcohol and substance abuse among Native American and Alaskan Native adults occurs at a rate that is 579% greater than the general population![33]
- Deaths as a result of alcoholism occur at a rate that is 440% higher than that of the general population!
- The rate of death caused by alcoholism among Native American young people is 5.2 per 100,000, which is 17 times the rate for White young people.[34]

So when Black people like yourself get 'licked' every weekend, remember that black, brown, yellow and red people have already done what you've done and screwed their lives up in exactly the same way that you're doing with the bottle. In the UK:

- 33,000 people die each year due to alcohol-related incidents or associated health problems. Alcohol is involved in 15% of road accidents, 26% of drownings, and 36% of deaths in fires.[35]
- In nearly half (44%) of all violent incidents victims believed offenders to be under the influence of alcohol.[36]

So when we say alcohol is more dangerous than you think, we really do mean that it's much more dangerous than you think.

c) **Black people don't have money to be wasting on**

frivolous crap. Black people in the UK earn on average £211 per week.[37] Compare this to White people who earn on average £256 per week.[38] So when you spend your whole paycheques in clubs on bottles of 'champers', it's almost like you're trying to replicate the **Slave Look** – making money for other people whilst you make nothing.

d) **You don't look good with it**. No matter how hard you try, no matter how much effort you put in, whenever I see you carrying that bottle of alcohol or that bag of draw down the street, you represent one of those dirty old people that hang around parks, drinking their can of White Lightning or Tenants Super, talking gibberish, and cackling insanely from noon to night. And that's because alcohol and 'green' coupled with a poorly paid job and living in an ugly area equals 'I'm-tired-of-being-trodden-on-so-I-have-given-up-on-life', a sentiment shared by those rowdy, haggard looking fellows who say stupid things to you outside Kings Cross station.

Candace: That's why we've decided that we want to try replacing your Bottle and Blunt with something totally different. We want you to carry something that works with your posture, with your history and with your level of intellect.

Kahina: That's why **Change Two** is giving you this Season's 'Must-Have' Accessory: the Savings Account Look.

The piece of fashionista worth its weight in Jimmy Choos. The reason? Because all smart people have at least three savings accounts. Without it, you're as stupid as a man who jumped out of a plane without a parachute who was hoping that he'd land on a giant marshmallow!

Why? Because 1) **what if you need cash ASAP**. Let's say (God forbid)[39] something terrible happens, like someone close to you dies and you need to pay for their funeral. Or let's say you suddenly lost your job and couldn't get another one for a while? Without any savings as back up, you'd be forced to borrow money from a bank somewhere, and be obliged to pay high rates of interest, financially screwing you.

Candace: That's right Kahina, according to research done by Combined Insurance, over half the population (52%) could only survive financially for 17 days, should they suffer an unexpected loss of income.[40]

Kahina: And sooner or later, with the pressure of a non-existent financial back up plan, you'll experience Money Sickness Syndrome, a condition which today almost half (43%) of the UK adult population is affected by. Nearly four million people admit money worries have caused them to take time off work and more than 10.76 million people suffer relationship problems because of money worries, with almost one in five complaining of a sex life slump.[41] Today, a quarter of those in debt are receiving treatment for stress, depression and anxiety from their GP.[42]

Candace: So it makes sense to save – to save your sanity.

Kahina: 2) **You need money when you get old.** The chances are that you'll live 'til around 79 years old.[43] The chances are (on average) you'll earn around £26k per year if you're a man, and 20k per year if you're a woman,[44] and the chances that you'll win the lottery are 1 in 13.6 million.[45] This means that you're likely to live a long life without becoming a millionaire. In other words, you need to start saving for your old age NOW! And when I say now, I mean NOW.

Let me show you something. Assuming that you save around £50 a month at a steady interest rate of 5% (ok, I know that nothing is ever steady in finance) and you retire at 65. If you start a pension when you're 25, your fund value at retirement would be £57,500...
— At 30, your fund value at retirement would be £44,600
— At 35, your fund value at retirement would be £34,000
— At 40, your fund value at retirement would be £25,000
— At 45, your fund value at retirement would be £18,100.[46]

That's how worthwhile it is starting your pension NOW! But check this. Because most retired folk alive today chose to start their pension late in life, right now 1.4 million pensioners (14% of the UK's pensioner population) live on an income of £5,000 or less each year. After council tax, water and electricity bills, this leaves on average about £3,092 per annum, which is the equivalent to about £60 each week or £8.49 a day. Do you really want to end up living like that?

Now I know that sometimes these pension funds go 'pear shaped' and you *could* totally dismiss our advice, spend your money now and be forced to work into your nineties when you're wrinkly like a prune, but wouldn't you much rather save now so that at least you have the chance to chill when you want to? 'Cos you should know by now that the reason why so many people got screwed in the Credit Crunch is 'cos they had no savings, and despite what the banks have done, every single financial expert right now is telling people that the key to avoiding financial ruin in the future is to save. Our advice is: don't be old, cold and poor living in this world.[47] And the only way to avoid it is to start carrying around the accessory of the moment. So drop the draw and the alcohol, and pick up the Savings Account.

Candace: It looks like the makeover is complete…almost…

DAY 5: (SHOP) COUNTER ATTACK
'Unity' Is The New Black

"Is White guilt supposed to make me forget I'm running a business?"[48]
Max Cherry (Pulp Fiction)

Candace: With your style sorted, we need only fix your physique.

Kahina: And boy doesn't it need fixing! I ain't gonna lie – you're pretty in the face but thick around the waist, 'cos your unathletic and overweight figure combined with your pasty, wrinkled hide is not buff by anyone's standards. So how are we going to rapidly transform the way you look? Nutriment Vitamin drinks? Botox? Fitness First gym membership?

Candace: The answer is simple. You need to start eating, dressing and shopping from the right people. And that's why our final day together may well be the most painful. **Change One** is not to buy from people who hate you, and **Change Two** is to buy from as many people who look like you as is possible.

Kahina: What d'you think, Kentucky Fried Chicken is probably a good place to start huh?

Candace: I think so.

Kahina: Kentucky Fried Chicken was started by the guy you see on the front of all their promotional material, the bearded guy wearing some 'old-school', 'deep-south' attire, a man called Harland David Sanders AKA Colonel Sanders. This is a man who has an interesting history, not least because of the people who he hung out with.

Get this. Many moons ago there was a man named George Wallace, born in the USA in 1919.[49] Wallace always wanted to be the Governor of Alabama, but he failed to be the Democrat candidate in 1958. He thought his policies were too soft on Black people and was quoted saying that "no other son-of-a-b**** will ever out-nigger me again".[50] That's why for the next election he hired a man call Asa Earl Carter to be his speechwriter.

Asa Earl Carter just happened to be the leader of the military wing of the KKK (you know, the fellas who went round castrating Black people).[51] This is perhaps why Wallace's most famous quote during the 1962 campaign to be Governor was, "Segregation now! Segregation tomorrow! Segregation forever".[52] Anyway, he certainly impressed the local rednecks and he won the 1962 election easily. He then cemented his place as a great American racist (joining the ranks of Ronald Reagan and George Washington) by blocking the enrolment of Black students at the University of Alabama in 1963.[53]

Now just so that you're not under any illusions as to the ethos of this person, this is a quote from the great man about his decision to close schools in Birmingham, Alabama to stop any integration in them: "The society is coming apart at the seams. What good was it doing to force these decisions [school integration] when White people nowhere in the South want integration? What this country needs is a few first-class funerals".[54] The reason why this statement was so shocking (apart from the obvious) is because he made this comment just three months after four Black schoolgirls were murdered when the KKK planted a bomb at a Black Church in Birmingham, Alabama.[55]

Candace: We're telling you all this because Mr Wallace had a rather important supporter: none other than Colonel Sanders, the granddaddy of KFC.[56] Colonel Sanders liked Wallace so much that he was even going to run with him during the 1968 elections. Yes that's right Colonel Sanders wanted to run with Mr George Wallace, a man who Martin Luther King described as "perhaps the most dangerous racist in America".[57] (Wallace instead chose a man called General Curtis LeMay of the US Air Force, famous for his stated desire to bomb Vietnam "back to the stone age".)[58]

And yet the funny thing is that today if all the KFC restaurants/laxative joints were closed down, the first people to fuss and fight would be Black people! Too many Black people love that damn chicken outlet and they don't care who knows it. The mere mention of that crusty old geezer's recipe gets our juices flowing! But buying stuff like those 'Bargain Buckets' full of birds who've spent their entire, pitiful lives living in a cage caked in excrement, being bred and drugged to grow so obese that they can hardly walk, becoming crippled under their own weight,[59] are exactly the reasons why you've a worse skin condition than a leper's.

Kahina: That's absolutely right, Candace.

Candace: Ok, I think it's about time that we went to the phone lines.

Kahina: Good idea. This is the part of the show where we let you, the viewers, ask us, the fashion experts, about inside tips and techniques to turn fatty into flattery. Following on from today's focus, this week's discussion is going to be about the types of products that you need to stay away from if you want to look Sleek and Unique.

Candace: Hi caller, you're on the air.

Caller One: Hi Candace. I'm a long-time listener, first-time caller. My problem is that I get tremendous backache and I'm wondering whether it's got anything to do with my fashion style.

Candace: I think I might have an idea what the problem is. Can I ask you what car you drive?

Caller One: Well right now, I'm driving a modest Ford Focus.

Candace: Well that's where you're going wrong darling. Don't you know that Henry Ford, the man who started up Ford Car Company, was a supporter of Fascism and wrote the book *The International Jew – The World's Foremost Problem*.[60] Luckily, he was around during the time that the German Nazis were around so he got the honour of being the first foreign backer of the Nazi party. He was so popular with the Nazis that Henry Ford's portrait was placed in Hitler's private office.[61] He was also awarded 'The Grand Cross of the German Eagle' and was named in Hitler's autobiography, *Mein Kampf* as the only man in America who was fully independent from Jewish control.[62] What a glowing endorsement! So my guess is that it's the car company that's affecting your health. What else do you expect if you spend before you study?

Kahina: Second caller, you're on the air.

Caller Two: Hi Kahina. I always seem to look like I have enormously fat thighs, even though they're not *that* big. What could be causing this? Is it perhaps something that I'm wearing?

Kahina: Ahhh…now this is something that I've had a problem with in the past too! So my advice to you, is to do some research about how and where your clothes are made – 'cos if you're trying to look hot for your new squeeze, the sweatshop look is by far the most unflattering look.

You see, when you buy clothes that are produced off the back of human starvation, misery and deprivation, you end up looking as nasty as the CEOs who set up this system. These are the inside facts about how your clothes are made:

• The People: Sportswear companies like to groom their factory workers from a young age. And that's why in Indonesia, they employ people as young as 14 in most of their factories. But they clearly like Pakistani children better, because they've been known to recruit people as young as 8 years old to make their footballs.

• The Plants: Yea I know officially the Vietnam war is over, but like Rambo said – nothing is ever really over. Vietnam is the host to many sweatshops, and in some of the plants, workers are routinely set unrealistically high daily quotas, meaning that they are forced to work overtime in order to meet them. It is standard for most workers to clock over 600 hours of overtime per year, well above the Vietnamese legal limit of 200 hours per year. Workers are only permitted one toilet break per 8-hour shift, and can drink water only twice a shift.

• The Pay: Workers at manufacturing plants in Vietnam earn 20 cents an hour and make as little as $1.60 per day. But don't be fooled into believing that $1.60 per day stretches a long way in this country. The average monthly pay for some sweatshop workers is around $37 per month whilst the minimum wage is $45 per month!

• The Punishment: Working at a sweatshop must be quite an experience. Men have been beaten over the head and hospitalised for poor sewing. Women have been forced to kneel down with their hands up in the air for 25 mins at a time as a result of lack of speed in their work, and workers at one factory in the 'Nam, were once forced to stand in the sun for half an hour for spilling a tray of fruit. One employee couldn't take the heat and walked back inside after 18 minutes. He was promptly fired.

From beatings and to forced abortions, to vermin-infested quarters and barbed wire, to armed guards and 12-hour working days seven days a week – this is the life of the person working to make your sweaters and your tracksuit bottoms.

Candace: OK, so who's the next caller?

Caller Three: How are you girls doing?

Candace: We're doing fine.

Caller Three: My question is this. How comes it seems like no matter what I do, I just can't find a wedding ring that I'm not allergic to? I've tried them all and within minutes of putting them on, they turn my hand red!

Candace: The problem is this – the rings that you've been wearing are probably encrusted with blood diamonds. You see, what happens is that when conflicts break out between different factions in African nations, these factions go on the hunt for arms to fight their battles. And in order to get these arms, they need money to buy them. Luckily for many of these factions, they are rich in resources. And some are luckier still and possess diamonds. And because the Candyman doesn't care much about Black people disfiguring, maiming, or killing other Black people, the Candy-companies are only too happy to buy their diamonds and provide them with the cash needed to buy their AK47s and rocket launchers.

And so whilst companies like De Beers, who control 80% of the world's diamond trade make millions every year, it comes at a costly price for the African continent.[63] From the 1,000 people killed in Ivory Coast to the 100,000 in Congo-Brazzaville, from the 200,000 in Sierra Leone to the 220,000 in Liberia, from the 800,000 in Angola to the 4.6 million killed in Congo-Kinshasa, the last twenty years has seen Africa ravaged by war, genocide, and tragedy.[64]

So if you want to find a diamond that doesn't make your finger look like you've just stepped out of the *Chainsaw Massacre*, it's probably a good idea to find some other type of wedding band.

Kahina: I think we have time for one more call.

Caller Four: Hi girls ... I just wanted to say that I watch your show every week and I just think that you two are great. My question is a simple one. Why is it that no matter where I invest my money, I always have cash problems?

Candace: Well here's the thing. If you invest your money in places that just love to incarcerate and murder Black people, it's gonna be hard to make Pz. Barclays Bank, for example, helped maintain apartheid South Africa, propping up the unbelievably racist government through loans until 1986 when protests forced them out.[65] This should come as no surprise since Barclays has a murky past, namely in the slave trade. In 1969 they merged with Martin's bank that had previously been part of Heywood's Bank,[66] which had become very wealthy through the slave trade by offering long-term loans to the owners of slave ships.[67]

And whilst we're on the slave trade subject, the JP Morgan Chase Bank, one of the largest banking institutions in the world today, merged with a bank that felt kinda like it was morally ok to offer insurance policies to the slave traders and their ships in case some of those malnourished slaves died on the way.[68]

Lloyd's Bank, formerly a coffee house, doubled as the place of return for runaway African slaves.[69] So if you were lucky enough to escape your captors, the bank that today helps you with all your financial needs, would hunt you down, and get you back to work on the plantation.[70]

Now I know some people like to forget about what happened during the transportation of slaves, but if you thought your last trip on Virgin Trains was bad, then think again. A conservative estimate suggests that 11 million Africans were transported to the Americas between 1540 and 1850.[71] In order to maximise their profits, slave merchants stacked, racked and packed as many Black people inside their ships as was 'inhumanely' possible; it was normal for ships to carry 150 people more than they were capable of taking.

A physician on a slave ship once reported: "the slaves...are locked 'spoonways' and locked to one another...they were often miserably bruised against the deck or against each other. I have seen their breasts heaving and observed them draw their breath, with all those laborious and anxious efforts for life which we observe in expiring animals subjected by experiment to bad air of various kinds."[72] Consequently, only 50% of the Africans that started the journey were able to work once they got to the Americas. The rest had either died from smallpox or dysentery, they committed suicide, or they were crippled for life.[73] As Olaudah Equiano said of his transportation:

> " ... with the loathsomeness of the stench, and crying together, I became so sick and low that I was not able to eat, nor had I the least desire to taste anything. I now wished for...death to relieve me; but soon, to my grief...on my refusing to eat, one (White man)...held me fast by the hands, and laid me across...the windlass, and tied my feet, while the other (White man) flogged me severely.[74] ...The air soon became unfit for respiration, from a variety of loathsome smells, and brought on a sickness among the slaves, of which many died. The wretched situation was again aggravated by the chains, now unsupportable, and the filth of the necessary tubs, into which the children often fell, and were almost suffocated. The shrieks of the women, and the groans of the dying, rendered the whole scene of horror almost inconceivable."[75]

Kahina: Now listening to all this, I'm sure you're feeling like us – that you need to start thinking about where you invest cash if you wanna stay trim. But forget Weight Watchers, the Atkins diet, or the Glycaemic Index diet – you need to use the 'Montgomery' diet!

Candace: …a diet with rapid results which instantly makes you look like you've hired Ciara as a fitness instructor.

Kahina: The 'Montgomery' diet is where you stop buying from those companies who treat you like a degenerate, and start buying from those companies who represent you.

Candace: You see, back in the 1950s, most bus companies in Montgomery, Alabama (the same US state that our good friend George Wallace ran), relied heavily on Black passengers to turn profit every year. However, at the same time, it was an enforced policy that Black people had to sit at the back of the bus and that they had to stand up if a White person desired their seat.

Kahina: Now I'm not a businesswoman, but surely that kinda goes against the principle of good business practice. Because surely if you're the director of your company, and you know that the thousands of Black people who use your buses are in effect putting your kids through university and are paying off your mortgage you're gonna wanna make sure that they remain happy so that they keep taking that bus to work. Yet they did the exact opposite. Do you know why?

1) **Because they hated Black people so much!** Their hatred for Black people was more powerful than their desire to make cash. Every time they sat at board meetings with the shareholders discussing how to maximise profits and increase their share of the market, all they could think about was how much they despised Black people.

2) **Because they thought Black people had an intellect that rivalled David Beckham's.** (And you gotta remember that this is a guy who once said of his son: "I definitely want Brooklyn to be christened, but I don't know what religion yet".)[76]

Yes that's right, the Candyman thought that Black people would use businesses run by racists regardless of how racist these racists were. And as a result, these racists treated Black people like racists do – like they were animals! But very quickly, Black people thought: This is ridiculous. Here I am spending my hard-earned money on a bus run by a man who in every way resembles a Swastika-saluting skin-head. Why am I putting a smile on his face every night?

Candace: And so in 1955, they refused to ride buses that treated Black people like idiots. Instead, in order to get to work, people would use car pools, receive free rides from volunteer drivers supporting the bus boycott, or they would walk![77] The outcome was inevitable. They crippled the bus companies, which crippled Mr Racist CEO and his crew of Redneck Corporate goons. The CEO could no longer buy that new action figure for his son's birthday, and he could no longer get that pony for his daughter's Christmas present.

Mr Racist CEO needed a solution to this debacle – fast. And as quickly as you can say 'Black Hair Product Shop' they changed their stupid bus rules and let Black people sit anywhere. The lesson we can all learn from this is simple isn't it K?

Kahina: It certainly is. Follow the fashion values that are in Vogue this year: **Buy Black wherever possible.**

Candace: I remember when the riots between Black and Asian people took place in the Lozells region of Birmingham in October 2005 – some Black people were complaining that Asian people ran all the businesses in their areas. What these Black people failed to realise was this. If they don't like the monopoly of Asian businesses, they need to either help Black businesses make more profit, or start up some businesses for themselves. Now I know that some Black shops are as welcoming as entering a Spanish Inquisition torture chamber, and I know that the style might sound a little 'Baroque', but it's worth remembering that the alternative is to buy from people who think of you in the same way that they feel about the slugs in their garden.

At the moment in London alone, there are more than 10,000 Black-owned private sector businesses, their annual turnover exceeds £4.5billion, and they provide up to 70,000 jobs in the capital.[78] From Ozwald Boateng jackets to Somali Saeed's Internet Café, and from Jonnies Barbers to Jackson's Catering – strengthen the community. Let's make Candy-people think differently about the 'Black Market'.

THE BLACK COLLECTION
'Having A GamePlan' Is The New Black

"Keep your mind on your money and your money on your mind."[79]
Snoop Dogg (paraphrased)

Candace: Take a look at yourself in the mirror. You look kinda showah now huh? Even we're impressed with the makeover that we've given you. Now you look B-L-A-C-K – a look that's been missing from your wardrobe for a while.

Kahina: But this isn't a regular docu-soap in which we change you for the cameras, and then we walk away while you slowly slide back into the pattern of life that we've just tried to alter. We're determined for you to keep this look.

Let me tell you a quick story. Legend has it that the first thing that Nelson Mandela did when he was imprisoned on Robben Island in the 1960s was to encourage his fellow inmates to give up smoking. His reasoning was that, apart from the obvious health implications, he, like the rest of his inmates, was subjected to living in a prison in which they had few rights. Since obtaining cigarettes depended on how much prison guards allowed them to have, and since smoking is as addictive as it is, smoking reduced the power and independence that the Black prisoners had over themselves. Nelson Mandela knew that power lies in the amount of self control that you are afforded and he wanted the Black people in prison to take as much power as they possibly could.

Like those prisoners, you live in a world in which your ability to think for yourself is constantly under threat. Don't give the Candyman yet another tool with which to control you. So stop handing them money to buy their country club memberships, whilst you slide further in debt and end up begging the very same people for help because you can't feed your kids. Instead, maintain control over yourself.

Candace: That's right. You need to work out what your priorities are, not what some suit in a boardroom wants them to be. So I don't wanna see Black people wearing £400 Christian Louboutin shoes and holding £200 Louis Vuitton handbags whilst living in a rented flat with furniture that looks like you robbed it from a crack den.

I don't wanna be hearing Black people talk about how much money they're making from hustling on the streets whilst being in arrears over their kid's child support. And I don't wanna know about Black people who are wearing Tiffany diamond encrusted earrings but still claiming job-seekers benefits.

Kahina: The Black Look is to buy Black, to have a University degree, to own your own home, and to have a savings account.

Candace: Let's roll this style out like Prêt-a-porter – ready for the Black masses to wear. *Black Is The New Black.*

> "Would you rather have a Lexus or justice
> A dream or some substance
> A beamer, a necklace or freedom"[80]
> *Dead Prez*

NOTES

1. Dead Prez, *Wolves*, (Loud Records 2000)

2. Dahia al-Kahina of Mauritania.

3. Candace, Empress of Ancient Ethiopia.

4. *Corporation*, (Big Picture Media Corporation 2003).

5. As featured in the film, *They Live*, (Universal Studios 1988).

6. Syson, Damon, Don't call us... ever, (*The Observer* 18/06/2004). http://observer .guardian.co.uk/review/story/0,6903,1263503,00.html (accessed 28 June 2008).

7. Shifrin, Tash, Rich-poor gap 'has widened under Blair', (*The Guardian* 02/08/2004). www.guardian.co.uk/society/2004/aug/02/socialexclusion.politics (accessed 28 June 2008).

8. Debt Facts and Figures, (02/06/2008).http://www.creditaction.org.uk/june.html (accessed 28 June 2008).

9. *ibid.*

10. Weissman, Robert, *Grotesque Inequality: Corporate Globalization and the Global Gap between Rich and Poor*, (Multinational Monitor 01/07/2003). http://www.highbeam. com/doc/1G1-108267313.html (accessed 28 June 2008).

11. Ignacio Ramonet, The Politics of Hunger, (*Le Monde Diplomatique* 11/1998). http://mondediplo.com/1998/11/01leader (accessed 28 June 2008).

12. Steward, Nkrumah, *The Nigga Kingdom raw dogma.* http://www.8bm.com/diatribes /volume02/032/661.htm (accessed 28 June 2008).

13. *Bankruptcy Cases on the Increase*, (11/08/2006). news.bbc.co.uk/go/rss/- /2/hi/business/4782987.stm (accessed 28 June 2008).

14. Rock, Chris, *Bring the Pain*, (HBO 1996).

15. As originally quoted by Harpreet (Tina) Daheley.

16. X, Malcolm, *The Autobiography of,* (Penguin Books 1968), Pg.164.

17. Check out Kosher's, 'The Reason' Workshop.

18. Lieutenant Colombo in full effect.

19. *The Black Inventor Online Museum.* www.blackinventor.com/pages/lewislatimer.html (accessed 28 June 2008).

20. *ibid.*

21. *The African American Registry.* www.aaregistry.com/african_american_history/2793 /Dr_Phillip_ Emeagwali_the_Father_of_the_Internet (accessed 28 June 2008).

22. *Dr. Mark Dean: Computer Scientist & Pioneer.* www.black-history-month.co.uk/articles /dr_dean.html (accessed 28 June 2008).

23. Marino, Kristin, *Ten Phrases Every Fashion Career Hopeful Should Know*, (12/09/2005). www.fashionschoolreview.com/news/2005/09/ten_phrases_every_fashion_care er_hopeful_should_know.html (accessed 28 June 2008).

24. Noubikko, www.noubikko.com/noubikkobody/tips/languages/languagea.htm (accessed 28 June 2008).

25. Rock, Chris, *Never Scared*, (HBO 2004).

26. Hill, Amelia, Council estate decline spawns new underclass, (*The Observer*

30/11/2003). www.guardian.co.uk/society/2003/nov/30/housing.uknews (accessed 28 June 2008).

27. Norwich Union UK: Communities in fight against crime, (31/07/2002). www.aviva.com/avivainvestor/index.asp?PageID=2&year=2002&NewsID=121 2&filter= (accessed 28 June 2008).

28. *Blackadder Goes Forth*, (BBC 1989).

29. Price warning to car owners, (23/07/2006). http://news.bbc.co.uk/1/hi/uk/ 847551.stm (accessed 28 June 2008).

30. Duffy, Simon, *Most Car Buyers Unaware of Vehicle Depreciation Rate*, (28/09/2007). www.buyingadvice.com/ownership-survey.html (accessed 28 June 2008).

31. *Introduction of Alcohol Through the Fur Trade: A Brief Overview.* www.montana.edu/wwwai /imsd/alcohol/Jessyca/furtrade.htm (accessed 28 June 2008).

32. *ibid.*

33. *Native American Youth Abuse of Drugs and Alcohol.* www.termpapergenie.com/youthabuse ofdrugs.html (accessed 28 June 2008).

34. *ibid.*

35. *Alcohol Deaths: Rates In UK Continue to Rise*, (National Statistics 1996-2001). www.statistics.gov.uk/cci/nugget.asp?id=1091 (accessed 28 June 2008).

36. *Crime and Victims*, (Home Office). www.homeoffice.gov.uk/crimevictims/reducing-crime/alcohol-related-crime/ (accessed 28 June 2008).

37. *Black and Asian workers 'underpaid'*, (BBC News 12/05/2002). http://news.bbc.co.uk/ 1/hi/uk/1924907.stm (accessed 28 June 2008).

38. *ibid.*

39. ...if you're religious.

40. Debt Facts and Figures, (02/06/2008).www.creditaction.org.uk/june.html (accessed 28 June 2008).

41. Debt Facts and Figures, (02/2006). www.creditaction.org.uk/assets/PDF/stats/ 2006/DebtStatisticsFeb2006.pdf (accessed 28 June 2008).

42. *ibid.*

43. *The average life expectancy of British citizens in 2007.* www.nationmaster.com/graph/ hea_lif_exp_at_bir_yea_tot_pop-expectancy-birth-years-total-population (accessed 28 June 2008).

44. 2007 Annual Survey of Hours and Earnings, (National Statistics 11/2007). www.statistics.gov.uk/pdfdir/ashe1107.pdf (accessed 28 June 2008). This is the average wage that a British citizen is expected to earn in 2007.

45. *Thirteen Point Six Million Chance Of Winning The National Lottery.* www.machinehead -software.co.uk/misc/lottery/chanceofwinninglottery.html (accessed 28 June 2008).

46. Figures provided by Prudential.www.pru.co.uk/retire/pensions/stakeholder/ (accessed 28 June 2008).

47. Taken from a phrase that Andrew Muhammad uses in his conversations.
48. *Pulp Fiction*, (Miramax Films), 1997.
49. George Wallace. http://www.spartacus.schoolnet.co.uk/USAwallaceG.htm (accessed 28 June 2008).
50. *ibid.*
51. *ibid.*
52. *ibid.*
53. *ibid.*
54. *ibid.*
55. *ibid.*
56. *Time* Magazine, (11/10/1968). www.time.com/time/magazine/article/0,9171,9 02367,00.html (accessed 28 June 2008).
57. George Wallace. http://www.spartacus.schoolnet.co.uk/USAwallaceG.htm (accessed 28 June 2008).
58. LeMay, (*Air Force* Magazine Online 03/1998). www.afa.org/magazine/March 1998/0398lemay.asp (accessed 28 June 2008).
59. *Kentucky Fried Cruelty*. http://www.kfccruelty.com/faq.asp (accessed 28 June 2008).
60. Ford, Henry Sr., *The International Jew-The World's Foremost Problem*, (Ford Motor Company 1920). http://www.biblebelievers.org.au/intern_jew.htm (accessed 28 June 2008).
61. Sutton, Anthony C, *Wall Street and the Rise of Hitler.* www.scribd.com/doc/2683369/ Wall-Street-And-The-Rise-OF-Hitler-by-Antony-C-Sutton (accessed 28 June 2008).
62. *Sal Vs BMW*, http://www.theawfultruth.com/salbmw/ (accessed 28 June 2008).
63. *Facts About Diamonds*. http://apscuhuru.org/analysis/diamondfacts/index.xhtml (accessed 28 June 2008).
64. Scaruffi, Piero, *Wars and Genocides of the 20th Century*. www.scaruffi.com/politics/massacre.html
65. Kollowe, Julia, *Barclays Faces Apartheid Court Action*, (21/01/2006).www.independent .co.uk/news/business/news/barclays-faces-apartheid-court-action-523883.html (accessed 16 August 2008).
66. Barclays Bank Website. www.aboutbarclays.com/content/detail.asp?NewsAreaID =138 (accessed 16 August 2008).
67. National Archives. www.nationalarchives.gov.uk/pathways/blackhistory/journeys /virtual_tour_html/liverpool/liverpool.htm#martin (accessed 28 June 2008).
68. *Leather Manufacturers' Bank Check 1850 Slave Insurance Bank*. www.scripophily.net/ checfromleat1.html (accessed 28 June 2008).
69. Walvin, James, *British History: Abolition of the Slave Trade 1807*. www.bbc.co.uk/history /british/abolition/building_britain_gallery_02.shtml.
70. *City of London Slave Trail*. www.heritagematters.org.uk/slave_trade_trail.html

(accessed 28 June 2008).

71. *Quick guide: The Slave Trade*, (BBC News 15/04/07). news.bbc.co.uk/2/hi/africa/ 6445941.stm (accessed 28 June 2008).

72. Slave Ships, (African Slave Trade). www.spartacus.schoolnet.co.uk/USASships .htm (accessed 28 June 2008).

73. *ibid.*

74. Equiano, Olaudah, *The Life of Olaudah Equiano*, (Dover Publications 26/01/1999).

75. *ibid.*

76. *Beckhams Host Glitzy Christening*, (23/12/2004). http://news.bbc.co.uk/1/hi/uk/ 4120477.stm (accessed 3 November 2008).

77. *The Montgomery Bus Boycott*, (A Brief History of Civil Rights in the United States of America). http://www.africanamericans.com/MontgomeryBusBoycott.htm (accessed 28 June 2008).

78. *The Rise and Rise of the Black British Entrepreneurs*. www.bl.uk/news/2006/pressrelease 20060418.html (accessed 28 June 2008).

79. Snoop Doggy Dog, *Gin and Juice*, (Death Row 1993).

80. Dead Prez, *It's bigger than hip-hop*, (Loud Records 2000).

CHAPTER SIX
For Kiyan, Jesse, Sunday and The Others

"Your kids can't play nowhere ... can't go to the movie the first week when it comes out. Why? 'Cos stupid ass niggers are shooting at the screen ... Every time Black people wanna have a good time, ignorant ass niggers have to f*** it up ... Can't keep a disco open more than three weeks: grand opening, grand closing."[1] *Chris Rock*

Hi guys. You might not recognise me. In fact you *definitely* won't recognise me, but **I'm your New Guardian Angel**. Now before you say anything, I know that our track record hasn't been so good of late what with the slave trade, the colonisation of Africa, apartheid etc. etc., but don't blame God for that. Your last Guardian Angel was extraordinarily incompetent, and screwed things up pretty badly for you guys.

Anyways, God was a bit concerned about you fellas so he appointed me to call a little 'Time Out' with you and talk to you on a level for a minute. I know what you're probably thinking right now, I can see it in your eyes: that 'get-outta-my-face-'cos-I-ain't-done-nothing' look. But before you get pranged, let me tell you why I'm here.

My official reason is...wait a minute...let me find the piece of paper: I'm here because of the needless, 'niggative', self-destructive, 'beef' that occurs between a minority of misguided people, particularly in the young Black community. I'm here because of the assaultitive, homicidal and suicidal violence committed *by* Black people *against* Black people in ways that are self and mutually destructive. I'm here because of the violence against Black people that is over-reactive, excessive, deadly, senseless, sadistic, unprovoked, or rationally unjustified by its cause, whether it be ghetto Vs ghetto, gang Vs gang, or being Vs being.

Basically, I'm here 'cos of Kiyan, Jesse, Sunday and the others – 'cos official reasons aside, I gotta lay it straight: from observing your community, it looks a lot like some of you guys really enjoy hating, hurting, humiliating, shooting, stabbing, robbing and killing each

172

other. And I mean let's be honest now, you're not robbing each other because you wake up every morning starving, on the verge of watching your mother die from hunger. You're not robbing each other because you, your baby mother, and your son are on the verge of being evicted from your council house 'cos you're in arrears over your rent. You're not robbing each other because your grandfather is terminally ill and you don't have the money to pay for pain-controlling drug treatment.

The reality is, you're acting this way towards other Black people because you don't like 'Harlesden mans', or because you don't like Kofi so you wanna jack his friend, or because you had a fight with someone in PYG and you've just seen someone wearing their colours.

Your beef is 'niggative', needless beef... and boy are the rest of the Black community getting bored of it! Bored of Black people too ready to pick on Black people. Bored of Black people too ready to jack Black people. Bored of Black people too ready to start trouble with Black people. Bored of having to worry about other Black people. Period!

Now before you start thinking that I'm picking on you, let me set things straight. I know that on Planet Earth, the media, particularly in the UK and USA, like to band around phrases like 'Black-on-Black' crime all the time, trying to convince every man and his dog that all Black people are crims.

And yet, you only have to look at 20th century history to realise, for example, that White-on-White crime is waaaaaaay more serious than anyone else's. In World War One (1914-1918), the British, French, Germans, Italians, Austro-Hungarians, Russians and the rest of the Europeans/Americans managed to kill well over 8 million European soldiers. Hitler, Churchill, Roosevelt, Stalin, Mussolini and their soldiers used a variety of methods to put an end to 28 million European civilian lives between 1937 and 1945. And in Spain during the Spanish Civil War, approximately 200,000 people were killed in combat. You see, from the Armenian Holocaust, to the Irish War of Independence, from Ceausescu's Romanian reign, to the Anglo-Boer War, from the 30,000 that died in the Finnish Civil War, to the 700,000 murdered in the Yugoslavian Civil War[2] – White people regularly go 'genocide' on other White people. After all, the UN was specially set up after WWII to stop White-on-White homicide!

The thing is, 'White-on-White' crime is a consequential effect of a racially homogeneous community and this is the same with respect to

'Indian-on-Indian' crime, 'Chinese-on-Chinese' crime and, 'Black-on-Black' crime. In other words, in Sunderland for example, where 98% of the population is White,[3] the White people who want to rob other people in Sunderland are likely to rob White people because obviously the majority of people available to rob are White. And that's why (obviously) in Black areas, 'Black-on-Black' crime is more significant. So I'm not down with the attitude that Black people are the *only* people with problems – but you definitely do have problems. Listen to this, in **London** (bearing in mind the Black population stands at 10.9%)[4]...

- 62% of people arrested for robbery are Black, compared with 27% who are White and 6% Asian.[5]
- 35% of burglary victims are Black.[6]
- 52% of GBH victims are Black.[7]
- 85% of homicide victims are Black.[8]
- 31% of all Black murder victims are shot, compared with 12% of Asians and 6% of Whites.[9]

In **Manchester** (bearing in mind that the Black population stands at just under 5%)[10]
- 8 out of 11 gun victims are Black.[11]
- 22 out of 35 attempted murder victims are Black.[12]
- Half of the victims of serious woundings are Black.[13]

And this ain't a recent thing neither! Before I got promoted to the Guardian Angel of Black people, I used to be the Guardian Angel of South London (it carries less pay and the job is far more taxing) and – if I'm honest – my experience of the Black community made me feel like you guys were in real trouble back then!

From the machine gun bullet holes in Angel Town to the blood stains in Kennington Park, in my experience a small percentage of you guys are messed up. In 2008, over 70% of all teenagers killed in London were Black.[14] In 2007 over two thirds of all teenagers murdered in London were Black.[15]

Now, let me talk specifically to the 'niggative' minority. After looking over your file, **I see why there is so much anger in your eyes**; it all kinda makes sense. I understand why you carry that screwface around with you all day. It's hard to wake up and feel positive about the world, when you're living in the conditions that you grow up in. I mean, sure there are people in the world who have things much harder than you, and things in Britain aren't *that* bad, but let's face it, they aren't *that* great either!

If you managed to make it past your first birthday, bearing in mind that infant mortality in the Afro-Caribbean community is 100% higher than for White children, there ain't much point in getting too excited. The majority of you live in areas in which your life expectancy is dramatically lower than the national average. But this shouldn't be too much of a surprise since Black people have a much higher rate of limiting, long-standing illnesses or disabilities than White people.[16]

But if you managed to stay healthy and well enough to make it to your fifth birthday **you have the educational system** to deal with. Black people are six times more likely to be excluded from school than White people.[17] Black students are second only to Pakistani and Bangladeshi students with the lowest GCSE results,[18] and if you wanna study subjects like Law you are 13% less likely to get a University place than your White counterparts[19] (just ask the 'Tell It Like It Is' Campaign).

Now, if you manage to crawl through the educational system, **you still need to get a job** that pays enough to keep you and your family alive. But since Black people have one of the highest rates of unemployment for any racial group at 13%,[20] you know it's gonna be damn hard. And if you *do* get a job, don't expect to get paid anywhere near what your White counterparts get paid. In hospitals for example, Black nurses are twice as likely as White nurses to be underpaid for the work that they do. And although Black workers make up 8.5% of the NHS workforce, they represent only 1% of hospital trust chief executives.[21] The fact that you live in one of the richest countries in the world means nothing. **You're still some of the poorest people in the Western Hemisphere.**

And because you're poor, **when you go home** after a hard day's work, you're likely to go back to a less than pleasant environment. 50% of Black African people live in socially rented accommodation,[22] and 23% of Black people are judged to be living in what are considered 'poor' housing conditions.[23] But if you don't have a home, don't be too surprised either. Black people constitute 10.3% of all homeless people in England, by far the highest BME group.[24]

And to make sure that your Earthly existence is totally crushing, **you have the police and the justice system to contend with**.

Black people are eight times more likely to be stopped and searched by the police than White people and Black people are still five times more likely to be arrested than White people. A study found that whilst the number of White people arrested actually fell by 1%, the number of Black people arrested rose by 12%. (This is after the McPherson report supposedly shook the system up.)

And when you do get arrested you have to make sure that you're careful, because over 1000 deaths have occurred in police custody since 1969, many of them Black people[25], and only one prosecution has ever been made. At present 18% of the male prison population is Black.[26] In the last few years, while the overall prison population rose by 12% the Black prison population grew by 54%!

Now let's say you've managed to live through birth, you've managed to survive the school system, you've managed to get a job, and you've managed to escape getting put in the slammer, you still have every chance of being **committed to a mental asylum**. Black patients are 44% more likely to be detained under the 1983 Mental Health Act than White people, and referral rates to Mental Institutes for Black people by the police are almost double that of White people.[27] But it ain't like when you get in these places you're free of abuse either. The use of control and restraints is 29% higher amongst Black patients than White patients and seclusion rates are 50% higher for Black men than White men.[28]

Boy, I'm not saying that there aren't opportunities for you in this country, but after I read all this, no-one can ever say to you "forget about it", or "don't be so upset", or "don't have a chip on your shoulder about racism". It's hard for you with a capital H! You get up in the morning and inside all you can think about are the days, years, decades, and centuries of political, social and economic mistreatment that you've experienced at the hands of the Candyman. You go through your day thinking about the life that you lead, you think about the injustice and prejudice that you receive, and you develop a personality that reflects this. You don't have anyone in your family that can help you. They're just as broken, as tired and as angry as you are, so you look for a family outside of your home and you find it with other young people who are on the street. But this street family is made up of young people who are equally as alienated. And although you find a sense of belonging with these people, neither you nor they have been given any direction, and neither you nor they have been given the chance to find a purpose in life.

So this crew of people becomes your family, and this unity becomes a way of you clawing back the power that you've been denied. Since you can't get power via education, via wealth, or via politics you take power in the one place that you can: on the street where people genuinely fear you.

So the next time you and your people 'catch eyes' with someone on road who refuses to look away, already feeling paranoid, already feeling hyped, already feeling disenfranchised, in your mind this person is posing a threat to your already beaten, battered ego in the last place that you feel like you have any power – and this makes you mad. That madness is channelled into violence which you're using as an attempt to re-establish your smashed self-esteem, your wrecked self-image and your destroyed self-confidence.[29] As Frantz Fanon put it: "violence is the expression of impotence grown unbearable[30] because absolute powerlessness, as well as absolute power, corrupts".[31]

After a study, the American Anthropological Association in 1988 concluded that people are not genetically predisposed to violence because violence cannot be scientifically related to natural evolutionary processes.[32] In other words, the cause of the violence that you exhibit has its base in the oppression that you suffer. And so time and time again, this raw anarchic anger goes on expressing itself violently against other people, without rhyme or reason, with no moral code nor any political motivation.

Now because Black people tend to live in areas surrounded by other Black people, all this anger, all these 'niggative' things you do, 'niggatively' affects other Black people. But it also means that when you move to someone, when you jack someone, when you shank someone, these same people are likely to live near you or know people who know you. And that means that they know how to get back at you. And if they can't get to you, then they'll get to someone you know. And that means your mother, your father, your son, your daughter, your brother, your sister, your cousin, your niece and your nephew are odds-on favourite to experience the same 'niggative' behaviour that is perpetrated by you.

And if that sounds bad, trust me, it gets worse. The Black victims who get terrorised are some of the poorest people in the UK. The rate of child poverty amongst Black Africans is now more than double that of White children[33] which is why it makes you and everyone Black around you extremely vulnerable to 'niggativity'.

177

You see, jacking someone's phone doesn't just affect them for that day; it affects the way they treat their families; it affects the way they go to school; and it affects the way they go to work. It is reported regularly that victims of crime experienced a loss of earnings as a direct result of that crime and many others change their jobs.[34]

Man it depresses me! **You just don't get it**. We created you the way we did specifically *because* we wanted you to succeed. We made you physically strong, we made your skin resistant to the sun. We made you healthy. We even gave you the best part of the world to live in. We gave you the longest rivers, the most diverse wildlife, the densest rainforests, the largest lakes, and the tallest mountains. We gave you untold vegetables, fruits and animals: from okra to hot peppers, from peaches to mangoes, from the zebra, to the lion. We gave you endless metals, fuels and precious materials: from gold to copper, from oil to uranium, from diamonds to cocoa. We gave you it all so that you could be set up for life. But then the Europeans came and screwed everything up...

Now I know that if things were better for Black people in this Candy-ruled world, you'd act differently towards your family, towards your friends and towards other Black people. But it's not and the Candyman will never *ever* make things better for you. (Believe me, I work with people who can see into the future and I know that it ain't ever gonna happen.) So since you can't change the way the Candyman treats you, you have one option and one option only: to change the way you treat each other.

And this is how we're going to deal with this Needless, 'Niggative' Beef. **1. Think before you act and look at the bigger picture**. Every time a Black person shows you a little attitude, bounces you in the street, looks at you strangely, or does anything else mildly disrespectful: **walk away, leave it alone and let it go**.

I know it hurts. I know that it makes you feel small. I know that it makes you feel like a fool. I know that it makes you feel inferior. I know that it crushes your pride. But let's be clear about this. Firstly, you ain't gonna feel much pride with a bullet to the head, or knife a in your back. Secondly, you ain't gonna feel much pride locked up in the Clink and thirdly, you need to work out what pride means to you.

You see, what I can't work out is why for some Black people, pride means one thing: stopping any Black person, and only Black persons from disrespecting them. I know what you're thinking: "But it ain't just Black people who I don't let dis me, no Candyman can *ever* disrespect me!" But let me ask you this. Look at where you live, and look at where the Candyman lives. Look at where you work and look at where the Candyman works. Look at where you go on holiday and look at where the Candyman goes on holiday. Look at where the Candyman sends your kids to school and look at where the Candyman sends his kids to school. How's your pride now? How do you feel inside now? So tell me, what crushes your pride more: a glaring look from a Black person or the Candyman screwing you over economically, politically and socially in every way?

In other words, forget the minor indiscretions that Black people do to you – deal with the more important issues. I know that some Black people walk around acting like the beef they have with other Black gangs/Black people in other postcodes is bigger than the Palestinian/Israeli debacle. Well I gotta level with those fugesi-living, phoney-Hollywood-dreaming, jive-talking, counterfeit-Gs. Your Black vs Black beef is a minor. The places that you're fighting over, the places that you're killing over – they don't belong to you. You don't own the lamp posts, the paving stones, the bus routes, the train stations, the parks, the traffic lights, the parking meters, the telephone poles, the water pipes or the trees. You don't own any part of 'the streets', so please stop going on about the 'road' like it's something that you need to protect.

That's why I'm saying to you: the next time a Black person kisses their teeth at you, ask yourself, "is it worth risking getting maimed or even dying to stop him from thinking he's better than you?" 'Cos don't forget, you know that they've had to endure the same existence that you've had to endure. So from today, be the first person to walk away from a Black person who challenges you to a fight over something worthless, be the first person to look away from the next Black person who looks at you aggressively, be the first person to apologise for brushing past someone. And the next time that a Black person treads on your shoes (no matter how hard those trainers were to find, or no matter how fresh they are), say "no problem" even if the person who did it doesn't say anything to you.

I know it ain't easy. And I know that in certain situations it's unavoidable. Some 'niggative' people give you no option but to brawl. Believe me, I know it! But let me make this clear to you ... I'm not asking you to be a coward. I'm asking you to be intelligent. I'm not asking you to humiliate yourself. I'm asking you to be Black. Because bottom line: Black people were not created to fear each other.

2. Take your anger out against those people who put you where you are. It doesn't take Hercule Poirot to work out who is responsible for every miserable aspect of your communities – and it ain't you. Let's break things down: Prime Minister 100% White; House of Commons 98% White; House of Lords 98% White; Bank of England Chairman 100% White; Lord Chief Justice 100% White; High Court Judges 99% White; Police Commissioner 100% White; Major Media Outlet owners 90% White and Weapon company owners 100% White.[35]

And over in the USA, every President prior to Obama has been 100% White; Senate 99% White; House of Representatives 92% White; Bank owners 99.9% White; Fortune 500 Company owners 99% White; Landowners 92% White; Hollywood studios owners 100% White; Major Media Outlet owners 100% White AND Arms Dealers 100% White.[36] And not just normal White people, not the 'Stacey-working-in-Ladbrokes-and-lives-in-Dudley' kind of White, we're talking about Candyman White.

Bottom Line: everything you're angry about you can be sure that the Candyman's to blame. So that begs the question: why is it I've never seen you lurking around the gates of Downing Street, yet I always see you ready to move to Black people who live in different areas to you? Why is it I've never seen you look up the address for Monsanto or for Nestle, yet you're over-keen to bottle a Black guy 'cos they're from another crew? The reason why, as Tupac put it, is because "you love to shoot a nigga but you scared to pop a cop."[37] You're cowards.

Question: Why do you think that in *Tom and Jerry* cartoons, when Jerry was being chased by Tom, you never heard Jerry say, "I can't stand being chased by this rotten cat, so let me go find some mice to violate?" Answer: Because Jerry wasn't stupid enough to attack mice who had nothing to do with his situation. Instead, Jerry tore up Tom's world by throwing anvils, washing machines and all kinds of household implements at him. Why? 'Cos he knew that no more Tom equals no more madness.

Question: Why is it that when Charlton Heston aka Moses and his crew of Jews were being chased by Ramses in the *Ten Commandments*, he didn't think to himself, "I'm gonna kill me a Jew". Answer: because it was the Egyptians who held his people in bondage, and so he asked God to swallow the Egyptians in the Red Sea.

Now don't get me wrong, I'm certainly not advocating violence.

But it's obvious really, if you want better jobs, less tacky estates, and better treatment from the police, you're gonna need to take some action against the players who hold all the cards. And no, the 'player with all the cards' ain't Jamal from Six Acres Estate who gave you that weird look last Tuesday, no it's not Tamika from Maiden Lane who thinks she's hot 'cos she's always wearing FM boots and a short skirt, and no it's not Adebola from Pemberton who wears a red bandana instead of the blue ones that most people in the area wear. The players who hold all the cards are the people at the top of the chain, the people who run the companies, the people who make the decisions – Not Darrell who works in the Chippie and gets lashed in the Nags Head every weekend. Not working class people, Black or White. So here's my suggestion:

1. Stay Angry: never forget that you have a right to be fuming about the condition that you're in.
2. Feel Aggrieved: never forget that you have a right to more than the lot that you were landed with.

Leave working class people alone, especially poor Black people, and seek to challenge those people who can change your life. For once, use the anger at your powerlessness to do something to empower yourself and take control from those who actually hold it. How do you do it? Well, that's for another chapter, I mean, another time... er...yea...that's for another time. Anyway, I gotta dash. I gotta twelve 'o' clock appointment with my line manager, Saint Peter and he can't stand lateness...so until I pass through again, take care of yourselves. **Power to the peaceful.**

This chapter is dedicated to the lives and memories of those young people who have been murdered as a result of 'Needless Beef'.

From 2007 in London...

Stephen Boachie, 17, stabbed on 1st January. Stephen, from Dagenham, east London, was stabbed on the forecourt of a petrol station in Barking. He died in hospital later that day from his wounds.

Dean Lahlou, 18, stabbed on 9th January. Dean, from Tottenham, north London, was attacked just after midnight near his home on Broadwater Road, Tottenham, after a night out. He later died in hospital.

Jevon Henry, 18, stabbed on 24th January. Jevon died in hospital after he was found on a street in St John's Wood, north-west London.

James Smartt-Ford, 16, shot on 3rd February. James, of New Malden, south-west London, was shot twice near to the entrance at Streatham Ice Arena, in south London. He died in hospital.

Michael Dosunmu, 15, shot on 6th February. Michael, from Peckham, south-east London, was shot several times at his home. He died in hospital shortly after.

Billy Cox, 15, shot on 14th February. Billy was shot at his home in Clapham North, south London.

Kodjo Yengo, 16, stabbed on 14th March. Kodjo, 16, died from a single stab wound to the heart in Hammersmith Grove, west London.

Adam Regis, 15, stabbed on 17th March. Adam was stabbed to death in Plaistow, east London, as he returned from a night out.

Paul Erhahon, 14, stabbed on 6th April. He died after being stabbed in the heart in the entrance to a block of flats in Leytonstone, east London.

Dwaine Douglas, 18, stabbed on 18th May. Dwaine, from Tulse Hill, south London, was stabbed during a row involving a number of males. He died in hospital after the attack in Thornton Heath.

Danielle Johnson, 17, stabbed on 28th May. Danielle died two weeks after being attacked in Palmerston Road, in Wood Green, north London. A post-mortem examination gave the cause of death as a stab wound to the chest and head injuries.

Sian Simpson, 18, stabbed on 19th June. Sian was stabbed in the heart during an attack by a group of teenagers in Mann Close, Croydon, south London.

Ben Hitchcock, 16, stabbed on 23rd June. Ben was stabbed in the stomach in Beckenham, south-east London, when a fight broke out at a party on 23 June.

Annaka Keniesha Pinto, 17, shot on 23rd June. Annaka, from Edmonton, north London, died in hospital after being shot at the Swan pub in Philip Lane, Tottenham, north London.

Abu Shahin, 18, stabbed on 26th June. Abu, from Newham, east London, was stabbed in Ilford and died shortly afterwards in hospital from stab wounds.

Martin Dinnegan, 14, stabbed on 26th June. Martin was stabbed in the chest during a dispute involving up to 20 youths in Islington.

Abukar Mahamud, 16, shot on 26th July. Abukar was killed by a single gunshot wound to the neck at the Stockwell Gardens Estate in south London.

Nathan Foster, 18, shot on 3rd August. Nathan, 18, was shot in Marcus Garvey Way in Brixton, south London. He died in hospital. He was with a group of 10 or 11 youths when they were approached by a male on a motorbike who opened fire.

Mohammed Ahmed, 17, stabbed on 30th August. Mohammed, from east London, was stabbed to death in Newham in Chesterford Street.

Edvin Johnson, 19, stabbed on 16th September. Edvin died after being stabbed in his leg on the stairwell of the Crawford Estate, where he lived, in Camberwell, south-east London. He was taken to hospital where he died soon after.

Rizwan Darbar, 17, stabbed on 7th October. Rizwan Darbar was stabbed in West Ham Park in Plaistow, east London, when he tried to stop a gang stealing a friend's phone.

Philip Poru, 18, shot on 14th October. Philip, a student, was sitting in a car with a friend in south-east London, when they were both shot. A post-mortem examination found Mr Poru died of gunshot wounds to the chest. His friend was also injured but survived.

Etem Celebi, 17, shot on 14th November. Etem, a semi-professional footballer, was shot as he sat on a wall near his home in Stoke Newington, north-east London.

Biendi Litambola, 17, assaulted on 17th November. Biendi, also known as Bobby, died after being assaulted in Canning Town, east London.

David Nowak, 16, stabbed on 15th December. David was stabbed to death following a mass brawl in Farleigh Road, Stoke Newington in north London.

Nassirudeen Osawe, 16, stabbed on 27th December. Nassirudeen was stabbed while out with two friends in Upper Street in Islington, north London. He and a friend were attacked after a row at a bus stop.

And In 2008…

Henry Bolombi, 18 years old. Stabbed on 1st January
Faridon Alizada, 18 years old. Stabbed on 5th January
Boduka Mudianga, 18 years old. Stabbed on 21st January

Fuad Buraleh, 19 years old. Assaulted on 26th January
Sunday Essiet, 15 years old. Stabbed on 19th February
Tung Le, 17 years old. Stabbed 23rd February
Ofiyke Nmezu, 16 years old. Assaulted 15th February (died in hospital 29th February)
Michael Alexander Jones, 18 years old. Stabbed 13th March
Nicholas Clarke, 19 years old. Shot in Stockwell 14th March
Devoe Roach, 17 years old. Stabbed in Stamford Hill 27th March
Amro Elbadawi, 14 years old. Stabbed in West Kilburn 27th March
Lyle Tulloch, 15 years old. Stabbed in Southwark 4th May
Jimmy Mizen, 16 years old. Slashed in Lee 9th May
Robert Knox, 18 years old. Stabbed in Sidcup 24th May
Sharmaarke Hassan, 17 years old. Shot in Camden 24th May
Arsema Dawit, 15 years old. Stabbed in Lambeth 2nd June
Ben Kinsella, 16 years old. Stabbed in Holloway 29th June
Shakilus Townsend, 16 years old. Stabbed in Thornton Heath 3rd July
David Idowu, 14 years old. Stabbed in Borough 17th June (died in hospital 7th July)
Melvin Bryan, 18 years old. Stabbed in Edmonton 10th July
Freddy Moody, 18 years old. Stabbed in Stockwell 17th July
Ryan Bravo, 18 years old. Stabbed in Walworth 6th August
Nilanthan Murddi, 17 years old. Stabbed in Croydon 16th August
Charles Junior Hendricks, 18 years old. Stabbed in Walthamstow 24th August 2008
Shaquille Smith, 14 years old. Stabbed in Hackney 30th August
Oliver Kingonzila, 19 years old. Stabbed in Croydon 13th September
Craig Marshall, 19 years old. Stabbed in Acton 25th September
Nabeer Bakurally, 19 years old. Stabbed in Forest Gate 8th November

NOTES AND REFERENCES

1. Rock, Chris, *Bring the Pain*, (HBO 1996).
2. *Twentieth Century Atlas: Source List and Detailed Death Tolls for the Twentieth Century Hemoclysm*, http://users.erols.com/mwhite28/warstat1.htm (12/02/2005).
3. Diversity and Integration. http://83.137.212.42/sitearchive/cre/diversity/map/

northeast/sunderland.html (accessed 13 July 2008).
4. *ibid.*
5. *Street Robbery: Fact sheet*, (Black Information Link 25/07/2002). www.blink.org.uk/ pdescription.asp?key=1021&grp=55&cat=199 (accessed 27 November 2007).
6. *The Experience of Gun Crime in London*, (Victim Support London 2006). www.vslon don.org/publications/gun%20crime_finalversion_06.pdf (accessed 23 June 2008).
7. *ibid.*
8. *ibid.*
9. McLagan, Graeme, *Guns and gangs – the inside story of the war on our streets*, (London: Allison & Busby 2006)
10. *Diversity and Integration.* http://83.137.212.42/sitearchive/cre/diversity/map.html (accessed 27 November 2007).
11. *The Experience of Gun Crime in London*, (Victim Support London 2006). www.vslon don.org/publications/gun%20crime_finalversion_06.pdf (accessed 23 June 2008).
12. *ibid.*
13. *ibid.*
14. *London's Teen Murder Victims.* www.capitalradio.co.uk/article.asp?id=532062 (accessed 23 June 2008).
15. *ibid.*
16. *Independent Inquiry into Inequalities in Health Report*, (1998). www.archive.official-docu ments.co.uk/document/doh/ih/part1b.htm (accessed 23 June 2008).
17. *Race, Crime and the Justice System.* www.smartjustice.org/yprace.html (accessed 23 June 2008).
18. Garner, Richard, *Black pupils begin to close the gap at GCSE*, (*The Guardian* 28/11/2007). www.independent.co.uk/news/education/education-news/black-pupils-begin-to-close-the-gap-at-gcse-760739.html (accessed 23 June 2008).
19. Curtis, Polly, *Segregation 2006 style*, 03/01/2006 www.guardian.co.uk/education/ 2006/jan/03/raceineducation.highereducation (accessed 23 June 2008).
20. *Labour Market* (National Statistics Online 2006) www.statistics.gov.uk/cci/nugget.asp ?id=462
21. Esmail, Aneez, Kalra, Virinder and Abel Peter, *A Critical Leadership Interventions Aimed At People From Black and Minority Ethnic Groups*, (University of Manchester 2005) www.aneezesmail.co.uk/PDF%20files/HealthFoundReport.pdf (accessed 23 June 2008).
22. Housing, (National Statistics Online 2001) www.statistics.gov.uk/cci/nugget.asp ?id=1699 (accessed 23 June 2008).
23. Housing and Black and Minority Ethnic Communities (Office of the Deputy Prime Minister 05/2003).http://action.web.ca/home/narcc/attach/Housing%

20&%20Racialized%20Communities%20Report%20%20UK%20(%202003%
20)%5B1%5D1.pdf (accessed 23 June 2008).

24. *Statistics About Homelessness*, (Crisis 04/2006). www.crisis.org.uk/pdf/HomelessStat
.pdf (accessed 23 June 2008).

25. Brown, Darren, *Deaths in custody film halted by legal threat*. www.Guardian.co.uk/uk
/2001/jul/07/prisonsandprobation.filmnews (accessed 23 June 2008).

26. *The Prison Population in 2001: A Statistical Review*. www.homeoffice.gov.uk/rds/pdfs
2/r195.pdf (accessed 23 June 2008).

27. Improving the mental health of the population. Towards a strategy on mental
health for the European Union. A response from the Green Paper (African and
Caribbean Mental Health Commission 03/2006). ec.europa.eu/health/ph_
determinants/life_style/mental/green_paper/mental_gp_co001.pdf (accessed
23 June 2008)

28. *ibid.*

29. Wilson, Amos N, *Black-on-Black Violence: The Psychodynamics of Black Self-Annihilation
in Service of White Domination*, (Afrikan World InfoSystems 1990).

30. Fanon, Frantz, *Terrorism: Concepts, Causes and Conflict Resolution* (Defence Threat
Reduction Agency 2003) www.scribd.com/doc/1470256/US-Air-Force-
terrorism-concepts (accessed 23 June 2008).

31. Wilson, Amos N, *Black-on-Black Violence: The Psychodynamics of Black Self-Annihilation
in Service of White Domination*, (Afrikan World InfoSystems 1990).

32. *Anger and predisposition to violence.* www.spiritus-temporis.com/anger/anger-and-
predisposition-to-violence.html (accessed 23 June 2008).

33. Delivering on Child Poverty: What Would It Take? www.dwp.gov.uk/publications
/dwp/2006/harker/harker-4newdeal.pdf (accessed 23 June 2008).

34. *The Experience of Gun Crime in London*, (Victim Support London 2006).
www.vslondon.org/publications/gun%20crime_finalversion_06.pdf (accessed
23 June 2008).

35. Information correct in 2006.

36. Information correct in 2002.

37. Shakur, Tupac, *Strictly For My N.I.G.G.A.Z*, (Interscope 1993).

CHAPTER SEVEN
The Street IQ Test

Greetings. *StreetSensations.com* welcomes you to the home of the unique and multi-faceted Street IQ Test – the only true way to test your Street Knowledge.[1] For years, the search for the core Street Values has eluded the most prolific social scientists, baffled the most incisive philosophers, and perplexed the fiercest gangsters.

But now, through this definitive examination, you have the chance to put your knowledge to the test and find out whether you truly possess the skills that are necessary to survive in the harsh environment that is most commonly known as 'The Street'. Developed by people who actually live on 'The Street', our test reflects the very finest research available in 'road' intelligence. And today, you have the chance to answer the question that has bugged you your whole life...**How street are you?**

Please Note.
1. This is a multiple choice test and contains a total of five questions.
2. Candidates have a total of 30mins to complete this test.
3. Conferring is strictly forbidden by candidates who are sitting this test.
4. You may only check your answers after you have completed each question.
5. There are no trick questions. The right answer is always the most logical. If you have a problem with logic, you may struggle with this test. However, if you have a basic grasp of common sense, a high score in this test is guaranteed.
6. If you have any issues with the answers, don't even think about challenging them. The answers *are* right. Anything else is just plain 'niggative'.
7. 'The Street' in this test is defined as an area that is populated by working class people of any denomination or cultural group.

Be ready to think fast and good luck!
THE TIMER HAS NOW STARTED

MODULE: STREET LAW
Question 1. The Definition Of 'Street Survival' Is:

a) To keep some form of protection with you at all times i.e a tool, a shank, a strap etc. etc.

b) To build up a reputation so fiercesome that no-one on the street will F*** with you

c) To make money by any means necessary

d) To stay 100% legit

Tick One Answer

Answer: 'D' to stay 100% legit.
And this is why. Because building a formidable reputation, making dodgy cash or carrying arms will leave you in a wheelchair, incarcerated, or in a pine box six feet deep.

First. If you carry some form of protection with you at all times, trust us – one way or another, you ain't gonna be on 'the streets' for long. We understand why you might feel the need to carry hardware around with you – it's a tough world out there – especially when there are plenty of people who carry hardware around with them too! But here are the reasons why it's pure trouble to do so…

Because i) **Carrying weapons means getting nicked**. If you're carrying a weapon whilst being Black – it's worth remembering this: Black people are eight times more likely to be stopped and searched under the Policing and Criminal Evidence Act than White people. That means that when, not if, you're stopped and searched and you're caught in possession of an offensive weapon – in the current climate, the police will do everything in their power to get you convicted. And trust me, the judge will have no difficulty handing down the mandatory four year minimum sentence – regardless of your excuse or explanation.[2]

Because ii) **Stabbing people isn't that easy**. Unless you're the Wing-Chun Grandmaster, have elite weapons training, or you're Jason Bourne – trust us – you will lose that knife. We know that in films it looks easy to stab someone, but it really isn't. What will happen is that when you pull that knife out, you'll lose control of it and will probably drop it. And that's when you need to start to pray. 'Cos when you lose it, and the person you tried to attack picks it up – HE WILL F*** YOU UP. And as a bonus, he doesn't have to worry about getting in trouble with the police either, 'cos since you brought the weapon to the scene of the crime, he'll probably claim self-defence and stands a chance of busting case.

Because iii) **People will always up the ante**. If you decide to start carrying a knife 'cos someone is after you, and those people find out, you can be sure that when they come for you, they'll carry something more serious – like a Beretta. And if you start carrying a Beretta 'cos someone is after you, and those people find out, you can be sure that when they come for you, they'll carry something more serious – like an automatic...and so on and so forth. Basically, whatever you got, the person who wants to take you out will go to the next extreme to slay you. So to conclude: on the face of it, weapons look like a smart choice. But any street professor will tell you that carrying arms is as clever as a guy bowling through Peck-narm with a sandwich board that reads: 'I-HATE-NIGERIANS'.

Second. It ain't possible to build up an 'untouchable' reputation. Sorry to disappoint. Let's say that you want to develop a name sooooooooo bad that people tremble when they see you and never ever think about f***ing with you. There's only one thing to do and that is to be the hardest, fittest, most skilled combatant who has ever lived on this planet. When I say the 'hardest', I mean harder than a T-Rex on anabolic steroids. When I say the 'fittest', I mean more fit than Haile Gabri Sellassie on a three month high altitude training binge. And when I say 'most skilled combatant', I mean more skilled than a shaolin monk who's won the world Martial Arts Championship Title for the 40th year running.

However, the problem is that this person has never, and will never exist. And d'you know why? 'Cos no matter who you are, how strong you are, who you've fought, or what you've been through – there will always, *always*, be someone harder than you in this world.

And how do we know this? Because every 'top dog' in the living history of the globe has been beaten, usurped, overturned, superseded or out-manoeuvred at one stage or another. From Don Corleone to Mike Tyson. From Carlito Brigante to Ivan Drago. From Tony Montana to Ming the Merciless. They all get banged up – either by the police, by enemies, or by someone simply wanting to find out if they really are invincible.

Third. To put it bluntly, making money illegally, either through fraud or theft, will land you in a cell with a butch geezer who calls himself Sally and who's just itching for you to drop the soap in the shower. 'Cos take a good look at your skin – if it's Black give up being a criminal. D'you know why? 'Cos Black criminals *will* get caught.

- Right now, the DNA of 37% of Black men is held by the police, compared with 13% of Asian men, and only 9% of White men.[3]
- Black people are 27.5 times more likely to be stopped and searched under section 60 of the Crime and Public Order Act.[4]
- Black people are more likely to be remanded in custody than other offenders charged with similar offences.[5]
- Black people are more likely to be given longer sentences than either White or Asian people.[6]

And even if you're not a crim, it matters not. If you're stopped and searched and they don't find anything that they can arrest you for, then they can normally rustle up a charge that's easy to get a conviction for: like 'assault of an officer of the law'. And when you get taken down the nick, your 'chump legal aid solicitor' will tell you, you have no choice but admit to it to get a lesser sentence. After all, you don't stand a chance of winning your case when the two arresting officers devise a story that Hans Christian Anderson would have been proud of. You see, nothing makes some police feel like they have justified their pay packet more than by fitting up a Black person, and nothing makes some judges sleep better at night than sending a Black person to the slammer. So to wrap up, either steal £60 million from a bank and make the crime worth it – or live a 'legit' life. It's that simple. **OK, now you know what ain't Street Smart. Let's take you through what Street Smart is.**

Rule Number 1: Staying alive. Yes that's right, the main rule to abide by when living on 'The Streets' is staying alive. Why? Because a dead man can't be on 'The Street'. That's why the "I don't give a f***" attitude ain't coming from the lips of a Street Soldier, 'cos if you don't care about life how can you survive? And as any Street Disciple knows, 'giving a f***' is an essential Street Attitude.

Rule Number 2: Not making enemies. Trying to stay alive in this world can be hard, what with the killers of Steven Lawrence still free. Now you can't do anything about killers like that, but there is a way to stop yourself from getting erased by your Street brethren and sistren. And the way to do this is not to make Street enemies 'cos enemies, by definition, are quite likely to do things to you that may affect how long you spend on this earth. And that's because (as we're sure you already know), when your enemy becomes 'an enemy', they'll probably want to injure you in some way.

But if you have an enemy like Bishop from *Juice* or Pinkie Brown from *Brighton Rock*, people who don't ramp or who'll jook you with a screwdriver, or blast you away with a converted replica gun just to see the expression on your face, then you're in serious trouble. 'Cos when these types of enemies are plotting how to injure you, they'll start to think about what you might do to them in retaliation. And it's at this point that your enemies are likely to come up with the idea of preventing you from retaliation by wiping you off the face of this planet forever. So the best thing to do is to avoid making enemies. This means a) try to keep yourself to yourself *and* b) choosing your friends and your associates carefully so that you're unlikely to find yourself involved with someone who has a knack for pissing people off. Basically, keeping yourself rival-free is a sure way of increasing your chances of staying alive.

Rule Number 3: Making money to take care of your family. Basic, but very important and not always easy to achieve. If you want to survive, you need to make some money. At the very least you need food, clothes and shelter for you and your family. Then you need to think about all the things that come with living life in England: your education; your kid's education; you and your family's travel to work; council tax; Christmas presents; mobile phone bills; television licence etc etc…but you *must* earn that money in a 'legit' way. Read the next rule to find out why.

Rule Number 4: Staying out of prison. Some people might say that the best way to make money is to jack someone's phone, others might say the best way is to hold up petrol stations. Some people might say that the best way to make money is to rob pizza deliverymen, others might say the best way is to sell draw. For those that have those kinda thoughts, it only indicates how tragically un-Street they are, 'cos none of those methods are gonna make you rich and, more importantly, they're likely to land you in prison. To be Street Smart, 'legit' money is the only money that can take care of you and your family. Because in order to be 'Street', you have to be *on* 'The Street'. And you can't do much on The Street when you ain't on 'The Street', and stuck in the nick if you get what I mean. **Bottom Line**: These are the Core Street Survival Rules.

MODULE: MONEY, POWER AND RESPECT
Question 2. A True Gangsta Is Someone Who:

a) Holds a gun whenever they walk road

b) Makes other people feel shook when they walk in a club 'cos of their affiliations

c) Terrorises their area

d) Has 'WANTED' posters of themselves all over town

e) Owns 51% of a multi-million pound company

Tick One Answer

Answer: 'E' Owns 51% of a multi-million pound company. And here's why. Any Street PhD Student will tell you that true Gangstas don't snatch mobiles phones on Kilburn high street, true Gangstas snatch multi-million pound corporations in hostile takeovers. True thugs don't drop college 'cos they wanna shank the teacher, true thugs drop 10,000 staff to increase their profits. True hustlers don't own marijuana plants in their loft, true hustlers own sweatshops in south-east Asia.

You see, when we talk about gangstas, we're talking about Gs like Jeroen van der Veer. While the local so-called Gangstas in Harlesden are making 15 year old kids stick cellophane bags of crack inside their buttocks just in case they get arrested, men like Jeroen van der Veer only worry about their police when they want some protesters arrested. This is a man who runs Shell and their operations in Nigeria and who's helped them gain over $400million profit from oil in the Niger Delta region over the last thirty years. This is a man whose desire for cash has increased the number of Nigerian people subsisting on less than one dollar a day from 36% to more than 70%.[7] You see, whilst 'North Weezy' *run* from the police, Jeroen van der Veer *runs* the police.

We're talking about Gs like Sir Richard Evans. The local so-called gangstas in Tottenham, whose converted replica guns might affect who wins the drug wars in the 'Murder Mile', are nothing compared to the British Aerospace CEO, Sir Richard Evans, a man who affects the outcome of billion dollar international conflicts. This is a man who's been knighted by the Queen, a man who mixes with Presidents, a man who can annihilate nations with his Hawk T1A Aircraft, his semi-autonomous ARVs, and his Sea-Dart Surface to Air Missiles. This is a man who runs the fourth largest defence contractor in the world.[8] So whilst the 'Man Dem Crew' are hiding their ex-Army revolvers under their beds, Sir Richard Evans is legally making missiles in his factory in Lancashire, and chilling in his plush office next to the River Thames.

We're talking about Gs like Rupert Murdoch. At present in Liverpool, so-called gangstas are getting worried about the new measures that the Prime Minister will bring in to reduce their criminal activities, but they're minor compared to Rupert Murdoch, a man so powerful he can decide who the next British Prime Minister will be. This is a man who can manipulate world opinion with a phone call. This is a man who owns *Sky News, Fox News, The New York Post, The Sun, The Times* and 175 other TV stations and newspapers. This is a man who owns MySpace, the Dow Jones, and 20th Century Fox Home Entertainment. So whilst the 'Norris Green Strand Gang' talk about the influence that they have over a few elderly residents in an area with a population of 18,000,[9] Rupert Murdoch talks about the influence he controls over the entire Western world.

Bottom Line: These men are true gangstas. They run the world. They ain't worried about ghetto power, driving round their area playing loud music from their car, robbing a phone here and there, buying a bigger gold chain to hang on their necks. Nah ... these are people with real power and wealth. These are people with armies, with billions of dollars at their disposal, who can pick up the phone and speak to the president of the United States any time they want. So the next time someone tries to convince you that they're a Gangsta, remember what it really takes to be a G.

MODULE: STREET REALISM (KEEPING IT REAL)
Question 3. My Ghetto Is:

a) The roughest, toughest, baddest place in the world

b) Not the roughest, toughest, baddest place in the world... but I say it is, because it provides me with an excuse when I flop my life

c) Not the roughest, toughest, baddest place in the world...so it's kinda wotless trying to glorify the badness in mine

Tick Any That Apply

Answer: 'C' Not the roughest, toughest, baddest place in the world... so it's kinda wotless trying to glorify the badness in mine.

And here's why. It's true, Black Britons have it hard. But if we think about things, just for a moment, we Black people, living in Britain, living in Europe, living in the western hemisphere, don't actually have it as bad as most Black people have it in this world. In fact, we have it nowhere near as bad as most Black people have it in this world. Whilst places like Lewisham, Newham, Middlesbrough and Salford are areas that have their fair share of roughness, they are nowhere near the roughEST!!!

And despite this, we hear some Black people go on about the UK Street Life like it's the nastiest, most horrific life in the world. The reason is because these people need an excuse. They need an excuse for the fact that they can't be bothered to utilise the opportunities that they've got to make something significant of their lives. Let us give you an example. Deborah wakes up one morning, she looks in the mirror – and suddenly she realises that she's 21, and that her life's a bit of joke. She flopped her GCSEs and she couldn't be bothered to re-take. She's got a criminal record because she robbed £5.23 off a young girl in her area. She's been unemployed and it hasn't even occurred to her to look for a job. And it dawns on her...She's – F***ing – Her – Life – Up.

Now most people at this point in their lives would think, "I'm tired of people looking at me like I'm a bum, a wasteman, and an idiot. So I'm gonna look for a part-time job, I'm gonna go back to college and I'm gonna get educated". But Deborah – she's a bit different – she starts to think, "I'm tired of people looking at me like I'm a bum, a wasteman, and an idiot. But I can't be bothered to change my life, so I'm gonna do something to change people's *perception* of my life".

And she devises this plan: She decides to make people think that she's been a victim of the worst persecution imaginable, so that it acts as an excuse for her f***ed up life. The next time she sees her friends, and they say – "how you doing Debs"...she lies and starts spinning them a yarn about all the hardships that she's faced, all the dreadful moments that she's experienced, and the difficulties that she's incurred…'cos that way, her friends start to say: "Whoa! Deborah's life certainly is f***ed – but when you think about the things she's had to deal with, you could never blame her for the way it is."

With the plan going so well, Deborah starts talking about her tragic life even before people ask her how things are going – kinda like a pre-emptive strike – just in case they were thinking anything bad about her. And after a while, she starts to actually believe her own stories – that she is the ultimate victim, that she's been held back from achievement at every juncture, that she can't be held responsible for any of her screw-ups, all because of the tragic set of experiences that she's faced in her life.

Basically, Deborah has no ambition, and can't be bothered to put any effort into having any ambition. But by telling people that the world is against her, that where she lives in the most f***ed up and dangerous place imaginable, that everything and everyone in her life has conspired to stop her from achieving anything, she has the perfect excuse for being a loser.

And the people who answered 'A', or 'B' are people exactly like Deborah. They are the people who like to make excuses all the time, for everything that they fail at. Nothing is ever their fault. Ever! If they didn't get that job, the people in the interview panel must have been racist, and the reason why they've never had a decent job up until now is because every interviewer they've ever had, has hated Black people. Even the Black ones! If they didn't get those grades, the teacher was against them, and the reason why they've never ever got good grades up until now is because all their teachers have hated them. Even the Black ones! If their son gets arrested, the police have always had it in for him – even the Black ones! Basically, any which way they f*** up is always someone else's fault.

Now although the Street Life is hard for Black people in Britain – it ain't *that* hard. And when I say it ain't that hard, I mean two things. First, Black people in Britain, despite the racism that exists, *do* have opportunities to do something constructive with their lives. Secondly, Black people in Britain got it much easier than a lot of other Black people have it in this world. And in order to prove this, we've developed a game called **Street Fighter II – The GhettoFabulous Tournament**. The game which pits ghetto against ghetto, hood against hood, and street against street to determine which vicinity has the right to call itself the most *Ghetto* on this planet.

We've taken the most talked about ghettos from Europe, the Americas and Africa and pitted them against each other in a straight up raw and bloody clash. The three ghettos featured are:

Brixton, London, England. *Information*: England's and perhaps the EU's most famous Ghetto, particularly after the riots in 1981, 1985 and 1995. It is internationally recognised as 'Britain's Black place to see', after receiving visits from Mike Tyson, Michael Jackson and Nelson Mandela.

Brief History Of Blackness: Black people started arriving in this part of London in the 1940s and 1950s and has remained Black ever since – despite the recent gentrification.[10]

Previous Tournament Record: Back in the 1980s they were unbeatable in Europe, and the recent emergence of gangs like PDC, OC and SMS have sustained their world ranking.

Special Weapon: Their reputation! Whenever anyone mentions 'Bricky' other areas still feel intimidated.

Major Weakness: They are under extreme pressure from St Denis in Paris as Europe's No.1 after the riots from Africans and West Indians kicked off in 2005.

Bronx, New York, USA. *Information*: Was the birth place of Hip-Hop, and is one of the grimiest places in New York ever since Italian heroin traffickers brought the southern part of the borough to ruin during the 1970s.

Brief History Of Blackness: Slaves began to arrive here from the West Indies in the late 1600s. And with the influx of Black people from the deep south in the 18th and 19th centuries, the Bronx has ever since remained home to a large African-American population.

Previous Tournament Record: With notorious and infamous areas like Washington Heights, it's no surprise that this Ghetto has a number of Championships titles under its belt.

Special Weapon: The fact that it has major White gangs like 'Satan's Soldiers' as well as old school gangs like the 'Black Spades' is a major plus point in its Street credibility.

Major Weakness: The reduction in crime since the late 1990s under Mayor Giuliani has drastically undermined its Ghetto rep.

Kibera, Nairobi, Africa. *Information*: The little-known squatter slum in Kenya is home to hundreds of thousands of people who, 60 years ago, settled here from the countryside in search of jobs.

Brief History Of Blackness: Well er…it's in Africa so it's pretty much always been 99.9% Black. Whilst Kenya does have significant Asian and White communities, during colonialism the Europeans were given the farmlands and the politics, whilst Indians were given a free licence to run the businesses which is why very few non-Blacks are found in Kibera.

Previous Tournament Record: This is the first time that the Street Fighter organisers have allowed them to fight for the GhettoFabulous Trophy. Previously many Black people in the West refused to appreciate just how ghetto some parts of Africa really were!

Special Weapon: They are an unknown quantity and no-one knows what to expect, or what stunts they'll pull. This is a major plus point for them.

Major Weakness: In many cases, the government can't be bothered to formulate statistics on how 'ghetto' the place really is. This could prove costly in the later stages of the tournament since it might be hard to justify just how impoverished the people in Kibera actually are.

OK, now that we've familiarised ourselves with the Ghettos, it's time to get started with the Tournament.

Round One. Where the Government at? In Brixton, if you're pregnant, and you've just been kicked out of home by your mum, the council will theoretically try to house you. We know that the waiting list is long, and we know that the service is woefully poor, but at least there *is* a system in place to provide things like hostels, bed and breakfasts, and council houses.

In the Bronx, if you're a recovering drug addict straight outta jail, the government will notionally try to house you. We know that the places they put you in are nasty, grimy and filthy and we know that New York is chronically short of social housing, but at least there is some government housing to offer people.

But in Kibera, the world's largest slum, there is not one house built by the government for people in need of housing.[11] In fact, the government recently bulldozed a number of houses in the slum,[12] which is why there's an estimated 30,000 street children in Nairobi sleeping rough.[13] So if you wanna live in a house in Kibera, you need to build it yourself. The problem is, due to the lack of house building resources, the average home size in Kibera is only 3m by 3m. With an average five people per dwelling, you can imagine how crowded it gets. But if you thought that was bad, remember that these houses have no amenities like toilets or drainage systems,[14] which is why when rain falls it turns the whole slum into the biggest, smelliest cess-pit imaginable.

Now when it comes to schooling in Brixton, if you're under 16, your education and your travel is free plus if you're at college, you can get £30 a week to study.[15] If you wanna get educated in the Bronx, it's also free and there are over 300 different schools in the area.[16] But in Kibera there ain't one government-run school,[17] which is why 75% of young people still receive no formal education.[18] So if you want help from the government, you may as well forget about getting it in Kibera.

Round Two. Where the money at? Brixton and the Bronx have abnormally high unemployment rates for a western nation at 9.8%[19] and 7%[20] respectively. But in Kibera the unemployment stands at well over 50%,[21] which means that getting a job in the Nairobi slums must be damn hard. And the thing is, regardless of how much you earn in the UK, or in the US, it can't be as bad as the majority of Kenyans who earn just over £1 a day.[22] As you can imagine, it means that every day is a struggle to afford money to buy food.[23] So that's why if you wanna earn money you would never move to Kibera.

Round Three. Where the lifeline at? (This is where things really get interesting.) Brixton is a cakewalk compared to living in the Bronx or Kibera. The life expectancy in Brixton is around 73,[24] whilst in the Bronx it's a measly 64.6,[25] which is shocking considering that America is one of the most developed countries in the world. But this doesn't even come close to the 47 year life expectancy for most people in Kibera![26] Let me explain why.

Murder: Regardless of what the Police tell us that 'Bloodset' are doing in Brixton, we don't have criminals nearly half as serious as the people in the Bronx or in Kibera. The murder rate in London is only 2.4 per 100,000,[27] whilst in New York it's slightly higher at 4.8 per 100,000.[28] However in Kenya, because murder is soooooooo regular, the government doesn't even bother to compile figures anymore. Gangstas like the Mungiki who run the Kenyan slums, punish enemies by whipping them in front of a large crowd, dismembering them, castrating them, dousing them in petrol and then setting them alight. Kinda different to the way gangstas deal with people in South London eh?

Hospitals: In London you're never more than a couple of miles from a hospital which will provide you with free healthcare treatment regardless of your financial situation, which incidentally is much better than in the Bronx. You see, if you have a really bad accident in the US, then it's time to whip your cheque book out 'cos you gotta pay for your health care out there. That's why 12 year old Deamonte Driver died in February 2007 of a tooth infection.[29] His family didn't have the $80 to pay for a routine tooth extraction, and his infection became an abscess which spread to his brain and killed him. And yes, you guessed it, he was Black. But it's far, far worse in Kibera where hospitals don't even exist. That's right, there are *NO* hospitals. And the things is, with Cholera rife and an estimated 440,000 people with HIV in Nairobi,[30] you kinda need hospitals pretty badly.

Prisons: If the UK ghetto 'mans' thought Feltham was tough, check out American prisons. There are at present 2.2milllion people behind bars in the USA of which 16% are regarded as being mentally ill. Nowadays, if you're convicted of three crimes you receive life imprisonment, which is kinda bad 'cos Black men in their early thirties are imprisoned at seven times the rate of Whites in the same age group.[31] But it's the death penalty that really separates the American penal system from the British system. With 2,000 people since 1976 being given 'the chair', a staggering 34%[32] of these have been Black, despite being only 13% of the population.[33]

However, this is nothing compared to a Nairobi prison – the world's genuine death trap. Why? 'Cos torture is rife from prison guards, prison cells are severely overcrowded and prisoners have limited access to medical care, which is why many contract life threatening diseases and illnesses whilst incarcerated. And to top it off, they're chronically short of clean water, clothes, food, and beds.[34] So you get to live in filth and get perpetually raped. Nasty eh? Hence, if you wanna stay alive, Kibera would be the last place on your list to take up residence. And that's why, after only the Third Round, Brixton and the Bronx are knocked the f*** out by Kibera. **The undisputed Ghetto Fabulous Champion is without a doubt K I B E R A!**

And the truth is, against most ghettos in the world, Brixton is way down in the rankings. The United Nations Children's Fund estimates that in Columbia, as many as 110,000 predominantly Black children[35] are living on the streets.[36] And that's because 'The Street' life for many people, literally means living on 'The Street'. In the slum Complexo Do Alemão, Rio De Janeiro, police raids have become so frequent, and their shooting has been so careless, that many parents have been forced to sleep on top of their children in the hope of protecting them from stray bullets.[37] In South Africa, the unemployment rate amongst Black people stands at 41%,[38] in Australia the life expectancy for male Aborigines is 18 years lower than it is for White Australians,[39] and for an island of only 2.7million people,[40] Jamaica is now the third most murderous country in the world.[41]

You see, true poverty is not about deciding what Nike trainers you should buy from JD Sports. True poverty is about having to make your own footwear from rags that you found on a rubbish dump. True poverty is not about coming home and having a warm shower in a house that's been given to you by the council. True poverty is coming home to a one room shack that *you* built with no toilet and no running water. True poverty is not about living in a society with a free National Health Service. True poverty is dying from diseases that don't even exist in Western countries any more. **Bottom line: Britain for Black people is not as bad as some want it to be.**

There are a lot of Black people in this world who know what true ghetto life is all about, and many even in Britain. But for the vast majority living on this island they're chatting s*** forever saying things like:

- You can't blame me for being a thief, I'm Black, I grew up in the ghetto.
- You can't blame me for dropping out of college, I'm Black, I grew up in the ghetto.
- You can't blame me for being unemployed, I'm Black, I grew up in the ghetto etc. etc. etc., whilst they wear a £70 jacket, play with a £90 PSP, use a £100 phone and dress in £120 trainers, pay minimal rent on a flat with full amenities, and get a £43 cheque every week off the government whilst they're unemployed.

We're not saying that things are easy for people in Britain, we're just saying that it's time we all put things into perspective.

MODULE: STREET PROGRESSION
Question 4. What Do You, As A Black Person, Fear The Most?

a) A Conservative Prime Minister coupled with a Republican US President

b) Being forced to read the *Daily Mail* ... cover-to-cover

c) Mistakenly walking into Millwall Football Stadium

d) Meeting a well-educated Black man or woman who leads a legitimate and successful life?

Tick One Answer

Answer: Anything But 'D'

And here's why. Because 'True Street' Black people never feel intimidated by well-educated successful Black people. In fact, research shows us that Black Street Brainiacs love Black people doing well, and especially love Street Black people doing well. And they love it 'cos:

a) Black people who live 'legit' will provide a positive role model for the 'youngaz' in their community, and give them the confidence that they need to work towards their aspirations

b) Black people who've got well paid jobs will make the area that they live in safer, 'cos when you've got lots of people with good jobs those same people ain't got time to turn to crime

c) Black people who've come from nothing and get well educated is something that makes them proud to be Black.

Yet there are some dumb Black people who answered 'D'. They say things like: "Look at him wearing that suit. Boy, he's sold out since he got that job in the city". Or "Just listen to her posh accent and her CD collection full of Orchestral music. Man, that girl ain't from The Streets". Or even "Check that cru who all got university degrees. Bruv, they ain't keeping it real". And d'you know why they say this? They hate it when Black people are anything *but* the stereotype. You would have thought that with the poverty and the exploitation that the Black community experiences on a daily basis, all Black people would resoundingly support all the legitimate academic, financial and career successes of all Black people.

Well, not for some Black people. Not for 'niggative' Black people. They resent, fear and hate anyone Black, who rejects the stereotype – (ironically) the same stereotype that the Candyman gave them. It just tears them up inside. They simply can't handle existing in a world in which there are Black people who listen to heavy metal music, or who talk without a street accent, or who make lots and lots of 'legit' wedge. The reason: because despite racism, these 'niggative' people have had scores of opportunities to do well for themselves. They come from a loving, generous household, they went to a reasonably good school, they live in an ok area, and yet they still f***ed their lives up.

Now don't get us wrong, we're not saying that just 'cos someone's had opportunities, they have to do well in their life. But what we are saying is that if someone doesn't do well, there's no need to resent Black people who have done well. These 'niggative' Dipsh*t Black people go around and make it their mission to convince the entire intelligent Black population of Britain that a) anyone who makes it out of the ghetto is a sell-out, and b) remaining impoverished and acting 'Ghetto' is the definition of 'Being Street'.

'Cos 'Being Street' in the Dipsh*t dictionary means cutting school classes, f***ing up your exams and not getting a job that requires you to wear a suit, doing petty crime, walking road with weapons, getting a criminal record, doing time in the slammer, maintaining a Street accent and dropping phrases like, "you get me", "man dem", "innit blood" and "what's gwaning" regularly into sentences.

In other words, Dipsh*ts try to make 'failure' an essential module in their 'Phoney Street Degree.' That's why Dipsh*ts cuss Black kids for answering questions correctly in class. After a while, these kids would rather act like school doesn't matter, regardless of how smart they are. That's why Dipsh*ts cuss Black kids for talking in anything less than a rudebwoy accent. 'Cos after a while, these kids would rather turn up to job interviews talking like they just come off the set of *Rolling with the Nines*, despite the fact that they went to a good school where no-one talked like that. That's why Dipsh*ts cuss Black kids for having never been arrested. 'Cos after a while, these kids would rather get nicked, in spite of the fact that it might get them a criminal record. The result of this 'niggative' assault on Blackness is that:

- Black pupils are excluded at three times the rate of White pupils in British schools.[42]
- Black people are the 'ethnic' group most likely to be studying for Advanced NVQs – Not GCE AS/A-Levels.[43]
- Only 11% of Black Caribbeans have a degree.[44]
- For every Afro-Caribbean man in university, there are now two in jail.[45]
- In America, about 1 in 3 Black people between the ages of 20 and 29 are either in prison, on probation, or on parole.

And these days, the only thing that Dipsh*t Black people won't cuss you for is getting involved in sports or music. Why? Because you don't need any academic qualifications to get into these professions. But as any Street Expert will tell you, aiming to be a sports player or a musician shows that you most definitely ain't Street. The reason:

1. *Because the chances of you making it in the sports and music industry are slim.* We know that you see people on the cover of *Vibe* magazine with more ice on their wrists than the polar caps, but what people don't tell you, is that your chances of making a comfortable living in sports or as

a musician are very, very slender indeed. And that's because the competition for places are very, very intense. The last time we checked, there were approximately 640 Premiership football players. Now with the male population of the United Kingdom at about 30 million that doesn't leave a lot of places available for you.[46] And in the music and entertainment industry, success usually depends on being in the right place and at the right time.

We're not saying that it's impossible to have a career in these fields. But we are saying that if do want a career in any of these areas, then get a degree first. 'Cos if you throw all your eggs into one basket, and forget to go to uni, you're gonna be flat broke in between the time that you get your big break. And if you don't get your big break – which in all honesty is extremely unlikely – then you're gonna end up spending your days serving fries in Sam's Chicken instead. But with a degree in the bag, you can always get a well paid job. Statistics show that with a degree, on average you're likely to earn over 50% more over your lifetime, than non-graduates.[47] This is why all Street Academics make sure that they get a degree before they head into the sports or music industry – 'cos it gives them something to fall back on if things don't pan out.

2. *Because you can make more money doing other things.* What people don't tell you is that the average life of someone in sports is just eight years,[48] and in the entertainment and the music industry it's much, much shorter. 'Cos just like Shola Ama, or Dane Bowers, one minute you're flavour of the month and then the music scene moves on, your record company dumps you, and you become a nobody. And when you're not popular anymore, and the money dries up, in no time you'll be serving customers at Pizza Hut.

However if you work in IT, Law or Medicine your shelf life is around 40 years, and you're looking at much, much more cash in the long run, because whilst we all know that the average wage of a premiership footballer is around £409k[49] per year, what a lot of people don't know is that most footballers will only get to a semi pro-level which pays around £25k per year. Not what you expected eh?

You're probably thinking, "but if I do make it I can make more money in sport and music than I ever could in anything else so it's worth the gamble right?" Wrong! The richest people in the world are typically in business or finance *not* in music or sport. In the last *Sunday Times* UK Top 1000 Rich List, only 22 were from the music industry, and only ten were from sports.[50] In other words, sports and music pays didley-squat compared to other professions.

3. Playing sport, producing tunes, and making people laugh is NOT all Black people can do – but it's all the Candyman wants Black people to do. The Candyman's dream is for *all* Black people to spend *all* their time and energy emulating Rio Ferdinand or Beyoncé 'cos:
a) It means that Black people can do what the Candyman wants us to do, which is entertain him on *Sky Sports* or *MTV.*
b) It means that the Black people who fail in music or sports will be forced to do all the crummy jobs they don't want to do.
c) It means that the Candyman, and his children, can take all the jobs that they want i.e. stockbroking, lawyering, doctoring etc.

You see, I don't know about you, but I think Black people are capable of much more than breakdancing and ball games.

To put it simply, Black Street Soldiers will always get a degree and move into jobs that avoid the stereotyped industries. But sadly, right now Dipsh*t people don't have to feel insecure about their lack of ambition anymore, because with so many Black people striving to win a MOBO or play for West Ham, many of us now work in Lidl or Morrisons.

Anyway the bottom line is: a Street Soldier's mission is not to be in competition. As a Mwanje once said, "don't blow out someone else's candle to make yours appear brighter." 'Cos every true 'Street Soldier' wants Black people to succeed.

MODULE: STREET COMMON SENSE
Question 5. When You Think You're Subjected To Racial Prejudice Or Discrimination, Do You:

a) Get upset and complain about it. Complain about it again and five minutes after that, complain about it again but never ever do anything about it

b) Get upset and say, "I'm gonna tear up the world", jack a Black person's phone, smash up a phone box, and hate everyone – especially Black people

c) Get upset and say, "I'm gonna prove to the world that nothing can hold me back"

Tick Only One

Answer: 'C' Get upset and say, "I'm gonna prove to the world that nothing can hold me back."

And here's why. Due to the lorry loads of prejudice, abuse and discrimination that Black people receive, the question of how a Street Soldier deals with prejudice is a vitally important one. And *StreetSensations.com* can categorically tell you that you have a 'StreetLess' mentality if you:

a) **Do nothing about it but complain**. Shakespeare once wrote "nothing will come of nothing."[51] Trust me, he was right. If someone treats you like a jerk, if it makes you upset, and if it affects your life, (I know it might seem blindingly obvious but) talking about it to your mates ain't gonna change anything. Sadly, a minority of Black people who've taken this test answered 'Get Upset and Complain...But Never Ever Do Anything.' And they're the people who stand around in the community centres, the schools and the bars and talk with their friends about their discriminatory experiences with an anger and a passion – but never do anything active to challenge it.

If you're a Black person who says to themselves, "I can't stand the fact that I get stopped in the street every friggin day, but I won't challenge it 'cos I've got too much to lose", then stop complaining about it. The system obviously can't be that bad can it? As Maya Angelou said, "if you don't like something, change it. If you can't change it, change your attitude. Don't complain."[52]

But, if you're a Black person who really gets affected by prejudice then you may as well take a chance and try to solve it. After all, apathy hurts no-one but yourself, and certainly not the Candyman who get haps by the fact that they can exploit people who can't be bothered to fight against it. The point is, it's gonna take effort to change things. The kinda effort that Rocky III put in for his rematch with Clubber Lang. So put up, or shut up.

b) **Go mental on the people who have just been racist to you without thinking about the consequences.** Lashing out, swearing and the rest of the emotional reactions as a result of receiving prejudice are understandable, but it's no way for a Street Soldier to survive. As any Street Lieutenant with an MA in Street Logic will tell you, every reaction to bigots should be well thought out. If, for example, a police officer stops you because 'someone of your description was seen robbing an old lady', reacting with 'get your f***ing hands off me...' is a bad move, 'cos it's only gonna get you booked. Whilst we appreciate why some people react like this, it ain't StreetSmart 'cos understand this: The police officer is the person with all the legal power, all the political power and all the physical power. And, therefore, your StreetSmart objective should be to stay out of trouble with the police, since a criminal record means game over for your employment prospects.

Now don't get us wrong, we know it's annoying being harassed by police, we know it probably happens to you all the time, we know that the last time they stopped you was when you were in a rush to get to work, and they made you late, which made your boss angry with you, which put you on your final, final, final warning ... but what you need to realise is that the moment you start swearing at a police officer, they'll book you for assault asap. So this is how you should challenge the System if you're sick and tired of being racially abused:

Rule One: *Drop some knowledge on them – Know your rights.* The next time you get 'randomly' stopped, show them that you know the law:

- Before you answer any questions, ask the police offier why you've been stopped.
- Ask for the police officer's name and number and make sure they give it to you.
- If they try to search you on The Street, make sure that they know that it's against the law to search you in public.
- Ask for a receipt for the stop and search, after all it's your right.

Once they can see that you're smart, they'll move on. Policemen on a hype tend to steer clear of intelligent Black people.

Rule Two: *Keep positive. Can't nobody hold you down but YOU.* If a teacher's treating you differently in class, banging up the teacher and getting excluded from school is not the way forward. The reason: because whatever you do to that teacher, they still get paid at the end of the month. But for you, it means permanent exclusion.

The only way that you can make this teacher feel like a chump is to keep doing the work, keep turning up to class and smash your exams. When your teacher sees that all their efforts to screw you up failed, they'll feel like a plum. And when you see them ten years later qualified, experienced, respected and doing what you always told them that you'd do, they'll be understandably irate that against all the odds, and despite their prejudice, they failed to f*** your life up. 'Cos living well is the best revenge. As Ludacris once said, "it's not the hand that you're dealt, but how you're playin' your cards."[53]

HOW WELL DID YOU DO?

NOTES AND REFERENCES

1. *IQ Test* www.iqtest.com. (accessed 24 June 2008).

2. *Tackling The Scourge of Knife Crime*, (31/05/2006).news.bbc.co.uk/1/hi/uk_politics/5032794.stm (accessed 24 June 2008).

3. Randerson, James, *DNA of 37% of Black Men Held by Police: Home Office Denies Racial Bias*, (*The Guardian* 05/01/2006). www.guardian.co.uk/world/2006/jan/05/race.ukcrime (accessed 24 June 2008).

4. *Engagement and Involvement of Disadvantaged Groups that Experience High Victimisation Levels, to Reduce Crime and its Impact.* www.londoncouncils.gov.uk/London%20Councils/Grants/Application%20 for%20funding/Service79.pdf (accessed 24 June 2008).

5. *Prisoners From Minority Ethnic and Religious Groups*, (Select Committee on Home Affairs).www.publications.parliament.uk/pa/cm200405/cmselect/cmhaff/193/19317.htm (accessed 24 June 2008).

6. *ibid.*

7. Watts, Michael and Zalik, Anna *Africa: The New Frontier for Imperial Oil* (06/05/2006). www.indybay.org/newsitems/2006/05/06/18214251.php (accessed 24 June 2008).

8. McNamara, Kirsty, *SDS to 'U': Sell Defense Stocks $7.3 million invested in Military Contractors*, (*Michigan Daily News* 15/03/07). www.michigandaily.com/news/2007/03/15/CampusLife/Sds-To.u.Sell.Defense.Stocks-2776751.shtml, (accessed 24 June 2008)

9. *2001 Census Profiles: The City of Liverpool.* www.liverpool.gov.uk/Images/tcm21-23030.pdf (accessed 24 June 2008)

10. *Brixton: A Short History.* www.urban75.org/brixton/history/history.html (accessed 24 June 2008).

11. Amanpour, Christiane, *World Fails To Save Africa's AIDS Orphans: Africa's HIV infected Children Also Ignored*, www.cnn.com/2006/WORLD/africa/07/17/amanpour.africa.btsc/index.html (accessed 24. June 2008) 19/07/2006.

12. Vasagar, Jeevan, *Bulldozers Go In To Clear Kenya's Slum City*.www.guardian.co.uk/international/story/0,3604,1195449,00.html (*The Guardian* 20/04/2004) (accessed 24 June 2008).

13. Low, Ula, *A World of Violence – The Daily Battles of Nairobi's Street Children.* www.europrofem.org/contri/2_04_en/en-viol/20en_vio.htm (accessed 24 June 2008).

14. *CSG Kibera.* www.csgkibera.org/ (accessed 25 June 2008).

15. Educational Awards and Benefits, (London Borough of Lambeth), www.lambeth.gov.uk/Services/EducationLearning/SchoolsColleges/EducationalAwards/ (accessed 24 June 2008).

16. Bronx Schools. www.greatschools.net/city/Bronx/NY (accessed 24 June 2008).

17. *White Mischief with Education in Kenya.* www.ncl.ac.uk/egwest/pdfs/White%20 Mishchief.pdf (accessed 24 June 2008).

18. *Slum the Size of Bristol,* (02/12/2003). archive.glastonburyfestivals.co.uk/news/article/+slumthesizeofbri/index.html

19. *About Lambeth,* www.lambeth.gov.uk/NR/rdonlyres/BA67FA12-CCA8-4F90AC 11-52FBABE1B2A4/0/Aboutlambeth.pdf (accessed 24 June 2008).

20. Rivette, Sarah Carrión, *Highlights Progress of the Borough,* (The Bronx Beat 11/02/ 2008) www.bronxbeat.org/cs/ContentServer?childpagename=Bronxbeat08% 2FJRN_Content_C%2FRW1StoryDetailLayout2&c=JRN_Content_C&page name=JRN%2FRW1Wrapper&cid=1175374073668&site=Bronxbeat08 (accessed 24 June 2008).

21. Facts and Information About Kibera, (Kibera UK - The Gap Year Company). www.kibera.org.uk/Facts.html (accessed 24 June 2008).

22. *The Dynamics of Returns to Education in Kenyan and Tanzanian Manufacturing,* Global Poverty Research Group, (04/2005). www.gprg.org/pubs/workingpapers/pdfs/gprg-wps-017.pdf (accessed 24 June 2008).

23. Steward, Nkrumah, *The Nigga Kingdom,* (Raw Dogma), (accessed 24 June 2008).

24. OMS, *Life Expectancy at birth by health and local authorities in England and Wales, 2000-2002,* (National Statistics Website Release 06/11/2003). www.statistics. gov.uk/downloads/theme_population/Life_expect_birth_h-la_E-W_00-02.pdf (accessed 24 June 2008)

25. Miringoff, Marque Luisa, *The Social Health of the Nation: How America Is Really Doing,* Oxford University Press, USA (07/06/1999).

26. Pambazuka, Soren Ambrose, *Preserving Disorder: IMF Policies and Kenya's Health Care Crisis,* 01/06/2006.www.globalpolicy.org/socecon/bwi-wto/imf/2006/0601imf health.htm (accessed 24 June 2008).

27. Bone, James, *US Murder Rate Sinks as Zero Tolerance puts Gangs on Run,* (Times Online 03/01/2005). www.timesonline.co.uk/tol/news/world/article407900.ece (accessed 24 June 2008)

28. U.S. FBI, *Crime in the United States, annual. From Statistical Abstract of the United States, 2006* www.disastercenter.com/crime/nycrime.htm (accessed 24 June 2008).

29. Michandani, Rajesh, *Boy's Death Highlights US Health Debate.* http://news.bbc.co.uk/ 1/hi/world/americas/7018057.stm (accessed 24 June 2008).

30. Amanpour, Christiane, *World Fails To Save Africa's AIDS Orphans: Africa's HIV-infected Children Also Ignored* (19/07/2006).www.cnn.com/2006/WORLD/africa/ 07/17/amanpour.africa.btsc/index.html (accessed 24 June 2008).

31. DeParle, Jason, *The American Prison Nightmare,* (*The New York Review of Books* 12/04/2007). www.nybooks.com/articles/20056 (accessed 24 June 2008).

32. *Death Penalties at a Glance,* (*Los Angeles Times* 03/12/2003). articles.latimes.com/ 2005/dec/03/nation/na-execute3 (accessed 24 June 2008).

33. USA QuickFacts from the US Census Bureau 2006. quickfacts.census.gov/qfd/states/00000.html (accessed 25 June 2008).

34. Phombeah, Gray, *Inside Kenya's 'worst' prison*. news.bbc.co.uk/2/hi/africa/2816217.stm (accessed 25 June 2008).

35. *Colombia South America: A New Phrase of Waiting Begins*, (Hollis Adoption 05/03/2008). hollis-colombia.blogspot.com/2008/03/new-phase-of-waiting-begins.html (accessed 25 June 2008).

36. "Death? What Y'all Know About Death", said by Sergeant Barnes, *Platoon* (MGM 1986).

37. Alves, Maria Helen Moreira, *Public Security Or Genocide? The War In Rio Communities Complexo do Alemão and Penha*, 25/06/2007. www.comunidadesegura.org/?q=en/node/34592 (accessed 25 June 2008).

38. G. Kingdon and J. Knight, *Unemployment, Race And Politics In South Africa*. www.gprg.org/themes/t2-inc-ineq-poor/unem/unem-pov.htm (accessed 25 June 2008).

39. Maynard, Roger, Bleak Picture Of Aboriginal Life Expectancy, (*The Guardian* 21/06/2006). www.guardian.co.uk/world/2006/jun/21/australia (accessed 25 June 2008).

40. *About The People*, (CountryReports.org). www.countryreports.org/country.aspx?countryid=121 (accessed 25 June 2008).

41. *Crime, Violence and Development: Trends, Costs and Policy Options in the Caribbean*, (03/2007 United Nations). http://www.unodc.org/documents/data-and analysis/Caribbean-study-en.pdf (accessed 25 June 2008).

42. *Literacy and education levels by ethnic group and populations*, (National Literacy Trust). www.literacytrust.org.uk/Database/STATS/EALstats.html (accessed 25 June 2008).

43. *Youth Cohort Study: The Activities and Experiences of 17 year olds: England and Wales 2000*, (National Statistics: Department for Education and Skills 31/10//2001). www.dfes.gov.uk/rsgateway/DB/SFR/s000294/sfr42-2001.doc (accessed 25 June 2008).

44. *Education*, (National Statistics Online 2004). www.statistics.gov.uk/cci/nugget.asp?id=461

45. David Cracknell and Yuba Bessaoud, *Twice as many Blacks in Jail as at University*, (Times Online 14/12/2003) http://www.timesonline.co.uk/tol/news/uk/article1042543.ece (accessed 25 June 2008).

46. *United Kingdom*, http://www.worldstatesmen.org/United_Kingdom.html

47. *Parents Information*, www.keele.ac.uk/depts/aa/widening/downloads/Parents.pdf (accessed 25 June 2008).

48. Rogers, Andrew, *Prejudice, politics in England distort players' economic reality*, www.soccertimes.com/oped/2006/may29.htm (accessed 25 June 2008).

49. *The Chief Executive's Annual Report: Part II The Independent Newspaper Survey*. www.givemefootball.com/pfa.html?newsID=232 (accessed 25 June 2008).

50. *2008 Rich List*, (Times Online). http://business.timesonline.co.uk/tol/business/ specials/rich_list/rich_list_search/?l=17&list_name=Rich+List+2008&adv search=1&t=1&n=&k=&a=&r=&g=&i=&new=&x=34&y=2 (accessed 25 June 2008)

51. Shakespeare, William, *King Lear*

52. *Quote World*. www.quoteworld.org/quotes/444 (accessed 25 June 2008).

53. Ludacris feat. Young Jeezy, *Grew Up A Screw Up*, (Disturbing Tha Peace Recordings 2006).

CHAPTER EIGHT
The Immaculate Conception

Emma The Egg: Whoa, Whoa, Whoa! Where do you think you lot are going in such a rush?

Sammy The Sperm: Er, I woulda thought that was pretty obvious. We've just been given the go-ahead by both our Controllers so now us group of tadpoles are doing what we do best – swimming as fast as possible into you, and trying to find a way in!

Emma The Egg: Well sorry lads, but there's new rules. This is now a restricted area. And unless you guys can break out some ID, you're gonna have to step aside.

Sammy The Sperm: Didn't you understand me? Your boss and my boss have come to an agreement in the mid-section, and since we don't have much time, I'd advise you to fulfil your employer's wishes by letting me fulfil my employer's wishes so that you can start the ball rolling in the old 'fertilisation sector'.

Emma The Egg: Hey – it ain't all about you y'know. *I* decide who comes in my VIP area, so unless you start showing me some credentials, you and your friends are gonna have to find somewhere else to 'jam' for the night.

Sammy The Sperm: Girl – with an attitude like that, if you weren't an Egg, I coulda sworn you were on your period.

Emma The Egg: Well I'm sorry to be so frigid, but in this day and age, I gotta be ultra-cautious when it comes to baby-making.

Sammy The Sperm: Jeeez, you're kind of a 'half-empty' kinda lady aren't you. Why don't you chillax a little!

Emma The Egg: Trust me, I would... but it's like this, and I gotta be straight…things are kinda 'niggative' these days. Too many Black men aren't taking the role of parenting seriously enough, and if I'm gonna expend all my energy creating a human being I'm gonna make damn sure that I do it with someone who's gonna take care of the thing. 'Cos right now in the UK, one in every two Black children are raised without a father,[1] and Black mothers are more likely than mothers from any other cultural group to be lone parents.[2] In America, as many as 70% of all Black children grow up with a lone parent![3]

Now I know that some Black guys don't really like to talk about this issue much, and I know that these stats are a bitter, bitter pill to swallow, but my concern ain't the emotions of a small group of Black men who can't be bothered to look after their children. My concern is that it's been proven that the more time a father spends with his child, the better he/she develops; and the less time a father spends with his child, the worse he/she develops.[4] So when I'm faced with an army of albino amphibians who think that they can just march in here willy-nilly, I get a bit jittery! 'Cos I'm wondering whether this is just a 'hit and run' for your boss, or whether he's playing for keeps – if you get what I mean.

Sammy The Sperm: Ok, I get it now. Yea, I heard those stats the other day too, and I was kinda wondering when someone would raise this issue with us. But before you start writing off Black men completely, you gotta understand that it's not always the man's fault. Sometimes the fathers who get called 'bad' fathers, are actually good fathers – in fact they're actually brilliant fathers. They're just men who unfortunately got involved with really, really bad women: the types of women who get pregnant with their man, and then use the child as a bargaining chip, as a way of getting what they want.[5] And when they get angry with their man, they'll prevent him from seeing his child and start claiming that their man is a bad father.

Emma The Egg: Yea, I know there are some messed up mothers out there who are equally as destructive as the men, but generally the opposite is true.

Sammy The Sperm: And what's the opposite?

Emma The Egg: That it's Black women's dedication, integrity and the tireless sacrifice towards their children, that are the only things saving thousands of children from ending up f***ed. For most Black lone mothers their day goes like this. At 7am she gets up and gets washed; 7.30am she gets their kid washed; 8am she gets breakfast ready for their kid; 8.30am she takes their kid to school; 8.45am she goes to work; 9am she arrives at work; 5pm she finishes work; 5.15pm she picks her kid up from after-school club; 5.30pm she cooks her kid dinner; 6pm she eats dinner with her kid; 6.30pm she drops her kid off to a babysitter; 7pm she arrives at evening school; 9pm she finishes evening school; 9.15pm she picks up her kid from the babysitter; 9.30pm she reads her kid a bedtime story; 9.45pm the kid goes to sleep; 10pm she goes to sleep! That's why it's no understatement to say that Black women are some of the hardest working, most under-appreciated members of British society.

Sammy The Sperm: Man, I get tired just thinking about that day!

Emma The Egg: 70% of all Black Caribbean mothers are employed during their pregnancy, the most likely of all cultural groups.[6] And two in every five Black Caribbean mothers continued to work from when their child was born, till when their child was three years old.[7]

Sammy The Sperm: I think I'm beginning to understand why you're so pranged.

Emma The Egg: But because of the immense pressure on single mothers, and the lack of support from a number of fathers, 40% of Black Caribbean families are on a low income.[8] Overall 72% of all lone parents live below the poverty line, compared with 32% of co-habiting parents, and a measly 14% of married couples.[9] This is probably why one in five poor children are from a cultural minority (double the rate for White children),[10] and 42% of all poor children live in one-parent families.[11]

So it doesn't take Sherlock Holmes to work out that much of the frustrations that exist amongst young Black people are as a direct result of the lack of guidance shown by Black fathers inside many households. After all, statistics do show that 70% of young offenders are from single-parent families.[12]

Sammy The Sperm: Wait, are you trying to tell me that *all* kids from lone-mothers are failures?!

Emma The Egg: Course not. But in the same way that smoking vastly increases your chances of dying from lung-cancer, though not everyone who smokes will die from it, being a lone mother doesn't mean that their children won't succeed, but it certainly increases the likelihood. Black people like the British Politician David Lammy and Olympic Gold medallist Denise Lewis were all raised by single mothers, but sadly they're in the minority. So you gotta understand my position. If I don't look for the **Immaculate Conception**, I'd be guilty of neglect of duty.

Sammy The Sperm: You know, you're starting to sound a bit pre…

Emma The Egg: …judiced? Listen, I'm all too well aware of the stereotypes that are associated with Black men, and don't worry I know that most of it's hype, but I gotta be honest with you a lot of Black guys ain't doing too much to challenge these stereotypes. I mean, the amount of tadpoles who come down here with bosses who've got kids from several different women is ridiculous! Things are so f***ed now that it's quite normal for some boys, when chirpsing a girl, to have to ask for their father's surname just in case they're not getting jiggy with their sister! And that's why I gotta be tight about this.

Sammy The Sperm: Alright, alright – here are our Identification Cards. Process them asap, and let us get back to the task at hand.

Emma The Egg: Let me just run this through the system. Hmmm … it looks like your boss has been rejected.

Sammy The Sperm: On what grounds?

Emma The Egg: I'm just waiting for the computer print-out…Ah…here is it…it seems like he's been rejected because he fails to comply with the Trinity…

Sammy The Sperm: … the Trinity? Are you, er, looking for a priest 'cos I'm sure they take a vow of celibacy.

Emma The Egg: Not the *Holy Trinity*, but the *Conception Trinity*. You see, the Conception Trinity (CT) are the essential criteria that I look out for when my manager's sizing up a man to be the father of her children. That way, I can reduce the chances of her being with the kinda guy who's gonna play the Invisible Man. I know that some women don't like to use the Trinity – they end up having a baby with a complete idiot – and then complain at the man for acting like an idiot. But that's kinda like locking yourself in a room with a tiger and then complaining when you get bitten. Basically, if they didn't wanna struggle for the next 18 years of their lives – giving up their studies, giving up their careers – they shoulda adhered to the CT. Sure, men can change their attitudes and things might not go as planned, but if more women followed the Trinity, they'd reduce the chances of being a single mum, and increase the chances of their child having two loving parents! Cool huh?!

Sammy The Sperm: Criteria for a baby?! That sounds a bit fascist if you ask me.

Emma The Egg: Yea but that's the thing, I ain't asking you. You need to pass certain criteria to give people damn tattoos in this country so it can't be that crazy that I'm asking your boss to comply with the CT, especially since having a baby is a teeeeeeeny bit more serious than getting your body painted on in Camden market.

Sammy The Sperm: So what are the three criteria?

Emma The Egg: The first one's quite simple. **Criteria One: Make sure the man has an up to date CV**. What I mean is *Make Sure He Has All The Correct Credentials For Being A Father.* And the correct credentials are as follows:
  A) **Being over 25 years old**. Since having a baby is a big thing, in fact, since it's probably one of the biggest things to ever happen to a man, there needs to be a certain level of maturity involved. Now I know that it's impossible to truly quantify the mental maturity of someone simply by judging their age...

Sammy The Sperm: After all it was Aaliyah who said that age ain't nothing but a number.

Emma The Egg: ...well...er...precisely. But with the help of sociologists and psychologists, it's fairly possible to predict people's

readiness for the certain things that they're allowed to do. That's why:
— Only at 15, can you see a 15 film without parental guidance
— Only at 16, can you have sex legally
— Only at 17, can you drive
— Only at 18, can you vote
And since having a child is far more important than *any* of these, the advisable age that I give is 25 plus.

Sammy The Sperm: 25 plus! But that's a bit late isn't it. I mean, I'm sure I read that back in the day everybody used to have children at an early age.

Emma The Egg: Yea, well times have changed my dear boy. Back in the old days, everything was done a lot earlier on account of the fact that people died far earlier than they do today. In the Victorian era, for example, people were allowed to have sex as young as 12, people could leave school at 13, people as young as 16 were joining the army and it was expected that people get married when they were between the ages of 18 and 22. Why? Because three out of every 20 babies died before their first birthday, the working classes ate a very poor diet and worked in inhumane conditions meaning that most people didn't see past their 40th birthday.[13] So people made the most of what life they had, particularly when it came to having children!

Twenty-first century UK life, however, is very, very different. Only five children in 1,000 die before their first birthday,[14] most life-threatening diseases have been cured or can now be treated, diets have massively improved and we haven't had to fight in any major wars for over half a century now, which is why most people now live well into their late 70s.[15] And because people live longer, they can wait until the time is right to have a kid. And the time is definitely *more* right after 25.

I say this for two specific reasons. First: because the younger you have kids, the poorer you're likely to be. Men who become fathers in their teens and early twenties are twice as likely to be unemployed, receive state benefits and live in social housing compared with fathers in their late 20s[16] and 69% of all mothers aged 20 or younger are living in poverty.[17] Second: because there are soooooooo many things to do in this world. You see, in the past, if you were a working class guy you worked, you drank, and you fornicated. And that was it. You might go to the seaside once in a while, you might watch a footie match occasionally, but there weren't that many leisure activities to participate in!

Nowadays, a man's got cheap flights to Ayia Napa, he's got the Premiership, he's got the Ministry of Sound, he's got Sky Digital, he's got *FHM* magazine, he's got *Halo* for the Xbox 360, he's got the *Godfather* trilogy on DVD. And with so much choice out there, he needs to experience and explore all this stuff before he's tied down with a kid. So it'd be advisable for any woman looking to settle down, to find a man who's spent a good few years travelling, drooling over football stats on soccernet, raving, vegetating in front of the TV, playing PlayStation, watching Gangsta films and having a fair amount of girlfriends. Once he's got most of this stuff out of his system (more or less, and particularly the girlfriend bit), then he's likely to be ready to dedicate his life to being a father, because the last thing a mother needs, is a father who feels like he missed out on his youth by having a kid when he was 'in his prime!'

B) **Make sure he has a degree.** This is a no-brainer. If a man doesn't have a degree, a woman should be fairly sceptical about his ability to be a father. Ok, if he took an apprenticeship, or he set up a successful company, or he's already got a decent job or he simply couldn't go to Uni, for whatever reason – his family needed him to work to bring money in 'cos they were flat broke, his mum was ill and he needed to take care of her etc etc – then you can let him off. But, if he hasn't got a valid reason (saying something like "I can't be bothered to go back to school" is not a valid reason), then the woman should *never* consider him as father material.

Now I know this might seem kinda harsh, but it's like this: when a man goes to an employer with a degree, it looks good because a degree shows that this man i) has a thirst for knowledge ii) can commit himself to something for at least three years and iii) can deal with a heavy workload.

So if a woman's with a man who hasn't got a degree, (and he didn't do an apprenticeship, doesn't have a good job, and has no valid excuse) he clearly has no interest in learning new things, he clearly has commitment issues, and he has no idea how to deal with a heavy workload: all of which are essential skills in raising a child! And anyway, if he's really keen on being a father to the woman's child, then he can always go back to Uni to prove himself. After all, it's never too late!

C) **Make sure he has a gameplan**. Yea that's right: you gotta have a J.O.B if you wanna be with me. There ain't no romance without finance.[18] A woman needs to look for a man with some sort of life strategy – that is to say, he needs to have an understanding of what he wants, and how he's going to get it. And the tell-tale sign of a gameplan in a man is whether he has a job that looks like it's going places or he has a passion for something that he plans to make into a career. If he has either of these, he's ripe to 'seckle' down.

Sammy The Sperm: But surely a man can develop a passion, or develop a career while he's got a kid?

Emma The Egg: You're right, he could. But it's just gonna be a lot harder. As soon as a man gets a woman pregnant, he needs to go to hospital with her for regular updates on the status of the foetus, he needs to go to pre-natal classes, he needs to read lots and lots of books written by lots and lots of wacky psychologists about child development, and he might even need to go to a couple of parenting classes. Then when the baby is born, he needs to take some paternity leave to spend some quality time with the child, he needs to go and show the kid off at relatives' houses on the weekends, and he needs to be prepared to be woken up at ungodly times of the night by their child screaming for...for...well...for anything!

And the thing is, all of this is gonna be mega-stressful. It's gonna be very difficult for a man to do all this, and think about what type of career he wants at the same time. But also, don't forget, if the man doesn't have a career, how in the hell is he gonna help pay for the mammoth list of things that the kid needs? It's estimated that on average, 23% of a man's earnings will solely go on his child's upbringing,[19] buying things like a baby seat for the car, nappies, baby clothes, toys, a crib, a high chair, bibs, baby wipes, and baby food.

Then, when they go to school, he needs to buy the school uniform, the sports wear, more toys, the Christmas presents, the birthday presents, the holidays, the pets, the clothes, the games, the food, and provide the lunch money and travel money. And when the kid becomes a teenager, you gotta be ready to buy the latest Xbox, the Adidas trainers, the Jacobs watches, the Ericsson phones, and the Stone Island jackets! Basically in order to pay for all this, especially post Credit Crunch, the man needs a decent job, charitable parents, or an extremely generous bank manager. 'Cos on average it costs £165,668 to raise a child from birth to the age of 21, which works out at £7,889 a year![20]

Sammy The Sperm: So what are you saying? If a man's poor he can't have a baby?!

Emma The Egg: Don't be silly, of course I ain't. I'm just saying that it's much easier if a woman gets with a guy who's got a job that brings in a fair amount of cash, so as to provide the stuff necessary to give their child the best start in life. And also, if a woman gets with a guy who ain't got a job, and who refuses to get a job, then he's clearly a wasteman. 'Cos if he can't take care of himself, you can be damn sure that he ain't taking care of his kid!

Sammy The Sperm: But what if it ain't his fault that he's flat broke with no goals. It's a hard, cold world out there y'know... especially for a Black man.

Emma The Egg: True, but being Black ain't an excuse for being broke. Being Black ain't an excuse for having no ambition. And being Black certainly ain't an excuse for being dumb. In fact, being Black means that he's got a responsibility to live up to the achievements of the Black people who came here with nothing and carved out a living for themselves – with more police brutality than there is today, with worse housing estates than there are today, and with more prejudice than there is today. You see, if a man really likes a girl and he tells her that he's ready to have a kid with her, then that should be all the motivation that he needs to go back to college, to make some Pz, and to make damn sure that he gives every last ounce of energy into giving his child the best chance in life.

Criteria Two: Make sure that he's got some morals. He needs to show that he's a man who 'comes correct' in the way that he lives. And he can do this by doing the following:

a) *Not participating in criminal activities.* I know that there are some women who date guys who rob, who carry arms, who deal drugs, but in all honesty this kinda attitude is f***ing dumb. 'Cos I know that initially it might seem cool to date someone who's got a little 'edge' to them, who's making Pz at a young age, who's kinda dangerous, but a man who's got a chance of going to prison or getting plunged with a knife is the worst type of father. 'Cos the last thing a woman should want is:

- To have to tell her child that their father is either in the nick or been murdered.

WHAT BEING BLACK IS AND WHAT BEING BLACK ISN'T

- To have a man who beats people up, who jooks people, and who jacks people. 'Cos this type of a man is unlikely to be a sensitive, kind, understanding father.
- To put their child's safety at risk because people are looking to do some damage to their father, as happened to Toni-Ann Byfield. When, in 2003, Joel Carl Smith came looking for rival drug-dealer Bertram Byfield, he killed both Bertram and the seven year old who was staying with him. 'Cos when someone wants to get to a man, his kids are an obvious place to start!

If the woman's in doubt about a man's career, i.e. how he makes his wads of cash, how he manages to get so many car stereos, why he's got four different mobile numbers, she needs to ask him what he does. If he can't give her a straight answer then he needs to go.

b) *Not acting like a player and having children from other women* – especially whilst he's with you. This is kinda obvious, yet you'd be surprised how many women fail to adhere to this vital rule. If the man acts like a player and checks nuff other women, then you can be sure that he'll be doing that kinda stuff even when he's got a kid with her. And if he's prepared to disrespect his baby mother so blatantly, then it's hard to see how he's gonna have much respect for the kid. And when you bear in mind that this kind of attitude is gonna be equally as painful for the kid as it is for the baby mother, then he needs to go.

If a man's got kids from a previous relationship, then his present girlfriend needs to be asking some important questions: like when, where, why, how many, and with whom he had his kids. Once the answers to these questions are thrashed out, a decision whether to progress can be made, but only *after* the answers have been thrashed out. 'Cos a woman needs to know whether the man's previous baby mother is a reasonable woman, whether the man takes care of his previous kids, and whether the man is capable of looking after two kids from two different relationships.

Now I know that this might seem kinda ruthless, but in this day and age, a woman's gotta have high expectations. You see, part of the reason why there are soooooo many Black women suffering is 'cos they don't have a lot of self-confidence, and have lowered expectations of what they want in a father. I mean think about it, if a man sells weed, if he carries a knife 'cos 'mans' are after him, if he's constantly flirting with other women, then it's quite obvious that he ain't gonna be a decent, reliable and worthy father – which means that any woman

THE IMMACULATE CONCEPTION

who shacks up with him can't have a lot of respect for herself, or high expectations of what she wants in a man. I know that she might love him, and if she does, there's no reason why she can't date him or even marry him…but for God's sake don't have kids with him!

Sammy The Sperm: But hold on… what if the man's done a few naughty things in the past, but has changed now?

Emma The Egg: I hear you. 'Cos of course people make mistakes when they are younger, and they shouldn't be punished for the rest of their lives. A woman might be dating a guy who got into a street brawl when he was younger and got pinched by the police, but has gone back to school, has got a degree, has got a job, and moved on from it. A woman might have fallen for a man who, by mistake, had a child with a woman when he was younger, but he plays a big part in his kid's life, and has a positive relationship with the mother.

But the point is, it's up to the man to *prove* to the woman that he can be a serious and reliable father to her children and not, as some men think, for the woman to prove to the man that he *isn't* a serious and reliable father! The problem with dating a man who hasn't proved that he's changed is that you're risking the future of your child's welfare.

You see, the implications of being with a man who doesn't act like a man – like only seeing his kids every so often, letting them out at all times of the night, putting them in front of the computer every night, cussing them, swearing at them, never having a positive thing to say about them, making them feel inadequate all the time, being physically abusive – is that the child suffers and, that's not what any loving mother should ever want… should they?

Criteria Three: make sure he is prepared to be married before having a baby. Now I know that this sounds a little scary which is why it's the last Criteria…

Sammy The Sperm: Did you say marriage, as in, like, permanent commitment?

Emma The Egg: Yep.

Sammy The Sperm: But isn't marriage, like, kinda 'old skool'. I mean, no-one gets married anymore.

221

Emma The Egg: And why d'you think that is…?

Sammy The Sperm: Well, take your boss and my boss for example. They wanted a child right?

Emma The Egg: Yea…

Sammy The Sperm: Now, at this moment in time, things are cool. But, well, you know what relationships are like – one minute it's Romeo and Juliet, the next it's Ike and Tina Turner! And the reason for that is because these days, you can't expect a man to settle down forever – but that's not to say that your manager's not a wonderful girl, 'cos she is, and she'd definitely make a wonderful mother, but I just can't see my boss being faithful to her for the rest of his life.

Emma The Egg: Listen, I'm a realist, and I know that millions of men go through exactly the dilemma that you're describing:
— Can I be faithful?
— Can I spend the rest of my life living with one woman?
— Can I resist the temptations of other women, especially when there are soooooooo many other gorgeous women in the world?
— Can I get a better looking woman? Is Mariah, or Tyra, or Vivica, or Alicia, or Janet gonna proposition me one day?

And that's why I appreciate that marriage is not everyone's cup of tea.

Sammy The Sperm: I'm glad you understand.

Emma The Egg: But unfortunately there's no getting around the third criteria and there are four reasons for this:
    1. **Children raised in a household with two married parents fare much better than the alternative.** In the US, children whose parents are married are statistically more likely to live a healthier life,[21] attend University, and be emotionally healthier. They are also less likely to abuse drugs or alcohol, less likely to commit offences, less likely to be the victim of physical or sexual abuse, less likely to be raised in poverty, and less likely to contract an STI.[22]
    In the UK, children who live with married parents stay in education longer, and get better grades.[23] And this is probably

because 33% of one-parent families live on gross incomes of merely £200 a week or less which compares with just 10% of cohabiting couples and a mere 3% of married couples.[24]

Now, if a man's serious about raising his child right, then it should be obvious that raising the child in a secure, settled and stable environment will improve his child's chances of having a happier existence. I know that some men might say, "but children who don't live in a married setting can still do well," and to an extent I agree, but the point is why take that risk? Why does he not just wait until he meets the woman he really wants to marry, and have children with her?

2. **Having a child means making a sacrifice**. If a man decides to have a child he needs to make sacrifices because, trust me, children require a lot of time: from walking them to school in the mornings, to having a chat to them before they go to sleep; from going through their homework with them, to watching them in the school play and from taking them on trips at the weekend, to taking them to the park across the road. And that's why when a man's got a kid, he's gonna need to reduce the amount of time he plays Championship Manager, reduce the amount of times he goes on the lash with the boys, and perhaps the most important thing – he's gonna need to give up the 'other' women. Why? Because a) no baby mother is gonna want a baby father who gets other women pregnant, b) no baby mother is gonna want a baby father who puts her through emotional stress by shagging other women and c) no baby mother is gonna want a baby father who stresses their kid by messing with their mother's emotions.

Now if a man knows and understands this, then marriage should be an obvious move for him. However, if he ain't keen on marriage, then quite clearly he's not serious about the sacrifices that need to be made to give his child 100% in life. And if he's not prepared to give 100% to his child's life, then that man needs to go – before she has a child with him.

3.**Marriage is a serious, serious thing.** When a man marries a woman who he's had a child with:
- Legally 50% of his possessions now belong to his wife
- If he ever divorces or separates, he will be required to pay maintenance to the child via the mother (who will most likely take custody)
- Getting a divorce is pretty difficult. So that means that for a man to marry his baby mother he's gotta be really serious about how much he wants her to be the mother of his children.

4. When a Black man doesn't marry his baby mother, it perpetuates the cycle of violence in the Black community. The phrase, "it takes a village to raise a child,"originally came from Africa. Why? Because, back in the day, people used to believe that children were the most important part of the community – and so anything and everything was sacrificed for the sake of every child's development. This is because young people were and are the fittest, the strongest, the smartest, the most motivated, and the most energetic people in society… and as a result, they were the ones who were gonna take care of the elders, they were the ones who were gonna protect the villages from invaders, and they were the ones who were gonna provide food for their peoples. Therefore it was perfectly logical that the whole village should work extremely hard to help *all* children become the most intelligent, the most socially aware, and the most physically powerful souls that they could be. Now, when the Candyman stepped onto the scene during slavery and searched for the most efficient way to break the Black community, he quickly realised that if he destroyed the ability for the youth to protect the community, then he could destroy the community. And the best way to destroy the youth was to dismantle and disassemble the Black family. So during slavery:

1. *They separated families.* Children were separated from their parents, husbands were separated from their wives, siblings were separated from each other and put to work on different plantations far, far away from each other. And so after a while, it became almost impossible to determine who was related to whom. As one slave put it: "Slaves was treated in most cases like cattle... it was pitiful to see children taken from their mothers' breasts, mothers sold, husbands sold from wives."[25]

2. *They raped Black women, especially if they were married.* Which caused Black men to resent their wives, and Black women to resent their children (since they were the result of a sexual attack), which created divisions between families.

3. *They forced slaves to have sex with other slaves in the same way that horses are put out to stud.* This happened regardless of their marriage to other slaves, regardless of their relationship to each other so that the notion of a 'relative' almost took on no meaning whatsoever, since everyone (seemingly) could be related to one another, and related to no-one at the same time. As Willie Lynch explained in *The Making Of A Slave*, (and yea I know that the authenticity of this speech might have been challenged, but it certainly helps to explain what happened):

"Crossbreeding niggers means taking so many drops of good White blood and putting them into as many nigger women as possible... varying the drops by the various tone that you want, and then letting them breed with each other until another cycle of color appears as you desire. What this means is this... You got a multiplicity of colours ...neither [slave] knowing where the other came from..."[26]

4. *They debased Black men.* Willie Lynch again explains:

"... in her natural state she [the Black woman] would have a strong dependency on the nigger male... we reversed nature bull-whipping the [Black man] to the point of death, all in her presence. By her being left alone, unprotected, with the male image destroyed, the ordeal caused her to raise her male and female offspring in reversed roles. For fear of the young male's life she will psychologically train him to be mentally weak and dependent, but physically strong... [But] she will train her female off springs to be psychologically independent. What have you got?... the nigger women out front and the nigger man behind and scared."[27]

This strategy has been replicated right up until the present day. Black families are separated. 30% of all children in care in London are either Black or mixed parentage.[28]

And Black men are dehumanised. The news perpetually portrays Black males as violent, out of control criminals. So that's why I can understand the attitudes of some Black men towards their families. But that doesn't make it right. 'Cos it's about time some Black guys went back to basics and understood that marriage is the only way to guarantee that their child will be best equipped to deal with being Black. 'Cos a child will, at least for the first 15 years of his/her life, depend on its parents for everything: financial support, guidance, love, and education. This requires two life long commitments from both parents. Marriage is the only way to cement this commitment.

Now when a man decides to have a child with a woman *without* making a life long commitment to that woman, he does exactly what the Candyman wants him to do – fracture the Black family, and fracture the Black community.

Because kids that are born into families whose parents are living separately are:
• Twice as likely to have mental health problems.[29]
• Three times as likely to score poorly on measures of self-esteem.[30]

- More likely to have behaviour problems or engage in antisocial behaviour.[31]
- And have higher risk of health problems.[32]

Which helps explain why Black youths are over-represented in the criminal justice system today.[33] 'Cos at the moment, the streets are raising too many Black kids. So when you see kids hanging outside on a 3°C, cold, dark, miserable November night, it's because they'd rather chill with their friends on the street than be at home. But the thing is, when you've got a group of young people, who've never been given much direction in their lives, who've grown up resenting the world, it's easy to see why they participate in activities that are less than positive.

And it's even more easy to see why they take a lot of their anger out on Black people just like themselves. Sure, the Candyman messes with them – when they get stopped and searched, when they get excluded from school – but they expect that from them 'cos they're not family! But when their own Black fathers treat them like a nobody, what's gonna stop them from taking their anger out on other Black people? After all, what good have Black people ever done for them?

So unless women want the street to raise their children – the best advice is to find a man who's prepared to be a man, and make a lifelong commitment to both her, and her child.

Sammy The Sperm: Whoa, you're kinda serious about this Trinity business ain't you.

Emma The Egg: 'Course. But I gotta be militant – you know how hard things are for young Black kids these days, especially in the current economic climate:
- Unemployment amongst young Black people aged 16-24 is around 40%.[34]
- And whilst Black youth offenders account for 6% of total offences, they receive over 11% of all custodial sentences.[35]

So it'd be kinda rude of me *not* to take things seriously!

Sammy The Sperm: Yea, well, if I'm honest, I always knew sooner or later someone was gonna pull me up on this.

Emma The Egg: You see, in the past Black women would *only* settle down with a Black guy, but nowadays, if they can't get what they want from a Black man they're going elsewhere to find it, which is why an increasing number of Black women are now dating White guys – and fair play to them!

Sammy The Sperm: I hear you, but it just means that my boss is pretty screwed, without getting screwed – if you get what I mean.

Emma The Egg: Look, all I'm saying is that it's about time that your boss treated Black women and Black children with a bit more respect. Anyway, I gotta repeat these rules to a whole heap of other albino tadpoles that I can see shooting towards me with exactly the same intentions in mind – so if you don't mind, I'm gonna have to leave it there.

> "They say family that prays together, stays together,
> And one that walks apart, just falls apart,
> So together we stand, divided we fall...
> ...and take on all..."
> *Juelz Santana*

NOTES

1. Palmer, Alasdair, *Failure Has No Father*, (*Sunday Telegraph* 15/04/2007). www.telegraph.co.uk/opinion/main.jhtml?xml=/opinion/2007/04/15/do150 7.xml (accessed 22 June 2008).
2. *Ethnicity and Patterns of Employment and Care*, (Equal Opportunities Commission 09/2007). www.cls.ioe.ac.uk/core/documents/download.asp?id=920&log_stat=1(accessed 22 June 2008).
3. Roper, Leo, *Children of Single Parents are Losing their History*, (01/11/2007). nwitimes.com/articles/2007/11/01/opinion/guest_commentaries/doc2abf103 f7024c710862573800003ee7d.txt (accessed 22 June 2008).
4. Horn, Blankenhorn, and Pearlstein, *The Fatherhood Movement*, (Lanham, Maryland: Lexington Books, 1999).
   — Peters, H. Elizabeth, Peterson, Gary W., et al, eds, *Fatherhood: Research, Interventions and Policies*, (New York: The Hawthorn Press, 2000),
   — *A Call to Commitment: Fathers' Involvement in Children's Learning*, (United States. National Centre for Fathering, Kansas City, MO. Partnership for Family Involvement in Education 06/2000). www.fathermag.com/204/fathering/index.shtml (accessed

23 June 2008).

5. *Black Women 'also cause splits'*, (24/10/2006). news.bbc.co.uk/1/hi/uk_politics/6080096.stm (accessed 22 June 2008),

6. *Ethnicity and Patterns of Employment and Care*, (Equal Opportunities Commission, 09/2007). www.cls.ioe.ac.uk/core/documents/download.asp?id=920&log_stat=1 (accessed 22 June 2008).

7. *Ethnicity and Patterns of Employment and Care*, (Equal Opportunities Commission, 09/2007). www.cls.ioe.ac.uk/core/documents/download.asp?id=920&log_stat=1

8. *ibid.*

9. Ward, Kelly, Alice Sullivan and Jonathan Bradshaw, 'Poverty' Taken from Ch.10 of *Millennium Cohort Study Second Survey A User's Guide to Initial Findings* (Centre for Longitudinal Studies Institute of Education, University of London 10/07/2007). http://www.cls.ioe.ac.uk/downloads/MCS2_Poverty.pdf (accessed 22 June 2008).

10. *Ethnicity and Patterns of Employment and Care*, (Equal Opportunities Commission, 09/2007). www.cls.ioe.ac.uk/core/documents/download.asp?id=920&log_stat=1

11. *One Parent Families*, (04/10/2007). http://www.oneparentfamilies.org.uk/1/lx 3x1olx20x1oix313x1oix1591x1/0/0/060905/0/0//lone_parent_facts.htm (accessed 22 June 2008).

12. Palmer, Alasdair, *Failure Has No Father*, (*Sunday Telegraph*, 15/04/2007) www.telegraph.co.uk/opinion/main.jhtml?xml=/opinion/2007/04/15/do150 7.xml (accessed 22 June 2008).

13. *Time Traveller's Guide To Victorian Britain.* www.channel4.com/history/microsites/H/history/guide19/part05.html (accessed 22 June 2008).

14. *Info Please Encyclopaedia: Infant Mortality and Life Expectancy for Selected Countries 2007*, (11/11/2007). www.infoplease.com/ipa/A0004393.html (accessed 22 June 2008).

15. HighField, Roger, *Life Expectancy in Britain falls behind other Western Nations*, (*The Telegraph* 10/05/2002). www.telegraph.co.uk/global/main.jhtml?xml=/global/ 2002/05/10/nold10.xml (accessed 22 June 2008).

16. Berrington, Ann, Ian Diamond, Roger Ingham, Jim Stevenson, Riccardo Borgoni, M. Isabel Cobos Hernández and Peter W.F. Smith, *Consequences of Teenage Parenthood: Pathways which Minimise the Long Term Negative Impacts of Teenage Childbearing Final Report*, (University of Southampton 2005). www.dfes.gov.uk/research/data/uploadfiles/RW52.pdf (accessed 22 June 2008).

17. *ibid.*

18. Guthrie, Gwen, *Ain't Nothin' Goin' On But The Rent*, (Polydor 1986).

19. Average U.S. Family Will Spend $215,000 (23%) of its Total Income to Raise One Son to Age 22, *Family Planning Perspectives*, Vol. 15, No. 3 (May- June, 1983), pg. 131 and 136. http://www.jstor.org/pss/2134732 (accessed 22 June 2008).

20. Smithers, Rebecca, £165,000: *The Cost of Bringing up a Child.* www.guardian.co.uk

/money/2005/nov/25/childcare.schools (accessed 22 June 2008).

21. Curtis, Polly, *Marriage still the best way to play happy, healthy families*, (*The Guardian* 05/10/2007). http://www.guardian.co.uk/society/2007/oct/05/health.socialtrends (accessed 22 June 2008).

22. US Department of Health and Human Services: Administration for Children and Families. http://www.acf.hhs.gov/healthymarriage/benefits/index.html (accessed 22 June 2008).

23. Curtis, Polly, *Marriage still the best way to play happy, healthy families*, (*The Guardian* 05/10/2007). http://www.guardian.co.uk/society/2007/oct/05/health.socialtrends (accessed 22 June 2008).

24. *One Parent Families*, (04/10/2007). http://www.oneparentfamilies.org.uk/1/lx3x1 olx20x1oix313x1oix1591x1/0/0/060905/0/0//lone_parent_facts.htm (accessed 22 June 2008).

25. Julia Brown, aged 85, Atlanta, Georgia, interviewed as part of the Federal Writers Project in 1937. http://www.spartacus.schoolnet.co.uk/USASseparation.htm (accessed 22 June 2008).

26. Lynch, Willie, *The Making Of A Slave*. www.thetalkingdrum.com/wil.html (accessed 23 June 2008).

27. *ibid.*

28. *Care Matters White Paper: Equality Impact Assessment* www.dfes.gov.uk/publications/ timeforchange/docs/timeforchange_EIA.pdf (accessed 23 June 2008).

29. *ibid.*

30. *ibid.*

31. *ibid.*

32. *ibid.*

33. House of Commons Home Affairs Committee: *Young Black People and the Criminal Justice System, Second Report of Session 2006/2007 Volume I*, (Ordered to be printed by The House of Commons, 15/06/2007).

34. *Nacro: Youth Crime Briefing Document*, (10/2001). www.nacro.org.uk/data/resources/nacro-2004120244.pdf (accessed 22 June 2008).

35. House of Commons Home Affairs Committee: *Young Black People and the Criminal Justice System, Second Report of Session 2006/2007 Volume I*, (Ordered to be printed by The House of Commons, 15/06/2007).

CHAPTER NINE
Black Actually

"Blackness is a responsibility, not an excuse." *Biscuit*

I closed my front gate, and walked through the park...

"What's goin' on Ben? How you doing?"

"Cool nuh," replied Benjamin. He was the old, Jamaican guy who hung around the park bench. "Hey, you don't got no spare change you could lend me, do you?"

"Yea no probs." I put my hands in my pockets and tried to grab as much shrapnel as possible.

"You still do youth work? I heard things are serious," he asked.

"Yea they're kinda mad, but it's cool though," I answered nonchalantly.

"You know, I was watching the tv, about that young bredren, Shakilus Townsend who was stabbed back in July 2008. I remember thinking about what things were like for the Jewish community back when I was a youngster living in Hackney..."

"...Yea, listen B", I interrupted, "I really gotta dash – I'm late for work. I'll pass through later and talk to you then..."

"My yute, stop your hurrying. Sit down and reason with this old man for a minute. Boy, you kids don't realise how much you'd actually learn if you observed the world, instead of running up in it all the time. You think I learnt to speak so well and know so much from rushing around all the time?"

Grudgingly, I walked over to the bench, and sat down.

"You see, I grew up in London's East End..."

I was struggling to find the relevance of this opening statement.

"Back in those days, a lot of Jewish people lived in the area, much like the way that Harlesden's dominated by people from back a yard today. Because when Jewish people were expelled from Eastern Europe during the 1880s, a whole heap of them moved to England. But because most of them arrived broke, they were forced to settle in one of the worst and poorest parts of the country – the East End.[1] And when I mean the poorest, I mean living next to open sewers with disease-carrying rats,[2] I mean living in huge tenement blocks with a whole family occupying a single room,[3] I mean working in factories from dawn 'til dusk all days of the week, and only being paid enough to save them from starvation.[4]

You see, way back in those days, 35% of the entire population of Tower Hamlets lived in utter squalor with another 20% on the brink, whilst in Bethnal Green the percentage of people living in poverty was as high as 44%![5] And that's why it was once said that:

> *"The East End of London is the hell of poverty. Like one enormous, black, motionless, giant kraken, the poverty of London lies there in lurking silence and encircles with its mighty tentacles the life and wealth of the City and of the West End."*[6]

Whilst the average death rate for Londoners was 18.4 per 1000, in the East End it was a massive 40 per 1000. Murder was such a regular crime in this part of London that in some cases, if you were arrested for homicide, you might only get charged with 'common assault'![7] Jack London wrote of the East End Criminal that:

> *"They possess neither conscience nor sentiment, and they will kill for a half-sovereign, without fear or favour, if they are given but half a chance. They are a new species, a breed of city savages. The streets and houses, alleys and courts, are their hunting grounds. As valley and mountain are to the natural savage, street and building are valley and mountain to them. The slum is their jungle, and they live and prey in the jungle."*[8]

Now because most of the Jewish community were new, because most of them were born overseas, because most of them spoke another language, and because many of them were extremely poor – they were an ideal scapegoat for the Candyman, who'd noticed that the White underclass were getting (understandably) agitated about perpetually living in absolute deprivation.

So from Conservative MPs raising and passing laws like the Aliens Act of 1905 to reduce immigration,[9] to newspapers like the *Daily Mail* (yep the same *Daily Mail*) running stories about Jewish people taking all the jobs away from British people[10] – the Jewish community were blamed for the poverty in the East End.

And as a result, Jewish men and women were attacked, the right-wing groups regularly marched through their area, and their homes and shops were smashed...(it almost reminds me of the way that the Teddy Boys attacked us in Notting Hill during the summer of 1958). And funnily enough, the Jewish community tried to tackle their poverty and persecution in exactly the same way that we did.

Initially, sport seemed like the best way to both make money and simultaneously gain acceptance in British society. Since Boxing was ultra-popular at the time, many Jewish people took it up...and very soon the Jewish East End community became renowned for producing world champions. Fighters like Daniel Mendoza way back in the 18th century, or Harry Mizler, Jack 'Kid' Berg, and Ted 'Kid' Lewis in the early 1900s,[11] helped inspire many young Jewish kids worldwide to take up the sport – which is why between 1910 and 1940, there were 26 Jewish world champions.[12] Because in the same way that most of the kids that you work with wanna be the next Ledley King, every Jewish kid wanted to be the next pugilist supremo.

But because not every kid was blessed with quick hands and an iron jaw, some resorted to petty crime as a way of surviving on the streets. Almost predictably, all Jewish people quickly became stereotyped as thieves, just like Black yutes are stereotyped as muggers today. Remember 'Fagin', the character in *Oliver Twist* – y'know, the man who got the Artful Dodger and Oliver to 'pick a pocket or two'. Well Charles Dickens originally intended for the character to be Jewish – because apparently, 'of the time to which the story refers, that class of criminal invariably was Jewish".[13] I mean, Jewish people were so badly pigeonholed, that even Jack the Ripper's murders were originally blamed on them.

So you can see that the Jewish community was pretty much in the same position that the Black community are now – if not much, much worse. And yet despite this, in just 80-odd years, they've transformed themselves into one of the most educated and financially secure communities in the UK! Today, Jewish people are the religious group most likely to own their own homes,[14] they are the religious group most likely to work in the banking, finance and insurance sector,[15] and Jewish women are the most likely religious group to hold managerial occupations.[16]

So the question is – how did they achieve this? I know that some people have suggested that the welfare state was responsible for pulling them out of poverty, but that doesn't explain everything. Because if the welfare can create wealth so easily, then surely every religious and cultural minority would be blessed right now."

"So what was it then B, what's the answer?" I asked, eager to hear the explanation.

"It was their *Pride* in who they were". Benjamin answered assuredly. "You see, for them, their identity was their source of inspiration."

"I hear you," I responded.

"To be Jewish meant something very special – it was like a badge of honour. Because in being Jewish, they believed that they had come from a very great and powerful people, who had overcome very extraordinary hardships to survive and exist today...and consequently, they felt like it was imperative that they respect the people who had taken them this far, by showing the UK what being Jewish meant. So they did three very important things:

1. **They set up their own businesses and worked damn hard on them**. Many Jewish people clocked, early on, that working for other people meant that they'd be creating profits for other people and not themselves. So they worked out that the best way to make money was to make money for themselves, by themselves. As a result, they set up their own companies and firms, initially setting up market stalls, selling used goods, and providing simple services like shoe-making, carpentry and tailoring.[17] And when they collected their profits each month, instead of buying fast cars, or gold chains, they either put it back into their community by building synagogues, private schools, and youth clubs or invested it in banks...

Alan Sugar, the guy off *The Apprentice*, the one who says, "You're Fired", is a good example of this. Starting out as a young Jewish kid from the East End, he originally started selling car aerials from the back of a van. And by investing his money safely, he had the funds to start up an electronics company and now has an estimated fortune of £800m![18]

2. **They made their children their no.1 priority**. It was clear to most Jewish people that the next best way to make money, was to get educated. Because once you got an education, you can get a good job, and when you get a good job, that's when the Pz start rolling in. And with schools more readily available in the 20th century, they made it very clear to their children that it was essential that they got as much out of education as was humanly possible. But if the state schools weren't up to the task, then they set up their own private schools to do the job instead – which is why at present there are 37 privately-run Jewish schools in the UK.[19]

3. **They saved until they had the cash to get out of the ghetto**. There was none of this 'keepin it real' attitude with the Jewish community. Their aim was to get outta the Ghetto – fast. They didn't care about 'knowing the streets', they didn't care about 'being true to the game', they didn't care about 'being close to the endz'. 'Cos they realised that the best way to represent who they were, was to be rich, to be successful, and to bring their kids up in a clean, safe environment so that future generations could take Jewish economic and social progression to the next stage[20] – which is why the majority of Jewish people in Britain now live in Barnet or Hertfordshire.

So you see, all you gotta do is simply do the simple things, simply. It's that simple…Anyway, I don't wanna keep you from your work. And since you're gonna donate me some silver, I'm gonna go down the newsagents and get me a nice cold can of Kestrel…"

I handed him what I had in my pocket.

"…Lickle more…", he shouted, as he stumbled off down the road.

I remained rooted to my seat. All I could think about was this line that I read in my English class by this poet John Keats:

> *"Beauty is truth, truth beauty – that is all*
> *Ye know on earth, and all ye need to know."*[21]

The truth is: we have problems. The beauty is: we can change them… …and those changes have to start with me. I got up from the park bench, and walked slowly towards Finsbury Park station. I tapped my Oyster Card on the reader and descended towards the platform. This is what I was gonna do:

One: I was gonna stop asking the Candyman for help.[22]
Because I'm not a child, and because I'm capable of getting rich by myself. You see, whenever I beg the Candyman for a better apartment, for more benefits, for better teachers – kinda like a child who's asking their parents for pocket money – I help re-enforce their superiority over me. Because the point is, I'm not dumb and I'm not stupid. I have enough intelligence to make Pz in this country, and I know for a fact, regardless of the racism, there are enough opportunities for me to be who I wanna be – it just all depends on how much work I'm prepared to put in. You see, making money is never easy. It's always hard work, it always takes time, and it always requires dedication. And like Robin Harris says, 'Job' ain't never gonna

come to my house and ask for a date – *I'm* gonna have to go look for a date with 'Job'!

So from today, I'm gonna stop trying to compete for the title of 'who's been the greatest victim'[23] and start to put some dedication into making Pz by myself, for myself. I got off the train at Holborn, walked past the fruit stand on Kingsway, and waited for a bus.

Two: I was gonna get educated by any means necessary. *Because poverty doesn't provide an excuse for ignorance; ignorance itself breeds poverty.*[24] I know that it used to be about 'being young, gifted and Black', but today it's all about being young, *educated* and Black. I have high expectations for myself. I wanna be successful, I wanna have a good job, and I wanna get rich – and the best way to do that, is to get 9 GCSEs, 3 A-Levels, and a University degree…'cos I know that people who have a degree earn on average £400,000 more in their lifetimes than people without a degree.[25]

And since I've got free schooling 'til 16, since I can get paid to go to college 'til I'm 18, since I can get a loan to go to University, since I can get untold courses for free if I'm unemployed, since I can borrow any book I want from my local library for free, and since I can get free internet access from a number of community centres, the only person who can make me screw up my education is me.

If I got racist teachers – then I need to spend more time studying at home. If I got peers who wanna cuss me for being smart – then I gotta take the cusses. If I can't afford the Uni fees – then I need to get another part-time job. 'Cos I'm not gonna let anyone or anything stand in the way of making money. And let's face it, while we all got hopes for what Obama can do for us, not even he can help us get a University degree. I could see the number 159 bus in the distance and held my hand out to signal…

Three: I was gonna get unified with all other Black people. *Because needless 'beef' is for people with very small brains.* From Toronto to Tottenham, from Toulouse to Temasi – I don't care how they look at me, I don't care what trainers they step on, I don't care how they brush past me, I don't care how they chat to my girl, or how gay they are ('cos homophobia's getting kinda boring now)…the next time I feel annoyance, anger, hatred or humiliation at the hands of another Black person, I'll swallow my pride and let it go.

It makes no sense for me to start 'beef' with them over utter and complete bulls***, repeating the cycle of violence so that I and we remain in this situation.'Cos only when we have some sort of unity,

like the Chinese, like the Gujuratis, like the Kurds, like the Greeks –
only then will I be able to study in peace, go to work in peace, live in
peace, and be all that I want to be. I stepped on the bus, searching
for a seat.

**Four: I was gonna condemn 'niggativity' wherever it
existed, whomever was the perpetrator.** *Because the more I stayed
silent about 'niggativity', the more that 'niggativity' f***s up my community.*
From the shootings, to the drug addicts, to the muggings, the only
reason why 'niggativity' continued was because people like me, in the
Black community, didn't speak up against them. For years, I'd
complained about the state of the Black community and yet at the
same time:

• I'd stay silent if I knew someone was carrying a gun
• I'd refuse to tell the police if I knew someone who'd committed a
  robbery
• I'd keep silent about people who were selling drugs.

But today I was gonna end this hypocrisy. From now on, if I know
anyone who carries a knife, or anyone who sells guns to people, or
anyone who sells heroin, or anyone who jacks phones from people,
I'm going straight to the police. F*** all the bulls*** about snitching.
The 'No Snitching' philosophy was designed by the Candyman to
keep us ghettoised and in this cycle of poverty and criminality. 'Cos
they know that the less we fight against crime, the more crime we get.
And the more crime we get, the less chance there is of the Black
community making legit Pz.

The National Liberation Front in Algeria chased out anyone who
pimped prostitutes in their community. The Black Panthers
threatened to kill anyone who sold drugs in their community. And the
IRA murdered anyone who committed robberies in their community.
Because if any community wants to get wealthy it can't afford to have
chumps running around, turning their daughters into whores,
turning their sons into drugs dealers, and turning their people into
gunmen.

But it ain't just that. I simply don't want anyone in my family to be
a victim of 'niggativity'. 'Cos the more I let criminality fester in my
area, the more likely that one day it'll come straight to me...whether
it's my mum who gets mugged, whether it's my brother who gets
stabbed, or whether it's my dad who gets beaten up. And that's why I
don't care who it upsets; if I find out that anyone acts 'niggative', I'm

going straight to the police. The bus sped down The Strand, over Waterloo Bridge, into south London.

Five and lastly – I was gonna love Blackness. *Because I'm so proud to be Black, it almost makes me look arrogant.* Regardless of how other Black people act, I'm gonna show the world what being Black is all about. So I wasn't gonna call Black people 'niggers' and I wasn't gonna tolerate anyone from any other culture calling Black people 'niggers'. I wasn't gonna call any Black women a 'b****' and I wasn't gonna tolerate anyone from any other culture calling Black women 'b****es'. I wasn't gonna say things like, "Black people are always late". I wasn't gonna say things like, "Black people only want things for free". And I wasn't gonna say things like, "Blackness is about being ghetto". 'Cos bottom line: **I wasn't gonna look down on Blackness.**

You see, when I think about things, it's kinda baffling where this low opinion of Blackness has come from. 'Cos when I really think about things, I have soooooo many reasons to be proud to be Black.

I was proud to be Black because the most powerful man in the world today is a Black man. I still can't get over it…it still boggles the mind…it still gives me goosebumps when I think about it. The transatlantic slave trade only ended 200 years ago. Slavery was only abolished in America 150 years ago. Goddamit, Black people were only properly allowed to vote 40 years ago and yet despite the f***ed up nature of American politics, Barack Obama managed to become president of the United States.

I was proud to be Black because Black people have almost independently defined the race-relations policies in the UK. The Race Relations Act of 1976 which prohibited racial discrimination in education, employment, housing and training came into play, partly as a result of Notting Hill Riots earlier that year.[26]

In 1981, the Brixton Riots were the basis for *The Scarman Report,* which invoked The Police and Criminal Evidence Act 1984, which set out new ways for police officers to carry out their duties, specifically when they stop and search people from cultural minorities.[27]

The Amendment to the Race Relations Act of 2001 came about almost entirely because of the tireless campaigning by Neville and Doreen Lawrence, the parents of the murdered teenager Steven Lawrence, which meant that public authorities, such as the Police and the Armed forces were now included in the Race Relations Act.[28]

It was also the murder of Steven Lawrence that prompted the *Macpherson Report*. This report found that the police were institutionally racist and forced them to hire many more people from the cultural minorities.[29]

Yea that's right, if it wasn't for Black people, you can be sure that things for *all* cultural minorities would be far more 'medieval' in the UK right now.

I was proud to be Black because, despite the prejudice and despite the single mothers, West Indian and African women earn more per month than any other racial group in Britain – and yes, that includes White and Asian women.[30]

I was proud to be Black because, despite the loan refusals and despite the stereotypes, there are more than 10,000 black-owned private sector businesses in London.[31]

And finally, **I was proud to be Black** because, despite everything that's happened to us over the last 400 years, despite being holocaust victims, we still exist! You see, despite the fact that we've had our names changed, our religion altered, our language erased, our history wiped, our peoples divided, our culture overturned, and 25 million enslaved[32] – we're still smashing it:

— from Tim Campbell, representing Jamaica, born in Plaistow, the winner of *The Apprentice* to Zadie Smith, representing Jamaica and raised in Willesden, the author of *White Teeth* and *On Beauty* and winner of the Whitbread First Novel Award.

— from Samantha Tross, representing Guyana, raised in East London, one of Britain's most respected orthopaedic surgeons to Ozwald Boateng, representing Ghana and raised in South London, the fashion designer for Keanu Reeves and Mick Jagger.

— from Baroness Patricia Scotland, representing Dominica, who grew up in Walthamstow, one of the youngest QCs ever to Tidjane Thiam, representing the Ivory Coast, the financial director of Prudential.

— from our domination of the musical world with Hip-Hop and RnB (and I only mention music because not only is the industry worth around £70 billion globally, but because the average American spends the equivalent of 41 days per year listening to music)...[33]

— to our complete domination of the genesis of the musical world, being the originators of the Blues, pretty much all forms of Dance music, Disco, Dub, Funk, Garage, Gospel, Jazz, House, Reggae, Rock, Samba, Ska, Soul and Techno, all the way (I'm embarrassed to say) to modern Pop music:

And don't even let me get started on Tiger, Hamilton, Ali, Jordan, Pele, Hanley, Powell, Ronaldinho and Sobers. I have every reason to be proud of all that we've achieved! It's also worth remembering that on top of being hugely successful, Black people are also some of the kindest people on this planet. 'Cos consider this:

- There are around 5,500 Black and Minority 'Ethnic' Voluntary and Community Organisations in the UK[34]...which means that there are tons of Black people who have dedicated their lives to helping their community.
- 55% of Black Caribbean women and 47% of Black African women[35] work in the public sector[36]...which means that there are tons of Black women who have dedicated their lives to helping the British nation.
- And over in America, around 20% of Black women and 7.3% of Black men are employed in the non-profit sector[37] – which is higher than any other ethnic group in this sector...which means that all in all, Black people are a damn sensitive bunch of people!

And aside from that, Black people are sooooooooo kind that they haven't massacred the Candyman yet. I know that sounds kinda harsh, and I don't mean it in a scary way. But all I'm saying is that after 400 years of some of the worst genocidal atrocities in living memory, Black people haven't gone on a mad, mental rage in a looooooooong time for which the Candyman should feel bloody lucky.

I only say this because when I see how Michael Caine AKA Jack Carter (from the film *Get Carter*) reacted when he found out that his brother was murdered in Newcastle or the way that Maximus Decimus Meridius (Commander of the Armies of the North, General of the Felix Legions, loyal servant to the true emperor, Marcus Aurelius. Father to a murdered son blah blah blah) sought vengeance on Commodus for murdering his wife in *Gladiator*...you and I both know that it's not unusual for wronged people to turn on their aggressors in a serious, serious way!

But UK Black people are sooooooooo chilled about their enslavement and oppression, that an estimated 50% of Black men and 33% of Black women are in relationships with White partners.[38]

In fact, Black people are even prepared to let non-Black people perpetually rip their music off, and still be prepared to be the backing singers for people like Amy Winehouse and the rest of the musicians who get rich from imitating Black sounds.

I mean, I don't remember many other groups of people engaging in a bit of 'truth and reconciliation' after they've been massacred for 300 years, like the South African's did! Now that's what I call a progressive bunch of people! I hit the request button, jumped off the bus, and headed to work.

I Love Being Black and I'm gonna make damn sure that for the next generation, the stereotypes of Black people are doctors, who live in big houses, who take care of their kids and who love their people...*and* who are on time!

Even if it's one step at a time, I just need to make sure that I take one step forward and not one step backwards.[39] And even if I can't do everything, I can at the very least do something.[40] As Oscar Wilde once said, 'We are all in the gutter, but some of us are looking at the stars". **I walked into the Youth Club**...and I'm definitely looking at the stars.

'It is not those who can inflict the most,
but those who can suffer the most who will conquer'
Terence MacSwiney

NOTES

1. *Jewish Encyclopaedia*. http://www.jewishencyclopedia.com/view.jsp?artid=533& letter=L (accessed 22 June 2008).

2. *Victorian Poverty and Disease*. www.barryoneoff.co.uk/html/squalor.html (accessed 22 June 2008).

3. *British History Online*, New Lond. Life and Lab. iii, 236, 251; Census, 1911-31' www.british-history.ac.uk/report.aspx?compid=22753 (accessed 22 June 2008)

4. John Law *Captain Lobe*, (1889). www.casebook.org/victorian_london/tower1888.html (accessed 22 June 2008).

5. *British History Online*, 'L.C.C. Housing of Working Classes in Lond. 1855-1912 (1913). www.british-history.ac.uk/report.aspx?compid=22752 (accessed 22 June 2008).

6. J.H. Mackay, *The Anarchists*, (Boston 1891), p. 152. www.casebook.org/victorian _london/tower1888.html (accessed 22 June 2008)

7. *British History Online*, 'The Times 11/03/1891, 3f.' www.british-history.ac.uk/ report.aspx?compid=22752 (accessed 22 June 2008).

8. London, Jack, *The People of the Abyss*, (1903). london.sonoma.edu/Writings/ PeopleOfTheAbyss/ (accessed 22 June 2008).

9. Shooter, Helen, Dispersing the Myths about Asylum, (*Socialist Review* 03/2003),

(accessed 1 Oct 2007). http://www.socialistreview.org.uk/article.php?articlenumber=8365

10. John Law, *Out of Work* (1888) p. 63-4. www.casebook.org/victorian_london/tower1888.html (accessed 22 June 2008).

11. UCL Bookshelf: *Fighting Back? Jewish and Black Boxers in Britain* 23/05/2007). www.ucl.ac.uk/news/news-articles/0705/07052902 (accessed 22 June 2008).

12. Bodner, Allen J and Ciulla, Joanne B, *When Boxing Was a Jewish Sport*, (Greenwood Publishing Group, Incorporated 1997). www.boxrec.com/media/index.php/When_Boxing_Was_a_Jewish_Sport (accessed 22 June 2008).

13. Johnson, Edgar, Our Mutual Friend: The Scholarly Pages, From *Charles Dickens: His Tragedy and Triumph* Part Nine, Chapter Four 'Intimations of Mortality' (Simon and Schuster, Inc 1952). dickens.ucsc.edu/OMF/johnson.html (accessed 22 June 2008).

14. ...along with Sikhs and Hindus. *Faith and Religion*, www.stockton.gov.uk/resources/council/edr/faithandbeliefprofile.doc (accessed 22 June 2008).

15. *National Statistics Online*, (2004). www.statistics.gov.uk/cci/nugget.asp?id=964 (accessed 22 June 2008).

16. *ibid.*

17. London. http://www.jewishencyclopedia.com/view.jsp?artid=533&letter=L (accessed 22 June 2008).

18. Dattani, Meera, *Sir Alan Sugar.* www.virginmedia.com/money/moneymakers/alansugar.php (accessed 22 June 2008).

19. Frean, Alexandra and Geldhill, Ruth, *More Faith schools are Planned in an Effort to Integrate Minorities*, (*The Times* 08/09/2007). www.timesonline.co.uk/tol/life_and_style/education/article2409948.ece (accessed 22 June 2008).

20. *Census 2001: Ethnicity and religion in England and Wales.* www.statistics.gov.uk/census 2001/profiles/commentaries/ethnicity.asp (accessed 22 June 2008).

21. Keats, John, 'Ode On A Grecian Urn' in *Selected Poems*, (Everyman 2001), Pg. 66

22. Interview with Wyclef Jean in the film, *Dave Chappelle's Block Party*, (Bob Yari Productions 2006).

23. Miles, Alice and Helen Rumbelow, *Thought for the Day: the Chief Rabbi Sir Jonathan Sacks is aiming to be Politically Incorrect*, (*The Times* 20/10/2007). entertainment.timesonline.co.uk/tol/arts_and_entertainment/books/article269 7509.ece (accessed 22 June 2008).

24. *Bad Rap for Malcolm X.* findarticles.com/p/articles/mi_m1282/is_n24_v44/ai_13326382 (accessed 22 June 2008).

25. Freda, Belinda, *Can't Work, Won't Work: Youth, Discrimination and the Labour Market: Problem or Stereotype?*, (University of Surrey May 2005).www.surrey.ac.uk/politics/cse/sequal-2005-YP-mick-final.doc (accessed 22 June 2008).

26. *NCVO: Race Relations Act 1976.* www.ncvo-vol.org.uk/workarea/linkit.aspx?Link Identifier=id&ItemID=179 (accessed 22 June 2008).

27. *The Scarman Report*, (27/04/2004). http://news.bbc.co.uk/1/hi/programmes/bbc_parliament/3631579.stm (accessed 22 June 2008).

28. *Race Relations (Amendment) Act 2000.* http://www.racialjustice.org.uk/RACE%20 RELATIONS2000.htm (accessed 22 June 2008)

29. Macpherson, Sir William, *The Steven Lawrence Inquiry*, http://www.archive.officialdocuments.co.uk/document/cm42/4262/sli-00.htm (accessed 22 June 2008).

30. *Black and Asian Workers 'Underpaid'*, (12/04/2002). http://news.bbc.co.uk/1/hi/uk/1924907.stm (accessed 22 June 2008).

31. *Redefining London's BME Owned Businesses*, LDA, (03/2005). www.lda.org.uk/upload/rtf/LDA_News_Issue_3_13_April_2005.rtf (accessed 22 June 2008).

32. *Quick guide: The Slave Trade.* http://news.bbc.co.uk/1/hi/world/africa/6445941.stm (accessed 22 June 2008).

33. *Statistical Abstract of the United States, 2008: The National Data Book*, (15/12/2006). www.guardian.co.uk/usa/story/0,,1972700,00.html (accessed 22 June 2008).

34. *Joseph Rowntree Foundation*, (report on the Role and Future Development of Black and Minority Ethnic Organisations, published 2001, ref 311). www.jrf.org.uk/knowledge/findings/socialpolicy/311.asp (accessed 22 June 2008).

35. ...of working age

36. David Owen, Anne Green, Jane Pitcher and Malcolm Maguire, *Race Research For The Future*, Minority Ethnic Participation And Achievements In Education, Training And The Labour Market, (Institute for Employment Research 06/10/2000). www.dfes.qbfox.com/research/rb225_bemg.htm?PHPSESSID= 129eadda2fd3a277ec (accessed 22 June 2008).

37. Burbridge, Lynn C., *Government, For-Profit and Third Sector Employment: Differences by Race and Sex, 1950-1990: Intersectoral Relations & Comparisons.* (1994). www.nonprofitresearch.org/newsletter1531/newsletter_show.htm?doc_id=9811 5 (accessed 22 June 2008).

38. John, Cindi, *Changing Face of Britain: Britain's Blurring Ethnic Mix.* ews.bbc.co.uk/hi/english/static/in_depth/uk/2002/race/changing_face_of_britain.stm (accessed 22 June 2008).

39. Andrew Muhammad, Personal Communication, (12/05/2006).

40. *ibid.*

..Outro

Thank you, thank you...Give praises...much appreciated for reading the book...I would take *all* the credit for it, but sadly I can't.Here are the people who've given me the thoughts, the ideas, the theories, the inspiration, the references, the style, and most importantly, the enthusiasm to write. Yes, here are the people who've really written this book! ...well, where do I start...?

Firstly, I know that I never say it enough but I'd like to thank my Mum, my Dad and my Brother. Not only for doing the washing up, the cooking, the cleaning, the hoovering, the shopping and everything else in the house, but for making me proud of my identity: being from two different cultural backgrounds. They are responsible for every smile, for every word written, for every step taken in confidence and they deserve my deepest gratitude. I must also acknowledge my extended family: the Ashbys, the Whittinghams, and the Vigors, from Jamaica, to South Africa, to Australia, to Northamptonshire to Somerset.

Secondly, I need to say a special thank you to my co-writers, Michael and Conan aka the Oracle. They probably don't think that they're co-writers, but these are two of the principal people in my life who've shaped my ideas and my philosophies. From the information, to the research, I could never have done this without them.

Thirdly, an unconditional thank you goes to all my friends, my mum's friends, my brother's friends and my dad's friends past and present. From Montem, Little Matt, Kishor, Winston, and Sherif. From 'The Endz', Big Matt, Tom, Michael and Ravi. From CH, Angus, Joe, Izi, Alex, Imo, Kirbal, Milky and Vaughn. From Brunel, Pascal and Hans. From Camden, Jon, Lisa and the rest of the Cantelocals. From Haringey, Suzette; from Streatham, Sandra; from Victoria, Nerina; from Primrose Hill, Sylvia and from Barnet, Tereska. From West London, Sati, Indy, Raj, Hrush, Mo and the rest of the Southall Soccer Cru. From East London, Bhamini and the whole Akhoonjee Squad; from North London, Derek, Shogun and the rest of the Thinking Team. From Gideon's side, Kofi, the Warren, cousin Kamali, Lee and Geoffrey. From the Rastafarians, Seymour, Bones, Yellowman, Fire, Rene, Lorraine, Cyrus and Bill Trojan. From California, Jasmin and the Kros family. From Ghana, Fafah and Courage. From Trinidad, Aiysha and Ryan. From Ukraine, Tanya and Oxana. From Macedonia, Meto; from Norway, Mads. From Sweden, Anna; from China, Jai. From Wembley, Neema; from Hackney, Marcia; from Harlesden, Noble; from North-West, Ruchi & Tina; from Brick Lane, Nick and too many others to mention. Some of you I see regularly, some of you I don't, and some of you I've lost contact with. But regardless, I salute all of you for the wonderful people that you are.

I would specially like to thank Ben, Paul, James, Cleon, Jigs, Baddar, Hassan and Peter for supporting me during 2000, and 2007 – the two most difficult years of my life.

Fourthly, I would like to thank those people who've educated me. And that's why I need to thank Christ's Hospital for giving me a totally different outlook on life; Mr Ward, Mr Shippen, Mr Tamvaikis, Ms Thornton, Mr Sutcliffe, Mrs Askew, Mr Dillow and in particular, Mr Holdsworth, who never gave up on me.

I also need to thank Fred Hampton, Paul Obinna Wilson-Eme, Tony Benn, Plato, Andrew Muhammad, Steve Garner, Khalid Abdul Muhammad, Dr. Lez Henry, Karl Marx, Neil from CCIWBS, Skeme, and especially Anser, whose panoramic thinking has taken my mind in a number of important directions.

Fifthly, I would like to thank those people who've led me into youth work. These people include Angela for telling me some home truths, Sofia who was the first person to suggest that I get into youth work, and most importantly Michael Douglas and Mark Whitlock, who gave me the inspiration to work with young people.

Sixthly, I want to thank the groups that I've worked with and who've genuinely made me feel proud to be a Youth and Community worker. Most significantly, SE1 United, but also SPACE, Blackfriars, Brent YOT, Islington YOT, Flipside and the Exit Programme, Let's Be Positive, Stockwell Gardens Youth Forum, The Hub, SOVA, SWP and the Two Parks Project in Belfast. In particular I wish to thank Natalie Bell (with her many hats) and Clifford Shirley from Waterloo, Jenny Hinds at Blackfriars, Jean-Michael in Ealing and Robert from DYP. I also want to thank all the Young People that I've ever worked with: for the cusses, the 'Biscuit', and the inspiration.

Seventhly, I must thank those people who gave me my writing style:

Michael Moore, Stephen Marlowe, Tom Wolfe and Richard Wright (the writer not the goalkeeper). I also need to thank Keith from Unheard Words who helped give me the confidence to write this book.

Eighthly, I need to give a shout out to all those friends and family members who have died in the last two years (man, it's been strange!!!)...my Dad, Paul Henrik, Tam Tran, Raj and Paula.

Ninthly, I'd like to thank my publisher, Hansib Publications, for believing in me! Arif Ali, Isha Persaud and Richard Painter. Thanks for being so patient with me and giving me the chance to put this into print!

Lastly, I gotta thank the people who inspired me to write about the subject matter. And they are Chris Rock, for having the guts to say what he said in his Niggas Vs Black people skit, Dead Prez for their straight up condemnation of 'niggativity', Machel Montano for keeping me positive, and most importantly Malcolm X for being my ultimate role model, keeping me forever political. Without these people, this book would be little more than a pamphlet.

Oh... and while I'm here, let me acknowledge the moments in my life that made me who I am. From the Michael Thomas goal against Liverpool in 1989, to reading those first few lines of 'Strength to Love'. From watching Brazil lose to Argentina in 1990, to listening to *Papa'z Song* in my room. From watching the *Godfather Part II* after seeing Peter, to waiting in Ealing on that fateful day. From meeting Bana in the Living Space, to having that conversation in Regent's Park on the 23rd June. They were some seriously emotional times – seriously, seriously emotional times!

It might sound a little weird but I need to thank my computer and the internet, 'cos we've had some late nights, some angry moments, and some tender moments (don't start getting the wrong idea). So I suppose I should really thank Konrad Zuse and Tim Berners-Lee!

And I suppose before I go, I should thank Me... and why not?! Yeah, I know it's kinda odd, but I have to thank myself for finishing this book. I had so many doubts. Am I wasting my time working with young people only earning £833 a month? Should I be out raving instead of staying at home and writing this book? Should someone educated outside of the state system talk so frankly about these issues? Can a mixed parentage person say what I am saying? But as Steven King says: "Talent is cheaper than table salt. What separates the talented individual from the successful one is a lot of hard work."

If you're still reading this, and you ever struggle to find some Black British role models, think about some of these...

In Sports

Lennox Lewis. Is one of only three boxers in heavyweight history to win the Heavyweight Championship on three separate occasions, and until recently, was the first British person to win a Heavyweight Championship Belt for nearly 100 years.

Louis Smith. Born of a Jamaican father and raised in Peterborough, is the first British athlete to win a medal on the Pommel Horse at the Olympics in 80 years at Beijing in 2008.

Jason Robinson. Brought up in Leeds, he was the only player to score a try in England's only ever Rugby World Cup win in 2003.

Kelly Holmes. During the 2004 Olympics, was the first British woman to win two Olympic gold medals at the same games.

Lewis Hamilton. The mixed parentage driving sensation came third in the 2007 F1 World Championship and won the 2007 Laureus Award for World Breakthrough of the Year. In 2008 he realised his ambition of becoming Formula 1 World Champion.

Theo Walcott. Born in Stanmore, is the youngest ever England player in a full international at 17 years old and 75 days, and in 2006 became the youngest player ever to score for the England Under-21s.

Linford Christie. Born in Jamaica. The only Englishman to win Olympic, World, Commonwealth and European 100m gold medals.

Ryan Giggs. From Cardiff, is the most decorated player in the history of the English Premiership and has taken over Sir Bobby Charlton's record as the most capped Manchester United player ever.

Denise Lewis. Raised in West Bromwich was the European, Commonwealth, and Olympic Heptathlon gold medal winner.

In Politics

Lord Morris. Bill Morris representing Jamaica, was the first Black leader of a British trade union (the T&G) and in 2007 was appointed to the House of Lords.

Baroness Amos. Valerie Amos born in Guyana and educated in Birmingham was the first Black woman to sit in the Cabinet of the government of the United Kingdom. Amos had previously been Leader of the House of Lords and is now a life peer.

Baron Taylor. John Taylor despite receiving a whole heap of racist discrimination at the beginning of his political career, he is now Baron Taylor of Warwick, a Conservative life peer.

David Lammy. Brought up by a single mother, is the first Black Briton to study a Master's at Harvard and is the first Tottenham MP to hold a Government position since 1945.

Paul Boateng. Half Ghanaian, was the UK's first Black Cabinet Minister in May 2002 when he was appointed as Chief Secretary to the Treasury.

Lee Jasper. Of mixed heritage, was the Senior Policy Advisor on Equalities to Ken Livingstone, the former Mayor of Greater London.

Oh, and here's a list of the UK's other Black MPs: Adam Afriye (Windsor), Diane Abbott (Stoke Newington), Dawn Butler (Brent South), and Mark Hendrick (Preston).

Now some people might say this is all expected, after all Black people have always succeeded in Sports and Politics. Here are the Black role models that some people didn't think existed:

In Law

Baroness Scotland. Patricia Scotland representing Dominica made legal history in 1991 when she became the first Black female QC and one of the youngest ever at the age of 35. She is currently the Attorney General.

Grace Ononiwu. Coming straight outta Africa, became the first Black Chief Crown Prosecutor in April 2005.

In Making Pz

Yana Johnson. Raised in Birmingham, is the founder of Yana Cosmetics and winner of awards such as Black Enterprise, European Federation of Black Women Business Owners, Global Women Inventors Innovators Award and Mahogany Brides.

Tim Campbell. Of Jamaican origin, was the winner of BBC2's *The Apprentice* in 2005 giving him an annual salary of £100,000.

Wilfred Emmanuel-Jones. Spent his youth in Birmingham. Founded his own food and drink marketing company, working with brands such as Loyd Grossman and Kettle Chips. He now owns a farm on the Devon/Cornwall border marketing The Black Farmer range of sausages and sauces. He's also set up the Black Farmer Rural Scholarship to give inner-city teenagers a taste of rural life under his personal mentoring.

In Being a Genius

Shaun Wallace. From Wembley and a barrister. He made television history in December 2004 by becoming only the second person from an ethnic minority background to reach the Mastermind finals, and the first Black person to win Mastermind.

Professor Stuart Hall. Originally from the West Indies, was appointed as a professor of sociology at the Open University from 1979-1997. His works have influenced the Labour Party, from Neil Kinnock to Tony Blair.

In Science

Dr Liz Rasekoala. Born in Nigeria, is a leading Chemical Engineer, and founder of ACNST (African-Caribbean Network for Science and Technology).

Professor Geoff Palmer. Born in Jamaica, was awarded the American Society of Brewing Chemist Award for distinction in research and good citizenship in science. Only three other scientists have ever received this award.

Samantha Tross. Of Guyanese origin, is one of Britain's most respected orthopaedic surgeons.

On the TV

Dame Jocelyn Barrow. From Trinidad and Tobago, was the first Black member of the Board of Governors at the BBC when she was appointed in 1983.

Rageh Omaar. Representing Somalia, has worked for the BBC and Al-Jazeera. Is one of the most respected journalists in the world.

Moira Stuart. Was the first female Afro-Caribbean newsreader on British television, and worked for the BBC for over 25 years.

Sir Trevor MacDonald. Trinidad born, self-made millionaire. Britain's first Black news anchor, and the face of ITN's Ten 'o' clock news.

Trix Worrell. Educated in south London, was the producer of Desmond's, Britain's most successful Black comedy.

Kanya King. Educated at South Kilburn High School, is the founder of the Music Of Black Origin Awards (MOBOs) who financed the first show by re-mortgaging her house.

Alrick Riley. Educated in Hackney, is a BAFTA-winning director and partner in Cinnamon Films.

In Fashion

Bruce Oldfield. Brought up in care. Now dresses a number of celebrities, including Sienna Miller, Jemima Goldsmith, Queen Noor of Jordan, and also the late Princess Diana.

Ozwald Boateng. Educated in Southwark College, owns a shop on Saville Row, and who designs clothes for Will Smith, Samuel L Jackson and James Bond to name but a few.

In Literature

Zadie Smith. Writer of the successful *White Teeth* at just 25 and the winner of the Orange Prize for Fiction for her book *On Beauty*.

Ben Okri. Educated in the University of Westminster and born in Nigeria, this writer and poet has won a number of awards for his works, including the Guardian Fiction Prize and the Booker Prize.

In the Arts

Ekow Eshun. Of Ghanaian heritage and educated at Kingsbury High School, has risen to be the Artistic Director of the Institute of Contemporary Arts (ICA).

Jo Arscott. Is of mixed parentage, raised in care, and educated in Gloucester. She worked her way to the position of Deputy Integrated Creative Director for Saatchi & Saatchi, and is now the Creative Director of 141 Worldwide.

Chris Ofili. Born in Manchester and of Nigerian origin, is a Turner Prize Winner who often uses his work to challenge Black stereotypes.

In the Youth Service

Jenny Hinds. Has worked with young people in south London for over 20 years, and was awarded a Lifetime Achievement Award at the Youth Oskar Awards 2007.

Arnie Reynolds. Born and bred in south London has assisted hundreds of kids to have a goal in life, and manages Waterloo FC, one of the most successful youth teams in London.

Lena Hartley. Born in Trinidad, is founder and director of Pyramid Health and Social Care Association (PHASCA). She has worked for much of her life on a voluntary basis, and has assisted the lives of many in south Tottenham.

Leroy Spence. Of Jamaican parentage. For over a decade has been a positive Black role model for young people in Lambeth, and is much admired and respected for his commitment to the welfare of the young people in his community.

In Disability

Ade Adepitan. From Nigeria, is a Paralympics Bronze Medallist. Despite contracting Polio at a young age, he has become one of the most recognised faces in the Basketball world and has campaigned for many years against race and disability discrimination.

And lastly ... don't be surprised

John Amaechi. A gay Black Role Model. Because it's about time! Raised in Stockport, played in the NBA as a centre from 1995 to 2003, and was the first player associated with the NBA to openly admit that he was gay. He is now studying a PhD in Psychology.

And if you want to keep learning and discover more about your world, refer to the following websites:

MY WEBSITE
www.jacobandbiscuit.co.uk

MY STUFF ON YOUTUBE
...search for 'No Niggativity, Pure Positivity'

MY FACEBOOK GROUP
What Being Black Is And What Being Black Isn't

BISCUIT'S MYSPACE
http://www.myspace.com/noniggativity

ROLE MODELS

www.ipa.co.uk/diversity/communities_intro.html
http://www.100greatblackbritons.com/home.html

HEALTH

http://www.itzcaribbean.com/health_revolution.php
www.mariandina.com
http://www.blackherbals.com/Articles_and_Reviews.htm
http://www.drafrika.com/
http://www.boydgraves.com/
http://www.afromerica.com/knowledge/psychology/

UK CURRENT AFFAIRS

www.blackbritain.co.uk
www.blink.org.uk/
www.blackinbritain.co.uk/
www.newsnow.co.uk/newsfeed/?name=Black+News
www.black-history-month.co.uk
www.blackpresence.co.uk/news.php
www.blackukonline.com/
www.ligali.org
http://www.ncadc.org.uk/index.htm
http://www.noborder.org/index.php

GLOBAL CURRENT AFFAIRS

http://www.indymedia.org.uk/
http://www.globalissues.org/
http://www.medialens.org/
http://www.black-collegian.com/news/
http://www.africasia.com/newafrican/
http://news.bbc.co.uk/1/hi/world/africa/default.stm
http://allafrica.com/
http://www.pacificmagazine.net/
http://www.southpacific.org/news.html
http://www.caribbeannewspapers.com/

BLACK NATIONALISM

http://www.assatashakur.org/forum/
www.finalcall.com
www.factology.com

http://www.dickgregory.com/index2.html
http://www.apspuhuru.org/
http://lemming.mahost.org/abr/
http://www.kingdomofyah.com/
http://www.theblacknationalist.com/news.html

AFRO-CENTRICITY
http://www.swagga.com/
http://www.ascac.org/scholars.html
http://www.geocities.com/CollegePark/Classroom/9912/kamguide
pg.html
http://www.yaaams.org/

SPIRITUALITY
http://rootsandrooted.org/ausar_auset.htm
http://boboshanti.com/
http://www.youtube.com/watch?v=KeZB2EsPqGE

HISTORY
www.chronicleworld.org/
http://100greatblackbritons.com/bios/olaudah_equiano.html
www.channel4.com/culture/microsites/O/organisation
www.vasili.co.uk/
www.blackwallstreet.freeservers.com
www.raceandhistory.com
http://www.trinicenter.com/
http://www.melanet.com/clegg_series/hoax.html
http://www.cwo.com/~lucumi/runoko.html
http://www.countercurrents.org/dalit-sikand140205.htm
http://www.historyforkids.org/learn/africa/history/index.htm
www.manuampim.com

WOMEN
www.bwrap.dircon.co.uk/
http://cambonli01.uuhost.uk.uu.net/forum/blackwomen/blado2.htm
www.megaessays.com/viewpaper/102450.html

HOMOSEXUALITY
www.ukblackout.com/
www.gingerbeer.co.uk/listing.php?ListingID=73&CategoryID=6

HOUSING
www.fbho.org.uk/site2/

MUSIC AND ENTERTAINMENT
http://www.daveyd.com/
www.kickgame.com
www.blackchat.co.uk/
http://www.afrocentriconline.com/phpBB2/
www.deephousepage.com
www.zulunation.com/afrika.html

GENERAL
You Tube www.youtube.com/ (for discussions and speeches)
...and just 'cos it's funny...http://www.blackpeopleloveus.com/

FILMS
1984
Animal Farm
Amistad
Bamboozled
Battle of Algiers
Biko
Bowling for Columbine
Boyz in the Hood
Bread and Roses
City of Gods
The Corporation
Do The Right Thing
Fahrenheit 9/11
Ghosts
Goodbye Uncle Tom
Hidden
Hoop Dreams
Hotel Rwanda
Jungle Fever
Lucia
Malcolm X
Once Were Warriors
Rize
Reds

Rosewood
Sicko
Soul Food
Spartacus
Sweet Sixteen
The Matrix
They Live
The Proud Valley
The Wind That Shakes The Barley
When We Were Kings

TV STATIONS
Channel 4, BBC2 and BBC4 (sometimes)
Al-Jazeera (Sky channel 514)

BOOKS
Africa
— *Assassination Of Lumumba*, Luto De Witte
— *Biko*, Donald Woods
— *Chief of Station, Congo: Fighting the Cold War in a Hot Zone*, Lawrence Devlin (1997)
— *Conversations with Ogotemmeli: An Introduction to Dogon Religious Ideas*, Marcel Griaule and Germaine Dieterlen
— *How Europe Underdeveloped Africa*, Walter Rodney
— *Next Gulf: London, Washington And Oil Conflict In Nigeria*, Andrew Rowell
— *The African Origin of Civilization: Myth or Reality*, Cheikh Anta Diop
— *The Algerian War And The French Army, 1954-62*, M. S Alexander
— *The Democratic Republic of Congo: Poverty in the Midst of Plenty (2006)*, David Renton and Frank Preiss
— *The History Of Africa: The Quest For Eternal Harmony*, M K Asante
— *Things Fall Apart*, Chinua Achebe
— *When We Ruled: A History Of African Civilisation & Achievement*, Robin Walker

Slavery and Black People In Britain
— *The Willie Lynch Letter and the Making of a Slave*, William Lynch (Author), Kashif Malik Hassan-el
— *After Abolition: Britain & The Slave Trade Since 1807*, Marika Sherwood
— *Capitalism and Slavery*, Eric Williams

— *Roots*, Alex Haley
— *The Black Jacobins: Toussaint L'Ouverture and the San Domingo Revolution*, C.L.R. James
— *The Overthrow Of Colonial Slavery*, Robin Blackburn
— *And Still I Rise*, Doreen Lawrence
— *Politics Of Windrush*, Peter Fryer
— *Staying Power: The History Of Black People In Britain*, Peter Fryer
— *There Ain't No Black In The Union Jack*, Paul Gilroy

Black People In America
— *Blood In My Eye*, George Jackson
— *I Know Why The Caged Bird Sings*, Maya Angelou
— *Last Year of Malcolm X: The Evolution of a Revolutionary*, George Breitman
— *Liberation, Imagination, and the Black Panther Party: A New Look at the Panthers and Their Legacy*, Kathleen Cleaver
— *Martin & Malcolm & America*, James H Cone
— *Redemption Song: Muhammad Ali & The Spirit Of The Sixties*, Mike Marqusee
— *Seize The Time*, Bobby Seale
— *Soledad Brother*, George Jackson
— *Soul On Ice*, Eldridge Cleaver
— *Strength To Love*, Martin Luther King
— *The Autobiography of Malcolm X*, Malcolm X
— *The Black Panthers Speak*, Phillip Foner

About 'niggativity'
— *Black Skins, White Masks*, Frantz Fanon
— *From Niggas To Gods Vol I*, Akil
— *Native Son*, Richard Wright
— *The Miseducation of the Negro*, Carter Godwin Woodson

Black People In The Caribbean
— *From Columbus to Castro: The History of the Caribbean 1492-1969*. Eric Williams
— *The Wretched of the Earth*, Frantz Fanon

About The Candyman
— *Dark Alliance: The CIA, the Contras, and the Crack Cocaine Explosion*, Gary Webb

— *How Capitalism Underdeveloped Black America: Problems in Race, Political Economy, and Society*, Manning Marable
— *The Assassination of Malcolm X*, George Breitman, Herman Porter, Baxter Smith
— *The Community Manifesto*, Karl Marx
— *The Judas Factor: The Plot To Kill Malcolm X*, Karl Evanzz
— *Whiteness Made Simple: Stepping Into The Grey Zone*, William (Les) Henry
— *When Affirmative Action Was White: An Untold History of Racial Inequality in Twentieth-Century America*, Ira Katznelson

International Issues
— *Che Guevara: A Revolutionary Life*, Jon Lee Anderson
— *If I Am Not For Myself: Confessions Of An Anti-Zionist Jew*, Mike Marqusee
— *Understanding Power: The Indispensable Chomsky*, Noam Chomsky

Women
— *Harriet Tubman: The Road To Freedom*, Catherine Clinton
— *Pankhurst*, Jad Adams

MUSICIANS
Alison Hinds
Common
Dead Prez
Erykah Badu
Jill Scott
Immortal Technique
India Irie
Jeru The Damaja
Machel Montano
Manraj
Mos Def
Nas
Talib Kweli
Tupac Shakur
Wu-Tang Clan

ORGANISATIONS AND INFORMATION
(dealing with international and Human Rights issues)

Action for Southern Africa
— *http://www.actsa.org*
African Liberation Support Campaign Network (ALISC-Network)
— *nkexplo@yahoo.co.uk*
Bankwatch Network
— *www.bankwatch.org*
Campaign Against the Arms Trade
— *http://www.caat.org.uk/about/about.php*
Death Penalty Info
— *www.deathpenaltyinfo.org/*
Ethical Consumer
— *www.ethicalconsumer.org*
FairTrade Foundation
— *www.fairtrade.org.uk*
Friends of the Earth
— *www.foe.co.uk*
Human Rights Watch
— *www.hrw.org*
Minewatch
— *www.eco-web.com*
New Internationalist magazine
— *www.newint.org*
War on Want
— *www.waronwant.org*
World Development Movement
— *www.wdm.org.uk*

NEWSPAPERS
Caribbean Times:
— *www.caribbeantimes.co.uk/*
New Nation:
— *www.newnation.co.uk/*
The Final Call:
— *www.fctp.co.uk/*
The Voice:
— *www.voice-online.co.uk/*

MAGAZINES
The Source:
— *www.thesource.com/*

RADIO STATIONS
Talk Shows:
Flames FM
— *www.flamesfm.com* with DJ Koolbreeze. Saturday 1am-7am.
Genesis Radio
— *www.genesisradio.tv* with Cosmic Warrior Sunday 10pm-Midnight
Galaxy Radio:
— *www.afiwestation.com/*
Colourful Radio
— *http://iamcolourful.com/radio/*

Finally, I hope that if you're young and you read this book you will keep reading, and maybe start writing yourself. As a form of expression nothing comes close. Now I know you might think reading's kinda long, and that most books don't really relate to many inner city experiences, but read the following five books – you might be surprised how much you like them:

1. *Street Boys: 7 Kids. 1 Estate. No Way Out. The True Story of a Lost Childhood* by Tim Pritchard. Looking at members of Peel Dem Crew (PDC) based in Angel Town, who changed their negative activities to become positive role models for young Black men and women growing up on the streets.
2. *Ugly & Beyond Ugly* by Constance Briscoe. The story of a young girl who, despite child abuse, poverty and every difficulty imaginable, manages to find a way through it to achieve her goals in life.
3. *Makes Me Wanna Holler: A Young Black Man in America* by Nathan McCall. A book about what it's like to be Black in a western society – the pitfalls, and the dangers.
4. *The Seven Principles of RESPECTisms: The Word on the Streets* by Ken Barnes. To put it bluntly, a book about how young people can be positive, get what they want, and do it all in the right way.
5. *Free Your Mind* by Andrew Muhammad. A book about understanding the system, and knowing how to make use of it for your own benefit.

Like Mr T eloquently says:

"...be somebody, or be somebody's fool..."

"We don't need no help or handouts, don't pull your grands out,
we can manage…"
Unorthodox Family

"...the thing that is missing, is not the genius that is present, or the genius that is absent. But the thing that is missing, is the unity of us as a people.

We cannot any longer depend on a benevolent White person...to look out for our needs. That responsibility is ours...

Power concedes nothing without a demand. But power won't even concede to a demand if the demand is coming from a weak constituency that looks like they've lost their testicular fortitude...

Our children cannot eat at the table of illusion and hypocrisy. Most of us who have access, who have wealth, who have quote unquote positions – we are like mannequins in the shopping malls of democracy. When you go to the shopping mall, you see the manikin – the manikin is dressed in what you would like to buy. The manikin can't talk. The manikin can't walk. We got Black people in power, but they got no power. We got Black people with money that we think are giants, but in the company of their White counterparts, they are midgets...

...if we wanna get where we wanna go, we can't focus on the house that has rejected us...we have to now focus on ourselves."

Louis Farrakhan

THE FUTURE AND WHAT TO WATCH OUT FOR...

The Artist...
Inderpal Virdi (representing Southall). This man was the main graphic/image designer behind this book. If you got time, check out his blog at http://heyindy.com. Trust me, this guy's stuff is incredible.
The Film Director...
Noble Fox, currently at the National Film and Television School, and documentary maker of films such as *Roads to Rotterdam* and *C.K.D.* This man's films are gonna be sik!
The Organisation...
The Youth Forum SE1 United based in south London AKA gs. Yea I know that the common perception of youth organisations are about table tennis tournaments and anarchic staff, but SE1 comes from a different angle. It was pioneered by young people aged between 13-19, who wanted 100% control over the way in which the youth provision in their area was run. So instead of just complaining about it and doing nothing, they set up their organisation, applied for funding, got an office, and hired staff to work for them. From the Youth Oskar Awards, to art exhibitions; from fashion shows, to mace debating; from being adopted by the Royal Festival Hall, to heritage trips to Egypt and Auschwitz – this organisation continues to vastly improve the environment and opportunities for young people in their area, and personifies the phrase 'youth-led' provision. In short, this is what youth work will look like in the future. Check out their website at www.se1united.org.uk for more information.
The Books...
Baddar Safeer, the soon-to-be author of a groundbreaking book – a no nonsense perspective from a British Pakistani's point of view on the little understood relationships between Asian cultures in the UK and around the world. From the myths and facts that surround intermarriage, sport, politics, and integration; to the over-hyped and so-called Muslim/Sikh, Sikh/Hindu, Hindu/Muslim animosity.

From the difference in treatment of Asian men, and Asian women in British society, to the fact that there are many things other than terrorism that British Muslims think about! This book will put the widely held beliefs and stereotypes about the Asian community in Britain to rest, provide a much needed fresh viewpoint on emotive and controversial subjects, and allow White and Black people to understand their Asian neighbours better.

WHAT BEING BLACK IS AND WHAT BEING BLACK ISN'T